mark

texts ● contexts

Athalya Brenner and Nicole Wilkinson Duran, Series Editors

Published and future volumes

mark

**Nicole Wilkinson Duran, Teresa Okure,
and Daniel Patte, Editors**

Fortress Press

Minneapolis

MARK
Texts @ Contexts

Cover image: Detail of *Forms of English Red* by Christian Hugo Martin
Cover design: Laurie Ingram
Book design: Perfectype, Nashville, TN
Chapter 6 translator: Leticia Guardiola-Sáenz

Library of Congress Cataloging-in-Publication Data
Mark / Nicole Wilkinson Duran, Teresa Okure, and Daniel Patte, editors.
    p. cm. — (Texts @ contexts)
  Includes bibliographical references (p.   ) and indexes.
  ISBN 978-0-8006-5998-1 (alk. paper)
  1. Bible. N.T. Mark—Criticism, interpretation, etc. I. Duran, Nicole Wilkinson. II. Okure, Teresa. III. Patte, Daniel.
  BS2585.52.M36 2010
  226.3'06—dc22
                        2010010074

The paper used in this publication meets the minimum requirements of American National Standard for Information Sciences — Permanence of Paper for Printed Library Materials, ANSI Z329.48-1984.

Manufactured in the U.S.A.

15 14 13 12 11 1 2 3 4 5 6 7 8 9 10

CONTENTS

Part Three
Putting Other Readings In Context

texts @ contexts
SERIES PREFACE

Myth cannot be defined but as an empty screen, a structure. . . .
A myth is but an empty screen for transference.

MIEKE BAL[1]

שבעים פנים לתורה

The Torah has seventy faces.

MEDIEVAL JEWISH TRADITION[2]

The discipline of biblical studies emerges from a particular cultural context; it is profoundly influenced by the assumptions and values of the Western European and North Atlantic, male-dominated, and largely Protestant environment in which it was born. Yet, like the religions with which it is involved, the critical study of the Bible has traveled beyond its original context. Its presence in a diversity of academic settings around the globe has been experienced as both liberative and imperialist, sometimes simultaneously. Like many travelers, biblical scholars become aware of their own cultural rootedness only in contact with, and through the eyes of, people in other cultures.

---

1. Bal 1993: 347, 360.
2. This saying indicates, through its usage of the stereotypic number 70, that the Torah—and, by extension, the whole Bible—intrinsically has many meanings. It is therefore often used to indicate the multivalence and variability of biblical interpretation. The saying does not appear in this formulation in traditional Jewish biblical interpretation before the Middle Ages. Its earliest appearances are toward the end of the medieval commentator Ibn Ezra's introduction to his commentary on the Torah, in midrash *Numbers Rabbah* (on 13:15-16), and in later Jewish mystical literature.

The way one closes a door in Philadelphia seems nothing at all remark-able, but in Chiang Mai, the same action seems overly loud and emphatic—so very typically American. In the same way, Western biblical interpretation did not seem tied to any specific context when only Westerners were reading and writing it. Since so much economic, military, and consequently cultural power has been vested in the West, the West has had the privilege of main-taining this cultural exclusivity for over two centuries. Those who engaged in biblical studies—even when they were women or men from Africa, Asia, and Latin America—nevertheless had to take on the Western context along with the discipline.

But much of recent Bible scholarship has moved toward the recognition that considerations not only of the contexts of assumed, or implied, biblical authors but also the contexts of the interpreters are valid and legitimate in an inquiry into biblical literature. We use *contexts* here as an umbrella term cov-ering a wide range of issues: on the one hand, social factors (such as location, economic situation, gender, age, class, ethnicity, color, and things pertaining to personal biography) and, on the other hand, ideological factors (such as faith, beliefs, practiced norms, and personal politics).

Contextual readings of the Bible are an attempt to redress a previous longstanding and grave imbalance. This imbalance rests in the claim that says that there is a kind of "plain," unaligned biblical criticism that is some-how normative and that there is another, distinct kind of biblical criticism aligned with some social location: the writing of Latina/o scholars advo-cating liberation, the writing of feminist scholars emphasizing gender as a cultural factor, the writings of African scholars pointing out the text's and the readers' imperialism, the writing of Jews and Muslims, and so on. The project of recognizing and emphasizing the role of context in reading freely admits that we all come from somewhere: no one is native to the biblical text, no one reads only in the interests of the text itself. North Atlantic and Western European scholarship has focused on the Bible's characters as individuals, has read past its miracles and stories of spiritual manifestations or "translated" them into other categories, and has seen some aspects of the text in bold and other aspects not at all. These results of Euro-American contextual reading would be no problem if they were seen as such; but they have become a chain to be broken when they have been held up as the one and only "objective," plain truth of the text itself.

The biblical text, as we have come to understand in the postmodern world and as pre-Enlightenment interpreters perhaps understood more clearly, does not speak in its own voice. It cannot read itself. *We* must read it, and in reading it, we must acknowledge that our own voice's particular pitch and timbre and inflection affect the meaning that emerges. In the past, and to a large extent still in the present, Bible scholars usually read the text in the voice of a Western Protestant male. When interpreters in the Southern Hemisphere and in Asia began to appropriate the Bible, this meant a recognition that the Euro-American male voice is not the voice of the text itself; it is only one reader's voice, or rather, the voice of one context—however familiar and authoritative it may seem to all who have been affected by Western political and economic power. Needless to say, it is not a voice suited to bring out the best meaning for every reading community. Indeed, as biblical studies tended for so long to speak in this one particular voice, it may be the case that that voice has outlived its meaning-producing usefulness: we may have heard all that this voice has to say, at least for now. Nevertheless we have included that voice in this series, in part in an effort to hear it as emerging from its specific context, in order to put that previously authoritative voice quite literally in its place.

The trend of recognizing readers' contexts as meaningful is already recognizable in the pioneering volumes of *Reading from This Place* (Segovia and Tolbert 2000; 2004; Segovia 1995), which indeed move from the center to the margins and back and from the United States to the rest of the world.[3] More recent publications along this line also include *Her Master's Tools?* (Penner and Vander Stichele 2005), *From Every People and Nation: The Book of Revelation in Intercultural Perspective* (Rhoads et al. 2005), *From Every People and Nation: A Biblical Theology of Race* (Hays and Carson 2003), and the *Global Bible Commentary* (*GBC*; Patte et al. 2004).

The editors of the *GBC* have gone a long way in the direction of this shift by soliciting and admitting contributions from so-called Third, Fourth, and Fifth World scholars alongside First and Second World

---

3. At the 2009 Annual Meeting of the Society of Biblical Literature, the Contextual Biblical Interpretation Consultation held a joint special session with the Asian and Asian-American Hermeneutics Group to commemorate the fifteenth anniversary of this three-volume project.

scholars, thus attempting to usher the former and their perspectives into the *center* of biblical discussion. Contributors to the *GBC* were asked to begin by clearly stating their context before proceeding. The result was a collection of short introductions into the books of the Bible (Hebrew Bible/Old Testament and New Testament), each introduction from one specific context and, perforce, limited in scope. At the Society of Biblical Literature's annual meeting in Philadelphia in 2005, during the two *GBC* sessions and especially in the session devoted to pedagogical implications, it became clear that this project should be continued, albeit articulated further and redirected to include more disparate voices among readers of the biblical texts.

On methodological grounds, the paradox of a deliberately inclusive policy that foregrounds interpretative differences could not be addressed in a single- or double-volume format because in most instances, those formats would allow for only one viewpoint for each biblical issue or passage (as in previous publications) or biblical book (as in the *GBC*) to be articulated. The acceptance of such a limit might indeed lead to a decentering of traditional scholarship, but it would definitely not usher in multivocality on any single topic. It is true that, for pedagogical reasons, a teacher might achieve multivocality of scholarship by using various specialized scholarship types together: for instance, the *GBC* has been used side by side in a course with historical introductions to the Bible and other focused introductions, such as the *Women's Bible Commentary* (Newsom and Ringe 1998). But research and classes focused on a single biblical book or biblical corpus need another kind of resource: volumes exemplifying a broad multivocality in themselves, varied enough in contexts from various shades of the confessional to various degrees of the secular, especially since in most previous publications, the contexts of communities of faith overrode all other contexts.

On the practical level, then, we found that we could address some of these methodological, pedagogical, and representational limitations evident in previous projects in contextual interpretation through a book series in which each volume introduces multiple contextual readings of the same biblical texts. This is what the Society of Biblical Literature's Consultation on Contextual Biblical Interpretation has already been promoting since 2005. The Consultation serves as a testing ground for a multiplicity of readings of the same biblical texts by scholars from different contexts.

These considerations led us to believe that such a book series would be timely. We decided to construct a series, including at least eight to ten volumes, divided between the Hebrew Bible/Old Testament (HB/OT) and the New Testament (NT). Each of the planned volumes will focus on one or two biblical books: Genesis, Exodus and Deuteronomy, Leviticus and Numbers, Joshua and Judges, and early Jewish novels (such as Judith, Susanna, and Tobit) for the HB/OT; Mark, Luke-Acts, John, and Paul's letters for the NT.[4] The general HB/OT editor is Athalya Brenner, with Archie Lee and Gale Yee as associate editors. The general NT editor is Nicole Duran, with Daniel Patte and Teresa Okure as associate editors.

Each volume will focus on clusters of contexts and of issues or themes, as determined by the editors in consultation with potential contributors. A combination of topics or themes, texts, and interpretive contexts seems better for our purpose than a text-only focus. In this way, more viewpoints on specific issues will be presented, with the hope of gaining a grid of interests and understanding. The interpreters' contexts will be allowed to play a central role in choosing a theme: we editors do not want to impose our choice of themes upon others, but as the contributions emerge, we will collect themes for each volume under several headings.

While we were soliciting articles for the first volumes (and continue to solicit contributions for future volumes), each contributor was asked to foreground her or his own multiple "contexts" while presenting her or his interpretation of a given issue pertaining to the relevant biblical book(s). We asked that the interpretation be firmly grounded in those contexts and sharply focused on the specific theme, as well as in dialogue with "classical" informed biblical scholarship. Finally, we asked for a concluding assessment of the significance of this interpretation for the contributor's contexts (whether secular or in the framework of a faith community).

Our main interest in this series is to examine how formulating the content-specific, ideological, and thematic questions from life contexts will focus the reading of the biblical texts. The result is a two-way process of reading that (1) considers the contemporary life context from the perspective of

---

4. At this time, no volume on Revelation is planned, since Rhoads's volume, *From Every People and Nation: The Book of Revelation in Intercultural Perspective* (2005), is readily available, with a concept similar to ours.

the chosen themes in the given biblical book as corrective lenses, pointing out specific problems and issues in that context as highlighted by the themes in the biblical book; and (2) conversely, considers the given biblical book and the chosen theme from the perspective of the life context.

The word *contexts,* like *identity,* is a blanket term with many components. For some, their geographical context is uppermost; for others, the dominant factor may be gender, faith, membership in a certain community, class, and so forth. The balance is personal and not always conscious; it does, however, dictate choices of interpretation. One of our interests as editors is to present the personal beyond the autobiographical as pertinent to the wider scholarly endeavor, especially but not only when grids of consent emerge that supersede divergence. Consent is no guarantee of "truth speak" (Bal: 2008, 16, 164–66 and elsewhere); neither does it necessarily point at a sure recognition of the biblical authors' elusive contexts and intentions. It does, however, have cultural and political implications.

Globalization promotes uniformity but also diversity, by shortening distances, enabling dissemination of information, and exchanging resources. This is an opportunity for modifying traditional power hierarchies and reallocating knowledge, for upsetting hegemonies, and for combining the old with the new, the familiar with the unknown—in short, for a fresh mutuality. This series, then, consciously promotes the revision of biblical myths into newly reread and rewritten versions that hang on many threads of transference. Our contributors were asked, decidedly, to be responsibly nonobjective and to represent only themselves on the biblical screen. Paradoxically, we hope, the readings here offered will form a new tapestry or, changing the metaphor, new metaphorical screens on which contemporary life contexts and the life of biblical texts in those contexts may be reflected.

Athalya Brenner
Nicole Wilkinson Duran

ABBREVIATIONS

AAR	American Academy of Religion
C&MA	Christian and Missionary Alliance
ELN	National Liberation Army (Colombia)
FARC	Revolutionary Armed Forces of Colombia
GBC	*Global Bible Commentary*
HB/OT	Hebrew Bible/Old Testament (written out except in preface)
ISEDET	Instituto Superior de Estudios Teológicos (Bolivar, Colombia)
KJV	King James Version
LXX	Septuagint
NASB	New American Standard Bible
NIV	New International Version
NJB	New Jerusalem Bible
NRSV	New Revised Standard Version
NT	New Testament
RSV	Revised Standard Version
SBL	Society of Biblical Literature
SNTS	Studiorum Novi Testamenti Societas
UNDP	United Nations Development Program

CONTRIBUTORS

Jin Young Choi is a Ph.D. candidate in New Testament and Early Christianity and a fellow in the Program in Theology and Practice at Vanderbilt University. Her dissertation applies Asian and Asian American feminist biblical hermeneutics to the Gospel according to Mark. She has published a number of Bible study books for church leaders and lay people in her native country, South Korea. Her research interests include cultural, postcolonial, and feminist studies in relation to the Synoptic Gospels and letters of Paul.

Sejong Chun is a Ph.D. student at Vanderbilt University, writing a dissertation on interpreting Galatians within the Korean American immigrant church context. He was born and grew up on a small island in South Korea. He received a bachelor's degree in theology and Master of Divinity at Presbyterian College and Theological Seminary in Seoul and a Th.M. from Duke Divinity School.

Nicole Wilkinson Duran grew up in Ohio and Pennsylvania and has lived as an adult in Thailand, South Africa, and Turkey. She is now an independent scholar living near Philadelphia. She has published two books, *Having Men for Dinner: Deadly Banquets and Biblical Women* (2006) and *The Power of Disorder: Ritual Themes in Mark's Passion Narrative* (2009) as well as various articles on Hebrew Bible and New Testament topics. She has also edited and coedited a number of other collections of essays and served on the editorial board of the *Global Bible Commentary* (2004).

Menghun Goh is a Ph.D. student in New Testament and Early Christian History at Vanderbilt University. He was born, raised, and educated in the Chinese education system in Kuala Lumpur, Malaysia, and graduated from the University of California and the Graduate Theological Union in

Berkeley. He served as a full-time Christian minister before embarking on his Ph.D. studies. Goh is interested in semiotics, apophaticism, and postcolonial theories.

Israel Kamudzandu is Assistant Professor of New Testament Studies in the Lindsey P. Pherigo Chair at St. Paul School of Theology in Kansas City, Missouri. He grew up in Zimbabwe and attended the University of Zimbabwe and Africa University. He received a Master of Divinity degree from United Theological Seminary in Dayton, Ohio, and the Ph.D. from Brite Divinity School.

Hisako Kinukawa is from Japan, and now serves as an adjunct professor at the Lutheran Theological Seminary and the Japan Nohden Theological Seminary; co-director of the Center for Feminist Theology and Ministry in Japan; and a board member of the Asian Women's Resource Center, serving on the editorial board of its journal, *In God's Image.* Kinukawa is the author of *Women and Jesus in Mark: A Japanese Feminist Perspective,* among other books.

Teresa Okure is Professor of New Testament and Gender Hermeneutics at the Catholic Institute of West Africa in Nigeria. A Sister of the Society of the Holy Child Jesus, Okure is also founding president of the Catholic Biblical Association of Nigeria (CABAN) and is well known for her contextual hermeneutics. She is a coeditor of this volume and the Texts @ Contexts series.

Daniel Patte is Professor of Religious Studies and of New Testament and Early Christianity at Vanderbilt University. A native of France, he received degrees in philosophy and theology from the Faculté de Théologie Protestante in Montpellier, France; the M.Th. from the University of Geneva, Switzerland; and a Th.D. from the Jewish Christian Center at Chicago Theological Seminary. Formerly the General Editor of the biblical studies journal *Semeia*, Patte was also centrally involved with the Society of Biblical Literature's Semiotic and Exegesis section as well as its section on Romans through History and Cultures, and, since 2007, the Contextual Biblical Interpretation group. Most recently he has been the general editor of the *Global Bible Commentary* (2004) and *The Cambridge Dictionary of Christianity* (2010).

Elsa Tamez currently serves as a translation consultant for the United Biblical Societies. Born in Mexico, Tamez received her Ph.D. in Theology from the University of Lausanne in Switzerland and her Licentiate in Literature and Linguistics at the National University of Costa Rica. She is Professor Emerita and a past president of the Latin American Biblical University in Costa Rica. Among her best known publications in English are *The Bible of the Oppressed* (1982); *The Amnesty of Grace: Justification by Faith from a Latin American Perspective* (1993); *Jesus and Courageous Women of the Bible* (2001); and *Struggles for Power in Early Christianity: A Study of the First Letter to Timothy* (2007). She has received several awards for her contributions to contextual biblical hermeneutics.

Osvaldo D. Vena is Associate Professor of New Testament Interpretation at Garrett-Evangelical Theological Seminary. Born in Argentina, he received a Master of Divinity from Bethel Theological Seminary in St. Paul, a Th.M. from Princeton Theological Seminary, and a Th.D. from ISEDET in Buenos Aires. He has published three books: *The Parousia and Its Rereadings: The Development of the Eschatological Consciousness in the Writings of the New Testament* (2001); *Apocalipsis* (2008); and *Evangelio de Marcos* (2008). He has also published numerous articles in both English and Spanish, as well as a music CD, *Still a Dream*, with original music and lyrics based on the poetry of Arab and Jewish children.

Introduction

Nicole Wilkinson Duran

The mysteries, lacunae, and silences in the Gospel according to Mark invite the reader's involvement, even insist upon it. The aim of this volume is to present a variety of this readerly involvement, discussing Mark's Gospel, with a consciousness on all sides of how our voices emerge from sociopolitical contexts. I am happy to say that not only are there exceedingly interesting voices with new and important readings in this volume, but these voices also seem in some ways to be in conversation with and learning from one another.

The chapters are arranged here in part according to focus and approach, in the hope that these groupings will evoke comparison and cross-fertilization among them. I trust that the groupings are self-explanatory, but more can be said in comparing the contextual approaches used in this collection. Sejong Chun and Israel Kamudzandu embrace the religious practices of their own very different contexts in order to shed light on Jesus' role as exorcist and shamanic healer. Jin Young Choi similarly affirms her own culture's communally oriented society and its ability to shed light on discipleship in this Gospel.

But we are not all ready to affirm either our own traditions or the effect those traditions have on interpreting the Gospel. Elsa Tamez may be affirming people's experience, but she is not lifting up or embracing an aspect of the culture in which she lives; rather in part she exposes the turbulent context

1

of war. Teresa Okure also is less affirming the role of children in her culture than awakening the reader to ugly realities that emerge there, and that also can be seen in the Gospel. These chapters in a sense use the biblical text to expose injustices in their particular context, while at the same time those injustices shed light on themes of justice in the Gospel.

Osvaldo Vena's take on discipleship makes for an interesting conversation with Choi but also bears some similarities to other chapters in the volume, since Vena is in part resisting the spiritualizing readings of his early context. Chapters by Menghun Goh, Hisako Kinukawa, Daniel Patte, and myself, like Vena's chapter, are not emphasizing the light our cultures shed on the text. Rather we bring out prominently the effect of our own traditions in obscuring certain aspects of the text and attempt in various ways to put together an alternative reading from that same (or from nearly that same) context. Patte's article in particular highlights, from the inside, the blindness to context on the part of what has been academic biblical criticism and its effect on meaning-making.

From and amid this variety of lenses and cultures, Mark's Gospel emerges here, in all its wealth of meanings and mysteries, speaking in a variety of tongues and even in meaningful moments of silence, all of which seem to be the Gospel's native language. Mark's Gospel ends with the un-witness of those who say nothing to anyone, ever. But clearly, the story of that silence reverberates, through language and experience, in the midst of tradition and culture, in the face of repression and violence, as mysterious and full of meaning as experience itself.

Part One

———

Jesus as Exorcist and Healer

CHAPTER 1

The Nature and Identity of Jesus in Mark 7:24-37

A Zimbabwean Interpretation

Israel Kamudzandu

Introduction

This reading takes into account the experiences of ordinary readers who form the majority of our parishioners in Africa, especially Zimbabwe. The focus of this essay is on the appropriation, reception, and contextualization of Jesus by Shona Christians during and after the colonial era. Thus, my task is to contend that the Markan Jesus should be understood in the context of a particular people, specifically, the Shona Christian people.[1] When missionaries came to Zimbabwe beginning in the fifteenth century, they succeeded in replacing the Shona religiocultural way of life with Euro-American religious institutions. To treat illness, Zimbabweans relied heavily on special people known as medicine specialists (shamans), people who were gifted in ushering in salvation through healing.[2] The resemblances between Shona shamanic practice and the healings of Jesus in Mark's Gospel are striking. Hence, a contextualized reading of Jesus in the Gospel of Mark during colonial and postcolonial era is in order.[3]

---

1. Shona people are part of the Bantu African group and are found in Zimbabwe.
2. Gordon L. Chavunduka, "Traditional Medicine and Christian Beliefs," in *Christianity South of the Zambezi,* ed. M. F. C. Bourdillon (Zimbabwe: Mambo, 1977), 132.
3. Contextualization is used in this essay to refer to ways through which postcolonial Christians were able to live out the gospel in obedience to Christ within their own cultures and circumstances.

Mark and his audience lived under the influence of Greco-Roman religion, in which the god Asclepius was believed to heal people and to perform various miracles.[4] Similarly, prior to the coming of the missionaries, African societies stood under the influence of both healers and miracles workers.[5] These gifted figures functioned as providers of salvation or wholeness to every aspect of community life. Not only did they bring physical healing to the community, but they also played a part in the political, social, and economic spheres: conferring authority on tribal chiefs, encouraging fertility, and blessing every undertaking. Healers were and still are the most powerful, influential, and complex religious figures in the Shona community. The word usually translated as "healer" can also mean priest, doctor, chemist, magician, visionary, and prophet. The translation "healer" suggests significant parallels between Jesus and the medicine shaman in the arenas of healing, miracles, exorcism, and clairvoyance.

Therefore, Jesus was appropriated as a shaman among Shona Christians; he was viewed as a medicine specialist, or *n'anga,* whose function was to offer salvation and social integration.[6] The healed person was to be integrated into the society or village life. The Gospels are replete with accounts of Jesus healing, in which he restores sick people to their relatives (Mark 1:31; 2:5; 5:19, 34; 10:52). More poignant is the incident in Mark 8:23: Jesus applies saliva or a mixture of saliva and dirt to the blind person's eyes. Similarly, in 7:32-36, he heals a deaf man by spitting on his finger and then touching the tongue of the man, uttering a noise that may have been interpreted as a sigh. By using these concrete means of healing—touch, breath, saliva, dirt—Jesus conforms to the practice of the medicine specialists of Zimbabwe.

---

4. Emma J. Edelstein and Ludwig Edelstein, eds., *Asclepius: A Collection and Interpretation of the Testimonies* (Baltimore: John Hopkins Press, 1945). A variety of tractates document Asclepius as the healer in the world of Greco-Roman antiquity, as well as cult centers in which Asclepius was hailed as the main representative of divine healing. See Simon Hornblower and Antony Spawforth, eds., *The Oxford Classical Dictionary,* 3rd rev. ed. (Oxford/ New York: Oxford University Press, 2003), 187–88.

5. In biblical times, especially in the New Testament period, miracles were referred to as "signs and wonders." The author of Acts 2:19 uses this phrase to refer to the mighty works, wonders, and miracles that God did through Jesus.

6. The word *n'anga* refers to a Shona medicine specialist who is endowed with a supernatural spirit and the ability to heal, exorcise, and diagnose various kinds of sicknesses. See Michael Gelfand, *Shona Religion: With Special Reference to the Makorekore* (Cape Town: Juta, 1962), 106–19.

This view of Jesus no doubt springs from the fact that my own mother was a sacred specialist in her own right. My mother, Esnath Kamudzandu, was known as a prophet and a healer who performed various functions of healing, prophesying, and even helping couples to conceive. While these practices were condemned in many Euro-American denominations, church members, including ministers, nevertheless came to consult my mother.[7] In the villages, a variety of sicknesses including paralysis, migraine headaches, anorexia, hemorrhage, mental problems, male and female infertility, as well as snakebites were common, and I witnessed my mother performing healings on all these ailments. This practice was common and is still carried out in many parts of Zimbabwe. All received healing at the hands of a simple and uneducated faith-healer woman.

The United Methodist Church and other denominations in Zimbabwe boast of a proud tradition of gifted women whose role and place in the church are basically to heal and offer salvation to those in need.[8] My mother was in this tradition—a prophet, healer, and nonconformist extraordinaire. As her phenomenal gift attracted more people, however, she was perceived as a threat by male preachers. The United Methodist Church did not officially subscribe to the spirituality of faith healing and was quick to point this out. In her spirituality, my mother offered a soothing balm of healing to those in need, particularly poor people. Her fame spread all over Zimbabwe such that even after independence, government officials in need of healing were frequent visitors at our farm. The purity of my mother's work, manifested in both the spiritual and the physical realms, received positive sanction from various important figures in the hierarchy of Shona chiefdom, and the Zimbabwean government awarded her a midwifery certificate in 1981. Clearly, my mother had a great impact on the lives of many people within the Shona culture. This is understandable, given the fact that most Shona people identified with her peculiar form of spirituality, manifested in God's self-disclosure to people in need. My mother offered spiritual healing to the wounded souls,

---

7. For an extensive discussion of similar practices, see Chavunduka, "Traditional Medicine," 131–43.

8. The meaning of salvation among the Shona people is different from the Western definition. In the entire continent of Africa, salvation is defined in practical terms such as the ability to produce children, healing from a variety of illnesses, harvesting, as well as the ability of cows to produce. See M. L. Daneel, *Old and New in Southern Shona Independent Churches,* vol. 1, *Background and Rise of the Major Movements* (The Hague: Mouton, 1971), 95–98.

and she offered physical healing to the stricken. She did this in ways that are parallel to Jesus' healings as recorded in all four Gospels. For the sake of our discussion and to help readers who are not familiar with tribal and village life, I will offer a brief definition of a shaman.

Definition of a Shaman/Sacred Specialist, or *N'anga*

Cultural anthropology defines shamanism as a "religious complex, found most commonly in band and tribal societies, in which specialists undertake to heal, guide, and prophesy through trance behavior and mystical flight." Hence, a shaman, whether a woman or a man, is characterized by trance, curing, and an ideology of cosmic flight; a shaman is an ecstatic individual believed to posses supernormal powers. In the African traditional religion, shamanism is not hereditary—one has to achieve it. Shamans are known to have extraordinary personalities; and at times they withdraw from the rest of the society in search of deeper wisdom and greater contact with the spirit world.[9]

In Shona culture, a shaman acts as a mediator who stands at the *axis mundi,* to communicate between the human world and the world of spirits, between the living and the living dead, and between animals and human society.[10] This worldview of shamanism sounds imperfect by Western philosophical and theological standards, but post-missionary and postcolonial Christians have come to affirm and believe in it, especially in times of crisis.

An encounter between Western missionaries, explorers, and colonialists with African traditional religion was a confrontation of religious values in which the latter was pushed to the margin by the former. Missionaries labeled the shamans as heathens, witches, witchdoctors, pagans—terms that made these gifted people appear to be evil in the eyes of local converts and Western Christianity. Yet, in reality, specialists or shamans were the greatest gift and played an important role in the life of African villages and communities. In order to clarify my contextualized readings of Jesus in the Gospel

9. Michael Bourdillon, *The Shona Peoples: An Ethnography of the Contemporary Shona, with Special Reference to Their Religion,* Shona Heritage Series 1 (Gweru, Zimbabwe: Mambo, 1982), 147–51.
10. See Gwinyai Henry Muzorewa, *An African Theology of Mission* (Lampeter: Edwin Mellen, 1990), 86–95.

of Mark, which is the subject of this paper, I need first to outline some of the qualities of shamans.

John Mbiti, a prominent African theologian of the twentieth century, wrote extensively on shamanism, and on African shamans in particular. In his writings he listed the qualities of these specialists: they are people who are expected to be "trustworthy, upright morally, friendly, willing and ready to serve, able to discern people's needs and not be exorbitant in their charges, and are influential to the society." I would add that shamans are concerned with salvation, and practical existential concerns. Endowed with clairvoyance and assisted by helper spirits, a shaman fills many social and religious roles, including those of soothsayer, therapist, and interpreter of dreams. As protectors of people, shamans also play an offensive and defensive role in guarding the group against natural and human-made disasters.[11]

In traditional Africa, especially in Zimbabwe, shamans are called by different names, such as medicine specialists/*n'anga,* tribal spirits/*Mhondoro,* ancestral spirits/*vadzimu,* and alien or patronal spirits/*masvikiro.* In all cases, shamans are believed to operate under the guidance of God, who is referred to as *Mwari* by the Shona people. It is worth noting that when missionaries came to Zimbabwe in the fifteenth century, they discovered that African traditional religion was equipped to deal with sickness and suffering by the use of miracles and magic.[12] Magical as well as spiritual beliefs and practices still influence the religious world of Shona people. The religious beliefs and practices of African people are interwoven with magic, and the distinctions that were made by missionaries between African culture and church did not exist among the people.

A religious and political fact hidden to many Westerners is that women played a crucial role in the liberation of Zimbabwe. Prophetesses and shamans were a common feature in the early days of missionaries and colonizers, and three national spirit mediums are believed to have prophesied about the coming of Western cultures. The leader and most influential among the three was a woman named Nehanda, who is known as the founder of the

---

11. Canaan Sodindo Banana, *The Church and the Struggle for Zimbabwe: From the Program to Combat Racism to Combat Theology* (Gweru, Zimbabwe: Mambo, 1996).
12. A good example of this is found in Mai Chaza, a healer and a shaman who later founded her own Independent Church specifically for healing purposes. Her story is well documented by Banana in *The Church and the Struggle for Zimbabwe,* 96–110.

independent Zimbabwe and is hailed as a spiritual prophetess and hero in Zimbabwe politics.[13]

In the school room, in parliaments, and in shrines, Africans always carry their religion for protection and success.[14] Thus, a shaman functions to bring salvation or wholeness to every aspect of community life. Like Jesus in the Gospel of Mark, a shaman plays a crucial role in human life; he or she confers authority on the village headman, heals infertility, and blesses every undertaking in the economic and political spheres. A shaman's healing differs from scientific medicine; it is holistic.

In Mark, Jesus' healing is basically holistic in that at every stage Jesus acknowledges the relationship between the spirit and the body of those whom he healed. In relation to healing, Jesus absolves the sick of guilt ("Your sins are forgiven" [Mark 2:5]), and in another healing event Jesus restores responsibility and status (10:52; cf. John 8:11). Even though Jesus was not a woman, it is nevertheless fitting to draw a shamanic parallel between healers in the African contexts and Mark's worldview. With this brief religious history, I will now discuss and analyze Jesus the shaman in the Mark 7:24-37.

Jesus Christ the Shaman/*N'anga* in Mark 7:24-37

The religious culture reflected in the Gospel of Mark is inescapably concerned with the forces of the universe—forces that could be dealt with only by a medicine specialist. In other words, Mark's evangelical environment was probably imbued with such ideas as the evil eye or witchcraft. Whether the evil spirits were there or not, religion was viewed as nothing but the awareness of and reaction against our dependence on the unfathomable scramble of energies coming out of the universe. Humanity seems to be nothing but marionettes, pulled here and there without their knowledge by invisible forces. It is at this point that the magician enters the picture. In a transitional culture such as the Greco-Roman, a religious functionary like Asclepius, who operated as a crisis manager, became a necessity in the lives of ordinary people. This role Jesus also was able to fulfill.

---

13. Edison Zvobgo, *The Struggle for Zimbabwe* (Harare: Zimbabwe Publishing, 1981), 66–77.
14. John S. Mbiti, *African Religions and Philosophy* (New York: Anchor, 1970), 2–3.

Mark records eight healing episodes, four exorcisms, and one raising from the dead. These stories are not peculiar to Mark but rather were common to his audience. While the genre of Mark 7:24-37 can be defined as exorcism, the language of the supplicant (the Syro-Phoenician woman) makes it a healing story, in which Jesus is portrayed as a popular medicine healer. In this context, Jesus enters the house; he wants to remain anonymous (v. 24) but is quickly noticed by people who are probably used to healers visiting their villages. The story reveals Jesus as a religious folk healer whose power heals and casts out demons to restore people to health and to a right relationship with society. In other words, Jesus enters a village where disease and misfortune are everyday religious experiences, and, as a medicine figure, he plays the crucial role of healing the sick.

In Africa, healing can be initiated either by a woman or by a man, and in the Gospel story the woman initiates the healing by approaching Jesus. She falls down at his feet as a sign of affirmation and respect for the sacred medicine specialist. Religiously, this woman has experience with shamans and she presents a petition on behalf of her daughter. She desires that the demon be cast out of her daughter, and she communicates her cultural and religious belief that the sacred specialist—Jesus—has the power to heal. It is probably true that the woman had some experiences with the cult of Asclepius or other healing specialists, and she saw the same powers in Jesus.

Thus, we can place Markan healing stories within the Greco-Roman healing and exorcism tradition. The story draws us further into other healing and exorcism experiences, especially the healing of a deaf man (7:31-37). The key character in this pericope is Jesus, the healer, who performs a ritual of healing. The ritual of removing the patient from the crowd is a common feature in healing practices in African traditional religion. The purpose is to give much time and personal attention to the patient, which enables the healer to penetrate deep into the psychological state of the patient.

The magical elements in this story persuade readers to contextualize these healing stories as part of an oral culture. Suffering, misfortune, and deafness are all caused by mystical powers as far as traditional societies are concerned. As long as people see sickness and misfortune as religious experiences, the shaman will continue to exist and thrive. Therefore in Mark, Jesus occupies a central shamanic role: he heals Peter's mother-in-law by grasping her hand and raising her up, and the leper with a touch of his hand (1:31, 41).

The saliva and water from the mouth of a sacred specialist are believed to possess healing powers, and thus Jesus' saliva is used as healing medicine. In Asclepius's testimonies, we read the story of a sacred dog whose saliva was used to heal a boy from Aegina. The boy had a growth on the neck, and when he came to Asclepius, one of the sacred dogs healed him by touching the growth with its tongue.[15]

The mixture of Jesus' saliva and a gesture of looking upward indicate a magical spell. Most Shona *n'angas* consult other higher diviners when faced with a serious illness. In fact, the man whom Jesus healed was perhaps believed to be under a magical spell. The statement that "the bond of his tongue was untied" implies that someone, probably out of jealousy, had cast a spell on this man. The verb used to describe his release from this spell is "loosened," meaning that the world of Jesus' ministry was aware of spells. In entering this culture of magic, sickness, and healing, Jesus was most likely viewed as a medicine specialist. In any case, the sickness of the man was solved by a sacred specialist (Jesus), as is the case in various testimonies to the healings and miraculous powers of Asclepius.

Like any other shaman, Jesus' popularity and identity cannot be kept secret as Mark wants us to assume. Instead, his healing stories are heard by those in need of healing, and many sick people are brought to Jesus. This is how a medicine specialist functions in traditional cultures. It is striking to notice that after Jesus raised Jairus's daughter, people were able to talk about salvation. In the Gospels as in African traditional religions, every healing concludes with an acclamation, as way of acknowledging salvation (Matt 14: 33; Mark 15:39). People can also sing hymns as a way of acknowledging the supernatural power of a shaman and consequently the divine power of God. In Wisdom 10:20–21, God is praised because of his defending hand whose power and wisdom opened the mouth of the mute and loosened the tongues of those who were not able to speak. Thus the healing we see Jesus perform in Mark 7 evokes God's power to heal; celebrating the healing involves praising God.

We may conclude this essay by summarizing a few major points. African Christians are aware of mystical powers in the universe. The source of this mystical power is ultimately from God, and is given to certain individuals

---

15. Edelstein and Edelstein, *Asclepius,* 234–35.

as a gift. In recent years, especially after independence, African Christians began to trust clergy with the ability to heal and ward off evil forces and sickness. For most Africans, the universe is not a static place but a dynamic living planet in which God directs everything. God has absolute control over it and the medicine specialists display their access to God in various ways, such as the ability to diagnose and prescribe herbs. Similarly, in Mark Jesus is portrayed as a miracle worker and a charismatic magician, acclaimed as the agent of the divine eschatological fulfillment.

Therefore, it is not a surprise that African Christians carry the Bible wherever they go and use it as a charm for protective purposes. Thus, Africans have various images and identities of Jesus that are not found in the Western world. This image makes a contextualized reading of Mark and the entire Bible possible.

CHAPTER 2

Exorcism or Healing? A Korean Preacher's Rereading of Mark 5:1-20

Sejong Chun

Shamanism is a paradoxical sociocultural reality in modern Korean society: "necessary but also despised."[1] Shamanism and shamanic rituals are still an important part of modern Koreans' lives. Some want to get advice from shamans for important events of their lives, such as moving or a wedding. Others hope to know the reasons for their misfortunes, such as illness among their family members, and possible solutions for them. The wide use of the Internet enables Koreans, especially younger generations, to contact shamans more easily by using websites designed for shamanic services and information.[2] Many Koreans, however, have despised shamanic rituals and shamans, especially from the time of the Chosun dynasty (1392–1897), whose main ruling philosophy was Neo-Confucianism. During that period, shamans belonged to the lowest social class,[3] and it was strictly prohibited

---

1. Chongho Kim, *Korean Shamanism: The Cultural Paradox* (Aldershot, Hants, England: Ashgate, 2003), 1.

2. For example, there is an Internet newspaper for shamans and their clients called "The Korea Shaman News." See http://www.musoknews.co.kr/.

3. In the early years of the Chosun dynasty (1392–1897), there were basically two different social groups: freeborn commoners (*yangin*) and lowborns (*cheonmin*). However, further stratification soon led to four distinctive classes: the elite (*yangban*), the professional class (*jungin*); the commoners (*sangmin*), and those who made up the largest group, and the lowest class (*cheonmin*). The *cheonmin* was made up of "house slaves, servants and maids, butchers, leather tanners, executioners, or shamans," who were engaged in "dirty and impure occupations." Hagen Koo, "The Korean Stratification System: Continuity and Change," in *Modern*

for the ruling elite, *yangban*, to get involved in any shamanic activity.[4] This culturally biased attitude toward shamanism and shamans is still very common among modern Koreans. For many Koreans, the expression "You are very shamanistic," may convey negative connotations, such as "you are like a savage."[5] In this perspective, shamanism has a contradictory position in modern Korean society.

Korean Christianity, which has become a very popular and powerful religion in Korean society during the last several decades, also has a paradoxical relationship with shamanism. Some accuse Christianity of being prejudiced against shamanism and even of persecuting shamans. In fact, many conservative Korean Christians regard shamanic rituals as something related to evil spirits, especially Satan. Others, ironically, argue that Christian rituals resemble those of shamanism and that preachers provide the same services that shamans do:[6] for example, Christian clergy might perform an exorcism rite using an ecstatic technique such as "fervent prayer."

In this essay, I attempt, as a Korean preacher, to understand the story of the Gerasene demoniac in Mark 5:1-20 from the Korean cultural perspective. I particularly try to create a constructive dialogue between the Markan narrative and the story of Korean shamanic ritual performed for Muno in Soy village in South Korea. The dialogue will help me read the Markan story differently from the existing interpretations by finding new "meaning potentials" in it. Before creating the dialogue, let me articulate my own context for reading.

Life Context and Intercontextual Dialogue

Biblical scholars have noted the importance of readers' contexts in their interpretations. One of them is Brian Blount, who believes that "language is potential" and creates choice: "Words . . . do not convey meaning: they convey meaning potential. That potential, that opportunity for choice, becomes

Korean Society: Its Development and Prospect, ed. Hyuk-Rae Kim and Bok Song (Berkeley: Regents of the University of California, 2007), 38.
4. See Park Ji-won's *yangban jeon* (The Tale of a *yangban*) in Chung Chung-wha, ed., *Korean Classical Literature* (London/New York: Kegan Paul International, 1989), 41.
5. About Koreans' negative attitude toward shamanism, see Kim, *Korean Shamanism,* 161–63.
6. Ibid., 37.

meaningful only when it is performed and accessed in a certain context."[7] In his book *Cultural Interpretation: Reorienting New Testament Criticism,* Blount insightfully articulates the impact of the sociocultural/linguistic contexts of readers on their interpretation of the text: "it must recognize that the language in the text can legitimately have different meanings for persons from distinct sociological and linguistic backgrounds."[8] According to him, "the social context of the reader determines which potential meaning is most appropriate."[9] As Blount argues, the social locations of readers often lead them to see a portion of large "meaning potentials" ignored by those who are in different contexts.

One of my main sociocultural contexts is my Korean culture, as a part of broader Asian cultures. In the book *Discovering the Bible in the Non-Biblical World,* Kwok Pui-lan, a leading Asian feminist theologian, proposes "dialogical imagination" as a new way of biblical interpretation, which is the result of her close observation of what other Asian theologians are doing.[10] She nicely articulates the challenges that Asian Christians are facing: "Asian Christians are heirs to both the biblical story and to our own story as Asian people, and we are concerned to bring the two into dialogue with one another." According to her, dialogical imagination "involves ongoing conversation among different religious and cultural traditions. . . . Dialogical imagination attempts to bridge the gaps of time and space, to create new horizons, and to connect the disparate elements of our lives into a meaningful whole." She suggests that there can be mainly two ways of combining "the insights of biblical themes with those found in Asian resources." One is to use "Asian myths, legends, and stories in biblical reflection" and the other is to use "the social biography of the people as a hermeneutical key to understand both our reality and the message of the Bible."[11] Kwok Pui-lan's idea of dialogue between biblical stories and Asian stories helps me find a way of reading the biblical text as an Asian believer.

---

7. Brian K. Blount, *Can I Get a Witness? Reading Revelation through African American Culture* (Louisville: Westminster John Knox, 2005), 2 (emphasis in original).

8. Brian K. Blount, *Cultural Interpretation: Reorienting New Testament Criticism* (Minneapolis: Fortress Press, 2005), 6.

9. Ibid., 16.

10. Kwok Pui-lan, *Discovering the Bible in the Non-Biblical World,* Bible and Liberation Series (Maryknoll, N.Y.: Orbis, 1995), 12.

11. Ibid., 12, 13.

I want to employ "intercontextual dialogue"[12] for my reading of Mark 5:1-20. Following Blount, I believe that socioeconomic, geopolitical, and cultural contexts of readers have a significant impact on their interpretations of biblical texts. However, the "meaning potentials" of biblical texts can be understood through a "genuine dialogue" between the contexts of readers and those of biblical texts. What I mean by "intercontextual" is a way of approaching two different contexts—a current situation and that of a biblical narrative—by reading one context through the insights of the other and vice versa. Therefore, intercontextual dialogue is an attempt to create a genuine conversation between the two different contexts.

I hope to make it clear that my focus on "context" does not mean to exclude "text," because "text" is a product of "context" in the sense that the latter shapes the former and "context" becomes "text." Tat-siong Benny Liew's explanation is helpful. He argues, "a so-called 'context' is also a text," because it is always "textualized" by sign systems. For him, the distinction between the text and the context becomes blurry.[13] That is why Benny Liew uses the term *context* with parenthesis: "(con)text reminds us visually that we are dealing with more than literary texts, and that literary texts are products of socio-political forces. At the same time, the parenthesis signifies that so-called 'contexts' are always already textualized and constructed, and that literary texts also have power to produce non-literary effects."[14] My intercontextual dialogue therefore includes various "texts" and "contexts."

In intercontextual dialogue, readers bring their own perspectives, issues, and sociocultural preunderstandings to their readings of biblical texts in order to formulate a dialogue with them. Through the dialogue, biblical passages

---

12. I borrow the term "intercontextual" from Tat-siong Benny Liew and Jean Kyoung Kim. See Tat-siong Benny Liew, *Politics of Parousia: Reading Mark Inter(con)textually*, Biblical Interpretation Series 42 (Leiden/Boston: Brill, 1999), 22–45; and Jean Kyoung Kim, *Women and Nation: An Intercontextual Reading of the Gospel of John from a Postcolonial Feminist Perspective*, Biblical Interpretation Series 69 (Leiden/Boston: Brill, 2004), 33–60.

13. Liew, *Politics of Parousia*, 25–27. Liew's idea of the blurry distinction between "text" and "context" is somewhat related to post-structuralists' understanding of the distinction between the text and the meaning. Terry Eagleton argues that there is no obvious distinction between signifiers and signifieds (*Literary Theory: An Introduction* [Minneapolis: University of Minnesota Press, 1983], 128).

14. Liew, *Politics of Parousia*, 33.

also interpret readers and their "texts" and "contexts." In intercontextual dialogue, therefore, readers and the text are dialogue partners who read each other.

I as a "flesh-and-blood reader"[15] attempt to read Mark 5:1-20 from my sociocultural context: a preacher in a Korean immigrant church in the United States. As Kwok Pui-lan suggests, I as a Korean believer hope to use the two different religious and cultural traditions that I have inherited: Christianity and shamanism. As a test case, I hope to create a genuine dialogue between Mark's narrative in 5:1-20 and the story of the shamanic ritual *kut*, performed for a boy named Muno.

Korean Shamanic Ritual and Its Characteristics

Chongho Kim, in his book *Korean Shamanism: The Cultural Paradox,* provides interesting observations on a Korean shamanic ritual, *kut,* performed for a fifteen-year-old boy named Muno in Soy village during his fieldwork in 1994–95. According to Kim's description, Muno was suffering from mental illness. His mother was unable to control him. He caused many problems in the village, including breaking into a neighbor's house and trying to rape a girl.[16] Muno became ill when he was around the same age at which his sister died. Muno's mental illness was regarded as a result of spirit involvement, possibly that of his sister, who died in misfortune.

> Muno often said that there was a baby in his body. Because he often repeated this nonsense, people interpreted it as spirit-possession. Also, on a couple of occasions, Muno, after running away from home at night, was found at his sister's burial place. Muno's mother was able to sense this connection as well.[17]

The shaman in the village also identified Muno's sister's anger toward her family as "the principal reason for Muno's illness." Muno's mother decided

---

15. Fernando F. Segovia argues that a "flesh-and-blood reader" is "always positioned and interested, socially and historically conditioned and unable to transcend such conditions" (*Decolonizing Biblical Studies: A View from the Margins* [Maryknoll, N.Y.: Orbis, 2004], 30).
16. Chongho Kim, *Korean Shamanism,* 42.
17. Ibid., 38.

to hold a very expensive shamanic ritual for him.[18] Kim describes the ritual in detail with his own interpretation:

> In the process of shamanic consultation concerning Muno's ill-ness, Muno's deceased sister emerged as the spirit the most strongly involved in the illness. She had died eight years earlier of an abdominal disorder. At that time her family was very poor, and the current medical insurance scheme for peasants had not yet commenced. Furthermore she was female, and the youngest daughter among three girls in her family. Consequently, her parents did not pay full attention to her illness: her father did not even permit her to visit a medical doctor at the initial stage of her illness. She was taken to a doctor only when she was suffering from such severe stomach pain that she doubled over and collapsed to the floor in agony, unable to rise. Her mother struggled a long distance to the doctor carry-ing the girl on her back, but medical intervention was too late and insufficient. Furthermore, she died unmarried and, because her life was incomplete, she had no right to a proper funeral. This resulted in her not receiving any *chesa* offering rites after death. Her parents buried her on the mountainside and did not even provide a tomb for her. . . . The first procedure was to invoke the spirit of Muno's sister. A shaman took this role and danced. It did not take long. As soon as the shaman became possessed, the spirit started to cry and shout, "Mommy, my resentment was so great that I had to annoy Muno. I could not bear your happiness. Don't you remember how badly you treated me! You didn't take me to the doctor even when I was crying from pain." In another session of the *kut*, a Spirit Stick was used. Muno's mother held it and was possessed. . . . During the possession, the mother was hit many times on her head and face by the Stick— or by the spirit of her deceased daughter with the Stick—although she was holding it herself. The shamans and participants consoled the spirit, "now your parents regret the matter thoroughly. Here is a nice wedding prepared for you. Forget the past and go to Heaven." However, Muno's sister was not easy to persuade, and it took the sha-mans quite a while before they could commence the main wedding

---

18. Muno's mother spent 1.75 million *won* (about $1,700), while she paid only 2,000 *won* (about $2) for psychiatric consultation and one month's medication for him (C. Kim, *Korean Shamanism*, 20–21).

ceremony. Eventually the wedding began with a bow between the miniature bride and the bridegroom. And then the shamans laid the two down on a mat and put a blanket over them. This represented the wedding night for Muno's deceased sister, who had suffered from a great deal of misfortune. My interpretation of this ritual is that the wedding was intended to make the life of Muno's sister complete, by resolving her attachment to This World through reaching a mutual understanding with her. Because of her inauspicious death, she had been doomed to wander as a ghost between two worlds, the world of the living and the world of the dead. This was why Muno's family and neighbours, and the shamans, believed that she was the cause of the misfortune which Muno and his family were suffering. Shamanism is a powerful theory of misfortune in Korean society, and, in the shamanic framework, a matter of misfortune does not occur independently, but is related to the misfortune of one or more wandering spirits.[19]

The shamanic ritual for Muno provides several interesting insights for our reading of the Markan story. First, there is "spirit talk" between the spirit of Muno's sister and living ones. Through the talk, the dead one and the living ones can communicate with each other for "mutual understanding." This "spirit talk" is a very unique phenomenon in the Korean shamanic ritual. Kim argues, "Among many forms of ritual existing in Korean society, *kut* is the only one in which spirits are enabled to speak. In other forms of ritual, spirits are silent and inactive."[20] He emphasizes this phenomenon as one of the most unique characteristics of the Korean shamanic ritual:

> In this ritual, shamans talked a lot with, or on behalf of, spirits. One of the shamans even provided her body for the spirit to be able to speak out about her wishes. They even cried for the spirit's misfortune. The shamanic healing ritual held for Muno was an attempt to heal the relationship of misfortune between him and the spirit of Muno's deceased sister through arriving at a mutual understanding. To achieve this mutual understanding it was necessary for the spirit to be able to speak.

19. C. Kim, *Korean Shamanism*, 38–39.
20. Ibid., 35.

The essential element in the Korean shamanic ritual is not ecstasy, but spirit talk.[21]

Second, the spirit-possession of Muno is related to Muno's sister's misfortune. Several factors are related to her misfortune. The first is that, as Kim mentions, her life is ended "incompletely": dying unmarried. In the traditional Korean culture, marriage is so important and is regarded as a way of becoming a social adult. Muno's sister, however, died unmarried, which means that she was not fully qualified either for a proper funeral or for a *chesa* ritual, one of the most common Confucian rituals to honor deceased ancestors. Shamans prepared a "ghost marriage" to solve the problem of the "incomplete life" of Muno's sister. Through the ghost marriage she could become a "social adult" and also be qualified for the *chesa* ritual. The second factor is related to her family's economic situation and her gender.[22] She was angry about her family's mistreatment of her, when she severely suffered from the pain. The mistreatment seemed to originate from the fact that the family was poor and that she was the youngest of the three daughters. Poverty and being a woman were the most common reasons for many Koreans' *han*. According to Suh Nam-dong, who laid the foundation of Korean *minjung* theology, *han* is "an accumulation of suppressed and condensed experience of oppression."[23]

It is commonly believed that in a patriarchal Confucian society such as the Chosun dynasty, being born a woman meant *han*. Kim articulates that Muno's parents' ignorance of their daughter's pain is related to her gender ("she was female") and the birth order in the family ("the youngest daughter among three girls in her family"). In Confucian culture, which often formulates a patriarchal and hierarchical social structure and worldview, the youngest daughter would be the weakest one in the family. In addition, her family was poor, which means that their limited material resources would rarely be used for the youngest daughter. Furthermore, in the ritual she is not

---

21. Ibid., 39–40.
22. On the subject of gender inequality in the traditional Korean culture, see Seung-Kyung Kim, "Family, Gender, and Sexual Inequality," in *Modern Korean Society: Its Development and Prospect,* ed. Hyuk-Rae Kim and Bok Song (Berkeley: Regents of the University of California, 2007), 131–57.
23. Suh Nam-dong, "Towards a Theology of Han," in *Minjung Theology: People as the Subjects of History,* ed. Commission on Theological Concerns of the Christian Conference of Asia (Maryknoll, N.Y.: Orbis, 1981), 64.

identified with her own name. She is identified only as "Muno's sister," indicating her relation to a male figure in the family. As the youngest daughter, she was not called by her own name. Because of these circumstances, Muno's sister must have died in misfortune; in other words, she died with *han*.

As Kim hints, this unfortunate death seemed to cause the soul of Muno's sister to wander around as a ghost. Many Koreans have believed that ghosts are the spirits of the deceased who could not enter "Heaven" because of their *han*. They are believed to wander around between the world of the living and that of the dead and to cause harm to the living ones by possessing them. The ghosts are often called "restless spirits." [24] They are different from household gods and ancestors who would be honored by *chesa* ritual. The series of misfortunes that Muno's sister experienced must have made her poor soul wander around between the two worlds and finally possess her brother as a medium to express her *han*. In this perspective, as Kim notes, shamanic ritual is a "cultural response to the experience of misfortune." [25] Then how can those insights from the Korean shamanic ritual be related to our reading of the Markan story?

Different Understandings of the Markan Story

The Markan narrative of the Gerasene demoniac has been regarded as a "tale," a "miracle story," or a "healing story." The most popular opinion, however, is to understand it as an "exorcism story," in which Jesus exorcises evil spirits. [26] Several scholars pay attention to the "development of traditions" within the text by proposing their own history of the text [27] (which is beyond my concern in this essay). I will briefly examine scholars' different understandings and hope to provide my intercontextual interpretation by articulating new "meaning potentials."

24. Laurel Kendall, *Shamans, Housewives, and Other Restless Spirits: Women in Korean Ritual Life*, Studies of the East Asian Institute (Honolulu: University of Hawaii Press, 1985), 86–110.

25. C. Kim, *Politics of Parousia*, 39.

26. For various understandings of the "genre" of the story, see Adela Yarbro Collins, *Mark: A Commentary* (Hermeneia; Minneapolis: Fortress Press, 2007), 266.

27. Rudolf Pesch suggests a four-stage development ("The Markan Version of the Healing of the Gerasene Demoniac," *Ecumenical Review* 21 [1971]: 349–76). See also Robert H. Gundry, *Mark: A Commentary on His Apology for the Cross* (Grand Rapids: Eerdmans, 1993), 266.

One interpretation of the story is that it shows Jesus' superiority over evil powers. Scholars who prefer this option attempt to connect this narrative with Jesus' silencing of the violent sea (4:35-41) in the previous chapter. In that story, Jesus calms the storm with a simple order: "Be still" (4:39). They argue further that the uncontrollable conditions and the extraordinary strength of the demoniac rhetorically emphasize the greater power of Jesus who can control "the uncontrollable." Through these two stories, Mark is presenting Jesus as "the powerful one" who is the central character of the two stories.[28] From this perspective, the demoniac's action of "bowing down before Jesus" (5:6) and the spirits' revealing Jesus' identity as "Son of the Most High God" (5:7) should be understood as an acknowledgment of Jesus' superiority.[29]

A second option is that this story reveals a severe battle between God's power and the destructive power of evil spirits. According to this interpretation, the demoniac's encountering Jesus should be understood as "the confrontation of powers."[30] The power of the unclean spirits also implies the power of death.[31] The demoniac runs to Jesus not to greet him but "to get rid of him."[32] The spirits' revealing Jesus' identity is an attempt "to exorcise Jesus out of exorcising" them.[33] Mark shows that unclean spirits are already worried about Jesus' destruction of them (1:24), and the worry becomes reality in the current story: "The destruction of the pigs perhaps indicates the destruction of the unclean spirits."[34] In this understanding, the story shows that the confrontation of the powers is concluded with the victory of God's power over the evil powers.

A third interpretation is that this story is to show Jesus' boundary-crossing ministry. From this perspective, the focus of the story is on the issue of purity/impurity or clean/unclean. Important terms are the territory of *Gerasa* (Gentile region), *unclean spirit,* dwelling among *tombs,* and a large herd of

28. John R. Donahue and Daniel J. Harrington, *The Gospel of Mark,* Sacra Pagina 2 (Collegeville, Minn.: Liturgical, 2002), 170.

29. Herman C. Waetjen, *A Reordering of Power: A Sociopolitical Reading of Mark's Gospel* (Minneapolis: Fortress Press, 1989), 114–15.

30. Gundry, *Mark,* 248.

31. Ibid., 249.

32. Ibid.

33. Ibid., 250.

34. Morna D. Hooker, *The Gospel according to Saint Mark,* Black's New Testament Commentaries (London: A. & C. Black, 1991), 141.

swine, which, from the Jewish cultural perspective, represent impurity. Jesus enters that "impure territory" and conducts his ministry among the unclean by healing a man who is possessed by unclean spirits. In this understanding, the story is about God's kingdom, which tears down earthly barriers. Through Jesus' kingdom ministry, the traditional sociocultural boundaries between the Jews and the Gentiles are overcome,[35] and the Gentiles begin to join in God's kingdom. The recovered man's proclamation in the Ten Cities indicates the beginning of the boundary-crossing Gentile mission.

A fourth approach is to see this story from the sociopolitical perspective. Ched Myers, who initiated a so-called sociopolitical interpretation, wants to see the "symbolic" connotations of the story. He argues that the story is filled with military images: *Legion* refers to a division of Roman soldiers; the term *herd* (5:11) is not proper for pigs but is often used to indicate "a band of military recruits"; Jesus' "dismissing them" (5:13) is a military command, and the pigs' "charging" into the lake (5:13) "suggests troops rushing into battle."[36] For Myers, the demon represents the Roman powers, and the demoniac "represents collective anxiety over Roman imperialism." Therefore, the story is about Jesus' symbolic action of liberation for the colonized from the colonial oppression of the Roman powers.[37]

Richard A. Horsley develops the sociopolitical implications of the story with the help of Frantz Fanon's social-psychological insights. Horsley argues, "not only that the demon's name is symbolic, indicating that the Roman army is the cause of the possessed man's violent and destructive behavior, but that the man also is symbolic of the whole society that is possessed by the demonic imperial violence to their persons and communities."[38] He believes further that the demon possession not only is closely related to the Roman military violence and economic exploitation but also represents the embodied anti-Roman resentment of the colonized.[39] In this perspective, the unclean spirits represent the violent Roman domination, and the man who is

---

35. Pheme Perkins, "The Gospel of Mark," in *The New Interpreter's Bible,* 12 vols. (Nashville: Abingdon, 1995), 8:583–84.

36. Ched Myers, *Binding the Strong Man: A Political Reading of Mark's Story of Jesus* (Maryknoll, N.Y.: Orbis, 1988), 191.

37. Ibid., 192–93.

38. Richard A. Horsley, *Hearing the Whole Story: The Politics of Plot in Mark's Gospel* (Louisville: Westminster John Knox, 2001), 140.

39. Ibid., 145–46.

possessed represents the horrible situation of the colonized. Therefore, Jesus' exorcising the unclean spirits exemplifies the establishment of God's rule, the kingdom of God, by destroying "all the demonic forces,"[40] especially the Roman Empire.

John R. Donahue and Daniel J. Harrington, however, reject this understanding because they believe that the term *Legion* is "simply a colloquial expression for a large number of demons." They argue, "The problem with this socio-political explanation is that Jesus is not expelling Romans from Jewish lands, since Gerasa was a largely Greek city in the Decapolis and would not have considered the Roman military presence as oppressive as many Jews did."[41] Nevertheless, we do not know exactly about the role of the Roman military in the Greek city (whether they were oppressive or not). How the inhabitants of the city felt about the presence of the military forces would be another issue to consider.

A fifth possible understanding is to bring some insights of "social-psychological theories of mental illness" into the reading of the story. Paul Hollenbach proposes that various exorcism stories in Mark mean that Jesus, an exorcist, "helped people who had various kinds of mental or psychosomatic illnesses."[42] He argues that social tensions such as "class antagonisms rooted in economic exploitation [and] conflict between traditions" can cause mental illness. On the other hand, mental illness "can be seen as a socially acceptable form of oblique protest against, or escape from, oppressions."[43] Hollenbach applies his understanding of mental illness to the reading of the demoniac story:

> It is likely that the tension between his hatred for his oppressors and the necessity to repress this hatred in order to avoid dire recrimination drove him mad. But his very madness permitted him to do in a socially acceptable manner what he could not do as sane, namely, express his total hostility to the Romans; he did this by identifying the Roman legions with demons. His possession was thus at once both the result of

---

40. Ibid., 138.
41. Donahue and Harrington, *Gospel of Mark,* 166.
42. Paul W. Hollenbach, "Jesus, Demoniacs, and Public Authorities: A Socio-Historical Study," *Journal of the American Academy of Religion* 49, no. 4 (1981): 567.
43. Hollenbach, 573, 575.

oppression and an expression of his resistance to it. He retreated to an inner world where he could symbolically resist Roman domination.[44]

Hollenbach's interpretation is fascinating, because he suggests that the very action of the demoniac could be understood as a symbolic resistance to the Roman imperial rule. However, if the demoniac resists the colonial rule of the Roman Empire by his bizarre and violent actions permitted through his madness, what would be the meaning of Jesus' healing of the man's disease? Is Jesus helping the oppressive imperial system by getting rid of the cause of the madness, the unclean spirits, which is the power source of his resistance against it? Probably not.

These five different understandings, in my opinion, are "legitimate" by being grounded in the Markan texts and "plausible" by making hermeneutical sense. They also have various weaknesses, however, because they focus on a certain part of the text and emphasize specific "meaning potentials" while neglecting others. I hope to add another option for reading the Markan story. I will use the two characteristic factors that we observed in the Korean shamanic ritual for Muno: "spirit talk" and "dying with *han*."

Intercontextual Dialogue

My reading of the Gerasene demoniac's story begins with three questions: Why does Jesus have a dialogue with the spirits? Who are the spirits and why do they possess the man? and Why does Jesus allow their petitions? By answering these questions, I will propose my own interpretation.

We can find something very interesting and unique in this story, if we compare it with other "exorcism" stories in Mark: (story A) a man with unclean spirits in Capernaum (1:21-28); and (story B) a boy possessed by a spirit (9:14-29). [45]. In these two stories, Jesus rebukes the spirits and commands them directly to come out: In story A, Jesus orders the spirits to "be silent" first and then "come out" (1:25). In story B, Jesus first says, "I command you" and then "come out of him and never enter him again." In the present story, however, Jesus does not say to the spirits to "be quiet" or

---

44. Hollenbach, 581.
45. Another "exorcism" story appears in Mark 7:24-30. However, there is no direct encounter between Jesus and the spirit who possesses the daughter of the Syrophoenician woman.

command them to come out.[46] As Donahue and Harrington point out, "It is the only exorcism in which the explicit command to 'go out' is not issued but is simply reported."[47]

Instead of commanding them directly to leave, Jesus begins a short dialogue with them. Geoff R. Webb also believes that "significant dialogue" is "taking place between Jesus and the other characters."[48] The short dialogue between Jesus and the spirits includes five different verbal and nonverbal exchanges: (1) Jesus asks the spirits' name (5:9); (2) the spirits reveal their name (5:9); (3) they beg not to be driven away from the region (5:10); (4) they beg Jesus to send them into the swine and to allow them to enter into them (5:12); and (5) Jesus allows their petitions (5:13).

Now, let me respond to my first question, Why does Jesus have a dialogue with the spirits? Even though it is a short dialogue, Jesus asks their name and the spirits beg Jesus for two things—that he not drive them away from the region but allow them to enter into the swine. If the verb "beg" (*parakaleō*) is "used often of a request made by a person in need,"[49] the spirits may have some sort of need or desire. Jesus' first action is to ask their name. Many commentators argue that to know a demon's identity is to have power over it; it is therefore a "typical exorcistic technique."[50] Asking one's name, however, could be a sign of good intention: to know something deeply about the person, therefore to hear his or her story. Jesus' question about the spirits' name provides an opportunity for the spirits to talk about themselves and what they want. By asking the name, Jesus seems to encourage them to speak out instead of silencing them as he does in other "exorcism" stories. During the exchange, the spirits speak to Jesus about what they want, just as Muno's

---

46. Even though Jesus speaks to the demoniac and he replies, the primary partner of Jesus' conversation is not the man but the spirits.

47. Donahue and Harrington, *Gospel of Mark,* 169.

48. Geoff R. Webb, *Mark at the Threshold: Applying Bakhtinian Categories to Markan Characterisation,* Biblical Interprettion Series 95 (Leiden/Boston: Brill, 2008), 92. Mary Ann Tolbert also sees the interaction between Jesus and the spirits as a "conversation." See Tolbert, *Sowing the Gospel: Mark's World in Literary-Historical Perspective* (Minneapolis: Fortress Press, 1996), 167. However, some scholars try to understand this interaction as a "bargain" between the exorcist and the demons. See Joel Marcus, *Mark 1–8: A New Translation with Introduction and Commentary,* Anchor Bible 27 (New York: Doubleday, 2000), 351.

49. Donahue and Harrington, *Gospel of Mark,* 166.

50. Yarbro Collins, *Mark,* 268; Waetjen, *Reordering of Power,* 115; Hooker, *Saint Mark,* 143; and Marcus, *Mark,* 344.

sister communicated with the living ones in the shamanic ritual. "Spirit talk" is happening here.

Let us move on to the second question: Who are the spirits and why do they possess the man? During the dialogue, the spirits say that their name is "Legion," because they are many (5:9),[51] which means that they are a community, not just an individual. If they are a community, what kind of community are they? Many scholars believe, as articulated above, that the term *Legion* implies the Roman army. I partly agree with them; however, the term may not refer to a division of the Roman army,[52] but may imply the cause of the spirits' current restless condition.

The spirits say, "for we are many" (5:9). In the shamanic ritual for Muno, the spirit that possessed him was his sister who "died with *han.*" The poor economic situation of the family and her parent's neglectful attitude toward her, which possibly resulted from the oppressive patriarchal culture, contributed to her misfortune and let her die with *han.* In my own understanding, *han* is a deeply repressed and accumulated emotion of sorrow, resentment, and helplessness under the situation of oppression. If we bring this idea to the answer of the spirits, we may think that they are souls of people who "died with *han.*" The main cause of their *han* could be the imperial rule of the Roman Empire through its military force against the colonized.

Frantz Fanon's description of the situations of the colonized in his book *The Wretched of the Earth* is very helpful in terms of understanding the systematic oppression of the colonizers, which often creates repressed emotions of anger, resentment, despair, and mental illness. Fanon explains how the colonial world is split in two: "The settlers' town is a strongly built town, all made of stone and steel . . . a well-fed town, an easygoing town; its belly is always full of good things. The settlers' town is a town of white people, of foreigners." The village of the natives, however, is "a place of ill fame, peopled by men of evil repute . . . a hungry town, starved of bread, of meat, of shoes, of coal, of light . . . a town of niggers and dirty Arabs."[53] He describes the use of violence in colonial society: "In the colonies, the foreigner coming from

---

51. Yarbro Collins thinks that the spirits are "at least two thousand demons" (*Mark,* 268). Gundry argues that they are "over six thousand" (*Mark,* 251).

52. Myers, *Binding the Strong Man,* 191.

53. Frantz Fanon, *The Wretched of the Earth* (New York: Grove, 1968), 39.

another country imposed his rule by means of guns and machines."[54] Just as the ancient Roman Empire used its brutal military forces to control the colonized, so the modern colonizers rule the natives with guns and machines.

Fanon also articulates how imperial oppression contributes to the mental illness of the natives:

> In the period of colonization when it is not contested by armed resistance, when the sum total of harmful nervous stimuli overstep a certain threshold, the defensive attitudes of the native give way and they then find themselves crowding the mental hospitals. There is thus during this calm period of successful colonization a regular and important mental pathology which is the direct product of oppression.[55]

According to Fanon's description, the natives who suffer under the oppressive social structure of the colony often formulate a certain emotional mentality that is similar to *han*. In the shamanic ritual for Muno, his sister's death with *han* as the result of the oppressive sociocultural environment is closely related to the mental illness of Muno.

From this perspective, it seems possible to say that the unclean spirits are the souls of the colonized who suffered from the brutal violence of the Roman imperial force, Legion. Their name, Legion, refers to the cause of their death: they could have been abused and murdered by the Roman army, Legion. If that was the case, they must have died with *han,* like Muno's sister. That is why they possessed a man as a medium through whom they could "speak out" to the living ones about the reason for their death and what they want. That could also be why the demoniac lived among the tombs and mountains. In shamanic understanding, tombs and mountains are often regarded as the places for wandering ghosts. The demoniac howls like an animal because the *han* of the spirits is too big and deep to be expressed in human language. The demoniac's action of bruising himself with a stone could be understood as the self-blaming and self-hatred of the colonized.[56] Therefore, from the

---

54. Ibid., 40.
55. Ibid., 250–51.
56. It is striking to find many similarities between the demoniac in Mark and a twenty-two-year-old Algerian in Fanon's book who became completely alienated from his family and suffered from mental illness because of his guilty feeling for not joining in the revolutionary activity. Fanon describes the patient: "The patient [young Algerian] was an emaciated man in a complete state of aberration. His body was covered with bruises and

perspective of the shamanic ritual and Korean cultural understanding, the "unclean" spirits could be the souls of the people who died with *han* under the oppression of Roman imperialism.

Lastly, let me respond to the third question, Why does Jesus allow their petitions? As briefly mentioned above, Jesus allows the spirits to submit two petitions: not to drive them away from the region and to let them enter into the swine. After hearing their petitions, Jesus accedes to them. If the spirits are evil enemies that Jesus must destroy, as in the second interpretive option above, why does Jesus allow their requests? Is it because Jesus knows that allowing their petitions will lead them to complete destruction by drowning in the bodies of two thousand pigs? Does "drowning in the sea" (5:13) mean the death of the "unclean" spirits? Maybe not.

Then another question is necessary: Why do the spirits not want to leave the area?[57] Is the region a hometown of the unfortunate souls where their family members are still living? Probably so. They may not want to be separated totally from the place where they lived and from the people whom they loved. They may want to remain around their own families as "extended family members." In Korean traditional culture, ancestors are often regarded as a part of an "extended family" that protects and blesses the living ones, their descendants. The living ones honor them by offering the *chesa* ritual, which is performed annually on the night of the day when the ancestor passed away. Koreans who perform it often believe that the deceased ancestors come closer to their offspring in order to participate in the eating table prepared particularly for them. A bowl of steamed rice and soup with a spoon and a pair of chopsticks will be prepared on the table for each ancestor. During the *chesa* ritual, ancestors are understood to join in the meal as the extended family members.

It is very interesting that traditional African culture also shares similar understandings. According to Peter J. Paris, "in the African experience death was not viewed as separation from the living but merely a transition of the

---

two fractures of the jaw made all absorption of nourishment impossible. . . . For three hours he heard all sorts of insults coming from out of the night and resounding in his head: 'Traitor, traitor, coward . . . all your brothers who are dying . . . traitor . . . he shut himself up in complete darkness . . . acting on impulse "like a madman"'" (*Wretched of the Earth*, 273–74).

57. Marcus tries to explain that "[t]he demonic, unclean Romans, like imperialists everywhere, do not want to be dislodged from the land they have occupied" (*Mark*, 351).

soul from the body to the realm of spirit. Accordingly, the so-called departed one is never separated from the family but always present and treated with great reverence by the daily offering of libations." Therefore, the ancestors are the "living dead."[58] In this perspective, the spirits in the Markan story may want to live as "living dead" among their own family members. That may be why they do not want to leave the area.

However, as hinted in the shamanic ritual for Muno, wandering souls as ghosts cannot become ancestors or house gods. In order to be ancestors, they should go to "heaven." That is why the participants of the shamanic ritual said to the spirit, "Forget the past and go to heaven." The ghost wedding for Muno's sister and the "spirit talk" through which Muno's sister can communicate with living ones during the ritual are tools for helping her enter "heaven" and, as a result, be qualified for being a part of extended family members as an ancestor.

The spirits in the Markan story communicate with Jesus by revealing the reason for their unfortunate death—the Roman colonial army—and their desire to be with their family members. Now one more thing is necessary for them as restless ghosts to be ancestors: entering "heaven." This can be why they ask Jesus to allow them to enter into the swine. It is interesting that in Korean shamanic ritual *kut*, a pig is the most common animal that is used as an offering, either its head or its whole body, for the spirits. It is not quite clear why the pig is employed for shamanic ritual. However, a practicing shaman named Kum-Kang-Jung-Sa[59] explained to me that during *kut,* the offered pig functions as the animal that takes *han* of a ghost. The pig is used as a tool to solve the problem of *han* that the ghost carries. By giving *han* to the pig, the ghost now can go to *Jeo-Seung* (the next world, the world for the deceased). In the Markan story, Jesus allows the spirits to enter into the swine that rush into the sea. As mentioned briefly above, the swine's drowning in the sea is often believed to be the total destruction of evil spirits. However, Korean shamanic perspective helps us imagine that drowning in the sea could be the way for the restless spirits to enter the next world for "rest." If this is the case, the swine can

---

58. Peter J. Paris, *The Spirituality of African Peoples: The Search for a Common Moral Discourse* (Minneapolis: Fortress Press, 1995), 47.
59. International telephone conversation, October 8, 2008.

be understood as the vehicles for the unfortunate spirits to enter the place of rest for the dead.

Conclusion: From a Demoniac to a Preacher for Healing

After the spirits left for "rest," the man who was possessed by them and used by them as a medium for their communication with living ones is restored. He wants to be with Jesus. However, Jesus sends him to his previous friends and family members from whom he has been alienated. The man who ran to Jesus for help (5:6) is now running away from him (5:20) to proclaim what Jesus has done for him, the gospel. The demoniac now becomes a preacher. The demoniac who harmed himself and caused problems among the people is now healed and begins to "heal" the wounded community under the colonial forces by proclaiming the gospel and sharing his own story. He becomes a "wounded healer"[60] and witnesses to the divine healing that he has experienced.

My intercontextual reading of the Markan story, with insights from the Korean cultural perspective in general and from the shamanic ritual for Muno in particular, lead us to understand this text as a healing and exorcism story. It is an exorcism story in that the spirits that possessed a man left him and the man is released from the captivity. However, it is also a healing story in which two different characters are healed: the possessed man and the unfortunate spirits that possessed him. God's healing power in Jesus cures not only the living one but also the spirits that died with *han*.

---

60. Henri J. M. Nouwen, *The Wounded Healer: Ministry in Contemporary Society* (Garden City, N.Y.: Doubleday, 1972).

CHAPTER 3

Other People's Demons
Reading Mark's Demons in the Disbelieving West

Nicole Wilkinson Duran

Reading from This Dominant Place

In Paul Hollenbach's 1981 analysis of Mark 5:1-20, he boldly draws on Frantz Fanon to establish the relevance of the Roman colonial situation to interpretation. His essay is an object lesson for me, as a Western reader of the Bible, full of good intentions, at least in my own mind. As we will see below, Hollenbach at least occasionally makes Fanon far more patronizing of the colonized peasant than he really was. But the really telling passage for me is somewhere near Hollenbach's conclusion. The reason that the former demoniac now frightens the townspeople, Hollenbach says, is that, freed from the demons of oppression, the man has been transformed "from a passive 'Uncle Tom' to a threatening 'John Brown.'"[1] It sounds liberating; no doubt it sounded liberating to Hollenbach. But upon closer examination, we realize that "Uncle Tom" was a black character in white fiction, unintentionally iconic for passivity and subservience, but someone who never in fact existed. John Brown, on the other hand, was a real, white revolutionary, frightening and angering to white slave owners, in part because he was one of their own kind. In Hollenbach's analysis, then, the demoniac is transformed from the

---

1. Paul W. Hollenbach, "Jesus, Demoniacs, and Public Authorities: A Socio-historical Study," *Journal of the American Academy of Religion* 49, no. 4 (1981): 581.

passive black man conjured up in the white imagination into a historical, revolutionary white man.

This is my people, and this is the problem of my context. Even when we can acknowledge Western dominance and its aftermath, we remain blind to our own involvement in that dominance. In trying to imagine the Gerasene demoniac as being released from colonial oppression and becoming a liberated and even violent threat to the colonizer, we end up with a picture of the fictional passive native who becomes an idealized version of, well, us. So I begin a Western contextual reading, realizing that while few Westerners have set out to acknowledge the shaping influence of our Western context, many have tried to step out of that context, without success.

Reading Scripture from a Western place, and trying to do so with visible intentionality, seems, on the one hand, superfluous and possibly arrogant, and, on the other hand, intrinsically doomed. The Western context, after all, has dominated biblical studies for its first centuries of existence. Born in Europe, the discipline continues to be framed by European-American concerns. Its predominant questions—the Bible's historicity and origins and the identity of the historical Jesus, for example—have been Western questions, emerging from an individualist culture with a linear sense of time, one that is capable of viewing both story and community as negative forces. To lift up my context, then, is to rub salt in the wound inflicted by a history of Western dominance. Readers may be African, Asian, or Native American, but they are reading this article in my native language and have been forced to learn my cultural values in the process of their education. Rather than needing to learn more of the Western context, many non-Western readers would like to unlearn its more damaging assumptions, a desire with which I sympathize.

But some Westerners continue to read the Bible, although Christianity's beating heart now resides in the two-thirds world. When we in the West read the Bible, like all readers we read it from our context. To deny that I read as a product of the West would not only be a lie, but potentially a disguise (though it may not fool anyone) that replicates the very repressive dominance it seeks to avoid. The denial of our own context has continually characterized Western readings of the Bible, and that is exactly the problem.

Every culture makes itself invisible to its own people. Culture appears to those immersed in that culture not as a series of social choices and constructions—not as a culture—but simply as the natural order of things, as common sense, as the way things are. Bible readers from around the world may initially experience their own culture's view of the Bible as the only view, but they are quickly and often rudely disabused of this notion in the process of education. To the extent that the biblical education is Western, it will insist that the reader discard his or her own cultural understandings and take on those of the educated West. The reader then sees two different cultural readings (whether or not they are presented as such), emerging from two different cultural contexts. Only Western readers have been able to continue in their blissful belief that they read the Bible without context, that they have no cultural prejudices, that what they read is the Bible and not the Western Bible. Just as native speakers of English often find it unnecessary to learn a second language, Western biblical readers can read biblical studies all their lives without ever learning a non-Western perspective. And just as for many native speakers of English, to speak is to speak English, for many Western readers, to read the Bible is to read the Bible from a Western context and in Western interests.

Largely as a result of having dominated academic discourse, Westerners continue to struggle (or not) with the urge to see ourselves as free from boundaries, as universal; as civilized rather than Western. Propagating the idea that our aims and thoughts are not grounded in a particular place or body has been part of the imperialist agenda. We believe we are promoting development and democracy when in fact we are promoting Americanism; and that bit of imperialist self-deception is a basic part of our cultural context. For white Americans, at least, *other* people have interests and colors, religions and causes; white Americans simply are. The sense that we are the center of the world has bred a sense that we are the blank spot in the world's cultures; we are the "plain" version of humanity's varied flavors, and thus the norm from which all others deviate.[2]

My effort here is to read the story of the Gerasene demoniac from a Western context that recognizes itself as a context. Ironically, though, the

---

2. I once worked conducting phone surveys in which I had to ask the participants' ethnic background. I asked one woman, "When I come to the name of the group that best describes you, please stop me: Caucasian, African American, Hispanic, Asian. . . ." She interrupted, "Oh no, honey, I'm just plain American." The response always struck me as a classic summation of white American identity: plain, without the flavors or colors added.

context from which I read is characterized by the above-mentioned lack of awareness of itself as a context. As ancient Israelite society was characterized by a concern for boundaries, bodily and social, American society likes to think of itself as disregarding ethnic and social boundaries. We are, in our own minds, a melting pot in which dividing membranes between groups happily dissolve, leaving us simply human and not American or Western or anything at all. Individuals should be individuals, in my culture, and not representatives of their culture, class, or gender. In order to read consciously from my context, then, from within my culture, class, and gender, I have to read against my context—against at least its insistence on being invisible.

Western Culture and Its Demons

In my white American, educated, and Protestant context, we do not believe in demons. Certainly, there are people in the West, particularly in the United States, who do believe in demons. But to believe in demons in the United States is to be marginalized by the dominant culture. To say from within the dominant American culture that you or someone you know is *possessed* by demons is to risk being institutionalized. For my own segment of American culture, there are few beliefs more anathema than the belief in demon possession.

White Americans like to see boundaries between groups disappear, but individuals should be firmly bounded. Individuals should be self-contained and not permeable to other subjects. Americans prefer to live in separate nuclear families, and we stand physically at a farther distance from one another than other peoples of the world—keeping four to seven feet between ourselves and strangers, while even Western Europeans keep half that distance.[3] Not only do we prefer that people should be separate, self-contained subjects, but we find it hard to see people any other way. The sense that every individual stands apart, literally, and can and must control his or her own fate, with the help of reason and hard work, is an essential tenet of Western culture. A possessed person is out of control and could not be expected to exert such control; therefore a possessed person simply does not exist.

3. Nina Brown, "Edward T. Hall, Proxemic Theory," http://www.csiss.org/classics/content/13 (accessed October 26, 2009).

In this dismissal of demons and possession, my segment of American society is at one with the broader Western culture that has dominated biblical studies and indeed the academy in general. Since its inception, biblical studies has read the Gospel's demons as something other than what the text assumes them to be. Rationalist interpretations in the nineteenth century saw biblical demon possession as misunderstood epilepsy or mental illness (indeed epilepsy was sometimes conflated with mental illness in the nineteenth century). These interpretations still hold sway with many Westerners, while others have refined the psychiatric diagnosis to schizophrenia, addiction, or multiple personality disorder.[4] Since Hollenbach, some biblical critics have begun to read demon possession as at once a symptom of colonial oppression and an oblique, allowable form of protest against the colonial power.[5]

Hollenbach and, more recently, Richard Horsley follow Frantz Fanon in seeing the phenomenon of demon possession as both an expression of the damage done by the colonial presence and an allowable, largely unconscious protest against that presence. The possession vividly embodies in the individual the pain and conflict that the empire causes to the society. Both Fanon and biblical critics influenced by his analysis assume that the demons themselves have no objective reality and that the people experiencing demon possession have been "mystified" by their own societies, so that the truths of colonized experience are hidden from them. The conflict is expressed through possession because other outlets, words, or actions of protest or resistance are unavailable; even a conscious sense that the oppression is wrong may be socially untenable. As Mary Keller points out, this kind of reading of possession phenomena attributes to the possessed "a kind of vulnerable, brute intelligence, in contrast to the scholar's critical, formal consciousness. By bringing their critical consciousness to the events, scholars can drag those bodies out of the obfuscation of their possessions, making sense of 'them' for 'us.' "[6]

---

4. Harry C. Kiely, "The Demon of Addiction: Jesus Answers Our Cry for Spiritual Deliverance: A Bible Study on Mark 5:1-20," *Sojourners* 25 (1996): 26–29; J. Keir Howard, "New Testament Exorcism and Its Significance Today," *Expository Times* 96, no. 4 (1985): 105–9.
5. Hollenbach; see also Richard Dormandy, "The Expulsion of Legion: A Political Reading of Mark 5:1-20," *Expository Times* 111, no. 10 (2000): 335–37; and Richard A. Horsley, " 'My Name Is Legion': Demon Possession and Exorcism as Responses to Roman Domination," paper presented at the Society of Biblical Literature annual meeting, 2007.
6. Mary Keller, *The Hammer and the Flute: Women, Power, and Spirit Possession* (Baltimore: Johns Hopkins University Press, 2002), 96.

What each of these explanations circumvents or translates is the reality of the demon or demons. Western thought cannot accept that there might in fact be a spiritual force (as opposed to a chemical or sociological force) acting upon this person. The West has been distinguished by its veneration of the (Western) subject. My predecessors and cultural ancestors believed in the ultimate control of the conscious, rational mind over the body and emotions, and in the possibility of rational individual subjects coming together to form an equally rational and sovereign government. Over the centuries before and since the Enlightenment, as the dominant culture developed rationalism, it simultaneously rejected the reality of demons and demon possession.

Possession is by definition the temporary dissolution of subjectivity. The possessed experiences an absence of self as a subject in charge of his or her own thoughts, words, and actions. Another force or forces take over, to such an extent that the possessed does not recall the experience; the conscious self, the subject, simply was not there.[7] Thus, by flying in the face of Western assumptions, possession became—along with cannibalism and human sacrifice—an earmark for the West of backward, "primitive" cultures. The peoples who claimed to experience demon possession were understood by Western rationalism to represent an earlier stage in the evolution of human culture. As Keller puts it, "the possessed person is treated as a signifier of regressive or repressive conditions."[8]

Keller writes of anthropological analysis, scholars who analyze the reports or incidents of spirit possession in a particular culture. But for biblical studies, the picture is somewhat further complicated by the issue of historicity. Keller emphasizes that, since the possessed person generally does not recall the experience, all accounts of possession are mediated. Observers report their interpretation of events—what the possessed person said or did—and no one can report accurately on what it is like to be the possessed person. In biblical studies we deal only with stories of possession, without the benefit of contact with the cultural context from which the story emerges. Yet, when it comes to accounts of demon possession, biblical scholarship has so far lacked an awareness of the mediated aspect of the story.

In the political as well as the medical and psychological translations of demon possession, there is an unstated tendency to see the text as a window

---

7. Ibid., 13.
8. Ibid., 57.

on a historical incident of possession. That is, critics see the experience or phenomenon of demon possession as an expression of psychological or socio-political realities, and they see the stories of demon possession in Mark's Gospel the same way. We forget, in analyzing these stories, that Mark is free to shape this account as he chooses, in order to make his point or simply to make it a good story. Perhaps because the Gospels' demon possession stories are so vivid, particularly in Mark's Gospel, the fact that these stories are liter-ary creations and not verbatim accounts gets lost in the analysis.

Paul Hollenbach is an excellent example of this conflation of actual pos-session with mediated possession account. "It is likely," Hollenbach says of the Gerasene demoniac, "that the tension between his hatred for his oppres-sors and the necessity to repress this hatred to avoid dire recrimination drove him mad."[9] If we are speculating on what drove this man mad, then we assume that the man has some existence outside of this story in Mark's Gos-pel. But we have no Gerasene man other than the one Mark hands us. He has no prehistory, no childhood, no family of origin, but begins to exist in chapter five, verse one, a full grown man running and screaming.[10] And this Gerasene man has not been driven mad by socio-political contradictions. I say that with confidence since the man in the text is not mad at all; he is possessed by unclean spirits! The political and anti-colonial elements in the story—and they are plentiful and powerful—are not an example of how society constructs and constrains mental illness; they are the values of the text or its author, emerging as embodied truth in the story. And whether or not Hollenbach or I believe that people can literally be taken over by spirits, Mark's Gospel certainly does.

Hollenbach quotes extensively from Frantz Fanon, to the effect that demon possession was, in French-occupied Algeria, at once an outlet for the aggressive response to colonial oppression and a breakdown resulting from inner conflicts caused by the oppression. But Hollenbach quotes what should be a troubling passage from Fanon's description of the colonized majority: "the cowering natives; the glance of the colonialist shrivels him up and freezes

---

9. Hollenbach, 581.

10. I am assuming that the possessed person is a man, although he is interestingly referred to as "the person," or "the human being"—*anthropos*—in verses two and eight. It is at least possible that the references to him as masculine are only grammatical—the word *anthropos* is grammatically masculine—and that the person's gender is not actually being stated.

him and the colonialist's voice turns him into stone."[11] In a more recent translation, Fanon seems to be emphasizing the newfound courage, rather than the timidity, of the colonial subject, "[the colonizer's] look can no longer strike fear into me or nail me to the spot and his voice can no longer petrify me. . . . In reality, to hell with him."[12] The main problem of the colonized is the channeling of his own forbidden aggressive reaction to the colonizer.[13] Full of aggression that he cannot express,

> [t]he colonized subject draws on the terrifying myths that are so prolific in underdeveloped societies as inhibitions for his aggressiveness: malevolent spirits who emerge every time you put one foot wrong, leopard men, snake men, six-legged dogs, zombies, a whole never-ending gamut of animalcules or giants that encircles the colonized with a realm of taboos, barriers, and inhibitions far more terrifying than the colonialist world.[14]

The sense that indigenous religions were webs of fear and superstition pervades Fanon's analysis.

A psychiatrist by training, Fanon's own experience of colonial oppression led him to point to social factors involved in mental illness and to analyze the psychology of the colonized subject. But he nevertheless operated strictly within the confines of Western psychiatry. That is to say, Fanon assumes rather than demonstrates that what Algerians experienced as demon possession was in fact mental illness. He then proceeds to point out the social aspects of mental illness: that the mentally ill, supposedly demon-possessed person is acting out social pressures, in ways that the society understands, accepts, and will not persecute.

Fanon's insight that mental illness is socially conditioned and socially expressive still sounds new and immensely useful in understanding how the

---

11. Hollenbach, "Jesus, Demoniacs," 573.

12. Frantz Fanon, *The Wretched of the Earth*, trans. Richard Philcox (New York: Grove, 2004; French original, 1961), 10. Even without reference to the original French, one can see that the translation has adapted to current understandings; earlier translations had "the native," Philcox uses "the colonial subject." Hollenbach cites a 1963 edition but does not name the translator.

13. I maintain the masculine here, since Fanon tends to portray the conflict as one among men and at times between masculinities—an intriguing subject for a different article.

14. Fanon, 18.

socially marginalized nevertheless are marginalized in culturally specific ways; those who reject or cannot live up to repressive social constraints cast off those restraints in culturally prescribed ways. Fanon's Western-educated prejudice against the religious beliefs and practices of colonized peoples, however, must be left behind. His sense, as well, that where religion and politics are found comingled, religion masks and mystifies political realities needs to be seriously questioned.

My own experience and a sense of epistemological justice urge me to take the religious experiences of others as religious experiences, and not as political or psychological expressions taking the form of religious experiences. The idea that religion is real and an active cultural force in itself may be somewhat more tenable now than it was in Fanon's time. I seek to read Mark's unclean spirits, then, as unclean spirits first and last—which is not to say that Mark's unclean spirits do not interact with postcolonial realities.

Yet, despite my urge to take the unclean demons on Mark's terms, I have to speak from my actual context. In contextual interpretation, a helpful question is often, What is at stake for me, or for my community, in reading the text this way? I can see that reading over the demons in the Gospels could have negative ethical effects, negating or patronizing the experience of many contemporary cultures as well as the ancient culture embedded in the text. But at the end of the day, I do not believe in demons. In fact, although I can sympathize with the belief in demons on an intellectual level, when I have encountered the actual belief in real people, it is probably as frightening to me as evidence of a demon's presence would be to the believer.

Though I do not believe in demons, and at some level share my culture's aversion to the belief, nevertheless I want to take the text on its own terms where demons are concerned, to recognize that possession is still experienced by many cultures, and to admit my own foreignness to the text as in some sense an inadequacy. Clearly, the Gospel writer believes in demons. They are alive and well throughout the story. They may very well be in league with the Roman occupation, and certainly they have what we would call psychological effects on the people whom they possess. But for the Gospel, they remain loose, unclean spirits, spiritual entities who take possession of people, polluting, sickening, and often attempting to destroy those people. The Gospel writer sees human life as plagued by unclean and malevolent spirits; as Keller has pointed out, I am not the first Westerner to feel strangely drawn to that vision, however untenable I may find it.[15]

Finally, Western thought, and perhaps particularly American thought, dislikes social boundaries and tends to applaud any transgression of them. The more educated, the more elite the Western intellectual, the greater the suspicion of boundaries, so that very well educated Westerners will often reject as definitive the categories of gay and straight, male and female—let alone racial, religious, economic, or national boundaries. I notice the boundaries in this story, no doubt, because I have a Western fascination for the idea of transgressing them. At the same time, I have to notice that the Gospel story for the most part sees boundary transgression as a problem as great as, or greater than, the boundaries themselves.

The Unclean Spirits, the Man, and the Boundaries

The man possessed by unclean spirits in Gerasa has no discernible subjectivity. Or, rather, whatever subjectivity he has, has very fuzzy edges. The initial encounter between the man with the unclean spirits and Jesus is one characterized by confusion in time and agency.

> [6]Seeing Jesus from afar, he ran and prostrated himself to him [7]and crying out with a great voice, he says, "What have you to do with me, Jesus son of God the most high? I adjure you by God, do not torment me!" [8]For he was saying to him, "Come out unclean spirit from the human being." [9]And he was asking him, "What is your name?" And he says to him, "My name is Legion, for we are many." (Mark 5:6-9)[16]

Our first contact with the possessed man is his running toward Jesus and throwing himself at Jesus' feet. Yet in this same act of passionate, respectful, desperate approach, the man or his unclean spirits are shouting at Jesus to leave him/them alone. And even this terrifically conflicted picture is further confused with the narrative's next piece of information—"for he was saying to him, 'Come out, unclean spirit, from the person!'" (v. 8). Mark is reshuffling narrative time, as he sometimes does. Jesus appears to have first ordered

---

15. Keller, *Hammer and the Flute,* 10.
16. All translations from the Greek are my own, unless otherwise indicated.

the spirit to come out, more than once (v. 8), and thus to have provoked the man and/or the man's possessing spirits to come running toward Jesus (v. 6), shouting to be left alone (v. 7). Just where Jesus' question as to the man's or the demons' name (v. 9) should be placed in the sequence of the dialogue is not at all clear. The overall impression is of Jesus and the possessed man shouting commands at each other—"Come out!" "Do not torment me!"—until the spirits begin to beg not to be sent out of the country (v. 10), signifying their acceptance of defeat.

Along with the confusion in time or in cause and effect of the dialogue, there is the already apparent massive confusion between the man and his demons. Jesus tells the unclean spirits to come out. Presumably it is the unclean spirits who, here as elsewhere, recognize Jesus as "son of the most high God," and command Jesus to leave them alone (v. 7). But was it the spirits or the man himself who ran toward Jesus and fell on the ground before him? Jesus may be asking the demons' name in verse nine in an effort to gain control of them, as is commonly understood. Or he may in fact be asking *the man's* name, in an effort to make contact with the being whose subjectivity has been so thoroughly obscured. It seems in either case that the spirits answer, not the man, managing to deflect Jesus' effort at clarification with an answer full of smoke and mirrors: "My name is Legion, for we are many."

The spirits are one being, and yet they are many, thousands, acting in concert as does a military unit. They act as one body, a *corps,* a body not their own. Indeed, if Jesus is asking the man's name, then the spirits' answer, "My name is Legion," becomes still spookier, since the singular "my" becomes the demons' claim that they have become the substance of the singular man.

The man himself, though, has not yet spoken and has no name. Indeed, the man never acquires a name in this story. Once the demons are gone, he becomes "the one who was demonized" and "the one who had the legion" (vv. 15, 18). His only speech is indirect and expresses less his own identity than the identity of Jesus. Initially asking permission to "be with" Jesus (v. 18), he instead does as Jesus commands and returns to the city "to proclaim in the Decapolis how much Jesus had done for him" (v. 20).

Without his demons, the man is anonymous and more or less passive, empty of all but the story of his own exorcism. But the man while he is being possessed is perversely fascinating to both the story and to me. Mark's description of the man's condition is vivid and extensive—for a Gospel of few words, the description here constitutes a diatribe. Most of the description has to do with binding and boundaries.

For Jesus and the disciples, the crossing over to Gerasa is both pointless and nearly fatal. In the Gospels and in biblical tradition, the sea is a great and treacherous social and physical boundary, crossed only for life-and-death reasons. But Jesus brings his disciples through their perilous crossing for no apparent reason. The disciples, at least, fear for their lives on the water, until Jesus rebukes them and the sea itself. Yet upon arrival, Jesus responds to the situation of the raving man at his feet, and then promptly gets back in the boat, leaving the cleansed man to preach in the Decapolis. They cross over, it seems, purely for the sake of the crossing itself, and everything about the crossing, everything about "the other side" (v. 1), speaks of boundaries— damaged or restored.

The man's own boundaries have been transgressed. He has been permeated, penetrated, by not one but thousands of unclean spirits. Mark's reference to the spirits as "unclean" evokes the purity system, and the system's categories and concerns suffuse this story. Uncleanness itself is about boundary transgression, so the man's possession by thousands is akin to a parasitic infestation; the destructive spirits make the man unclean—dirty himself and contagious to others.

The townspeople's solutions to the man's wild condition also focus on boundaries, or boundedness, or binding. The man was literally bound, hand and foot, but he has burst his bo[u]nds, so that no one can control him or tie him up any more (vv. 3-4). The fact that he cannot be bound renders the man the more disturbing to the reader, despite the fact that we have no sense of why he needed to be bound, no report that he was harming innocent people or destroying property before they tried to chain him. We hear that he has unclean spirits, but the unclean spirits' initial crimes seem to occur only in response to the people's effort to bind him. It is as if the man's main crime is resisting arrest—what was he being arrested for?

Whatever their reason for attempting to bind the possessed man, the Gerasenes are unable to do it with any long-term success. He or his unclean spirits are beings that cannot be bound; they have burst out of chains and shackles. The verbs with which the chain-breaking is described are particularly vivid and violent, having to do in both cases, appropriately, with disintegration. The word translated "wrenched apart" (RSV, v. 4; *diespasthai*) might also be read, "tore to pieces." Likewise, the verb "broke into pieces" (RSV, v. 4; *syntetriphthai*) has the sense of "shatter" and is used elsewhere of the alabaster jar (Mark 14:3) and of ceramic vessels (Rev 2:27). The chains and shackles, the very things that were to hold the man together and enable him to be present in society, have been so smashed as to become unidentifiable themselves, a collection of disintegrated pieces. Fanon wrote, "Such a disintegration, dissolution, or splitting of the personality plays a key regulating role in ensuring the stability of the colonized world."[17] The unclean spirits, like the occupying powers, are at home with disintegration.

The man or the spirits, having shattered the ties that bound them, now live outside the boundaries, among the tombs. The text makes sure we understand that the man is not just passing through the tombs; he lives there. The first thing we hear about the man, in fact, is that he is "in an unclean spirit, . . . having his dwelling among the tombs" (*en pneumati akathartō hos tēn katoikēsin eichen en tois mnēmasin,* vv. 2-3). While they are in one sense beyond the bounds, the tombs are also, like the sea, a dangerous boundary in themselves, a liminal place, between the living and the dead. Society generally abhors liminality, since it tends to weaken and call into question the categories that support and constitute the social order. But the possessed man lives in a liminal world, between physical and spiritual realities, between life and death, between subject and object of his own experience.

In this world, his every action seems designed to further break down the few remaining boundaries of his person. He bruises himself, or perhaps cuts himself (*katakoptōn*), with stones, apparently the closest weapons to hand (v. 5). Again, this action in the story may belong to the possessed man, tormented by the spirits and seeking to harm them by harming the body they possess. Or it may be that the spirits delight in doing harm, and, having broken apart the chains and shackles that bound the man to society, they now beat against his skin—the boundary that holds his very humanity together. This is perhaps the most graphic and terrible detail of Mark's description. Until now the townspeople's attempts at binding seemed the worst thing that could happen to the possessed man, but now we see that, free from all

---

17. Fanon, *Wretched of the Earth,* 20.

bindings, he is in danger of being painfully loosed from the bonds of life. Again, the text is ambiguous as to whether the spirits naturally destroy what they possess, or whether it is the overtaken and voiceless man who attempts with the stones to overthrow the thing possessing him.

The unclean spirits cross the man's boundaries inward, penetrating and inhabiting him. At the same time, in the form of their shouting, they cross the same boundaries—those between self and other, between life and death—in an outward direction. Among the tombs, while using the stones to burst the body's bounds, the man is always "crying out"—apparently wordless screams voiced ambiguously by the spirits and/or the man. Running full speed toward Jesus, the spirits do not simply speak or shout, but they "cry out with a loud voice" (*kai kraxas phōnē megalē*, v. 7). The phrase has a special weight in Mark's Gospel, occurring only when unclean spirits are exorcised from a possessed body (1:26) and then both when Jesus cries out from the cross, *"Elōi, Elōi, lema sabachthani?"* (15:34), and again in the same passage, when he breathes out his last breath (15:37). The phrase for Mark indicates the coming and going of spirit—synonymous with life, breath, and even soul—from the body. The spirits' exit seems to make this sound, this "great voice," as when Jesus' own spirit leaves his body in death. Indeed, the word translated *phōnē*, "voice," appears only three other times in this Gospel, outside of the phrase "crying out with a great voice." The voice crying in the wilderness (1:3) is its first appearance, and the divine voice that is heard at Jesus' baptism (1:11) and at his transfiguration (9:7) are the remaining two. The disembodied voice, certainly, seems to make known unseen spiritual realities in this Gospel. When such a spiritual reality crosses the boundaries of the human body, it never does so calmly or quietly; the "great voice" with which the spirits and Jesus cry out is loud and intense.

In this voice, as in the damaging of the body with stones, the demons transgress bodily boundaries, seemingly in an effort to dissolve them entirely. When they actually leave the body, they make no sound but, in apparent quiet, rush into the pigs and down the slope into the sea. This crossing from person to pigs and thence into the deadly boundarylands of the sea, seems less a transgression, a trampling of boundaries, than simply an exit, as through an open door. The danger was in the entrance of the demons and in the dissolution of boundaries that they sought to effect in the man as long as they stayed within. Again, like the Roman imperial presence, the crossing of boundaries represented in their leaving is not feared, but only the boundary transgression that constitutes their ongoing presence.

Once the spirits are gone, the man is seen "clothed and in his right mind" (v. 15). We had not heard that he was naked, but can only read it back in after the fact. But his clothing now reinforces his restored social and personal boundaries, the literal saving of his skin. The man's desire to go with Jesus across the liminal sea is refused. Instead, he must turn his back on both the sea and the tombs and return to the bound-up, binding, and categorizing town, to reenter the place from which both spirits and people expelled him.

Prometheus on the Rebound

Even while we insist on the boundedness of the individual—that the individual should be independent and sovereign unto herself—white Americans nevertheless love the idea of freedom from boundaries. When I googled the English word *unbound,* I found only positive references, all from my own context; namely, an energy drink and a software both go by this name, as do the student literary journal of the College of New Jersey and an online legal journal of Harvard Law School; an online Bible site named "the unbound Bible," an online medical resources site called "unbound medicine," and of course several references to the Aeschylus play turned Romantic literary myth, *Prometheus Unbound.* It appears that, with the internet and its globalizing impulses, *unbound* sometimes combines connotations of "freed from the necessity of bound books" with the older sense of hard-won freedom, including freedom of thought. In all cases, the idea of being unbound—not simply unconstrained by bonds, but uncontained by boundaries—emerges as entirely good.

Here I must read the Gospel against my context as best I can. It may be that only a prosperous and dominant people could believe that all boundaries are meant to be crossed. When no one threatens one's own boundaries, then boundary transgression seems liberating and empowering. Or perhaps this is more the doctrine of an imperialist nation, one that sees entry into new territory as its own manifest destiny, and so sees the boundaries that others have established—whether national, economic, or personal—as inapplicable to itself.

In the story of the Gerasene demoniac, the dissolution of boundaries is the problem, not the solution. Jesus' crossing to Gerasa has emphasized the danger of such crossings, a danger averted only by divine power. The situation in Gerasa is fraught with the in-between and unclean, characteristic of boundary-lessness.

What little information Mark gives us about this man's life before the story begins points to some kind of abuse of the man by his society; the townspeople try to contain him with sheer force and make no apparent effort to heal or help him. They seem to have accepted his outcast status, as evinced by the fact that they are shocked and frightened when he becomes again a clothed and socialized being (v. 15). To this extent, the story criticizes the maintenance of boundaries. Societies need outcasts. Outcasts define the boundaries of our societies; in the words of Peter Gabriel, "how can we be in, if there is no outside?"[18] The possessed man embodies the danger of being outside, the danger of the boundary and the boundary crossing, and he does so for the Gerasenes and the Jews within the story as well as for the implied Jewish Christian reader, and for me.

Mark's Gospel believes in the purity system, however much it may record Jesus as transgressing its categories. Jesus in this Gospel sometimes cleanses, sometimes protests the practice of the purity laws with respect to food; but he does not disregard the categories of clean and unclean. Gerasa in Mark's portrayal is unclean. It is a place between death and life, not unlike Hades or Sheol, populated by a tormented man, a herd of swine, an army of demons, and by people who seem to side with uncleanness.

In Mark's Gospel overall, the spirits are not usually called demons but "unclean spirits," and their uncleanness seems both literal and ritual in this story. Their presence induces the man to live among the dead and near the sea, and to be so unbound as to be in the act of disintegrating utterly. The spirits here evoke and embody a fear of borders disappearing or being smashed to smithereens, and the story believes that life requires borders.

Embodied in the disembodied and unclean presence of the spirits is the Roman presence. Fanon talks about the essential compartmentalization of colonial society; that there must be, in African colonies, a black city and a white city, and that the divisions must be fully apparent. But we never get a glimpse of the white city, the Roman city, in Mark's Gospel. We are, by

---

18. Peter Gabriel, "Not One of Us," from the third album entitled *Peter Gabriel,* Mercury Records, 1980.

analogy, among shades of black in the black city on both sides of the Sea of Galilee. What we see in Gerasa is not the other side, in this sense, but people who refuse to distinguish between sides, a city unclean not because it is Roman, but because it is not itself—it is in between and will not or cannot reject the Roman presence. There is, after all, almost nothing in the city but tombs.

However much I want to take the story on its own spirit-believing terms, the spirits taking a Roman military name for themselves is no accident. In fact, if the name came up only once in the course of the narrative, we might dismiss it as emphasizing only the great number of the spirits. But the narrator refers back to the formerly demonized man later, calling him "the one who had the legion" (v. 15). The name, or description, of the spirits is significant enough to remember, even after the spirits are gone.

Mark does not see the man being driven insane by the Roman occupation, but he does see the possessing unclean spirits as akin to the occupying Roman military. As swine transgress the boundaries and categories of livestock in Jewish law, and are categorized as unclean exactly because they cannot be categorized, the Romans and the demons are also characterized by their inability to be pinned down. They transgress all boundaries as though the boundaries did not exist, and consequently they are unclean themselves and they spread and foster uncleanness. Like the Romans, and like the Americans in recent history, the unclean spirits want both to control and to disappear, to brag of their empire and to deny the force of its presence, to institute the *pax Romana* by brute force. The demons do not wish to be accurately named, any more than does the empire.

Conclusion

I do not claim to be able to shrug off my Western or American identity, and indeed I live in fear that it will rear its ugly head in unanticipated, unconscious, and oppressive ways, similar to the Hollenbach citation with which I began this article. Yet I find myself drawn to see, in part, the un-Western side of this story; perhaps the converse of my own culture's values. That is, while my culture believes in freedom from boundaries, I cannot help but read in the text that boundary-lessness can be a form of oppression, that it belongs in the text to the demons and the Romans, that it is considered unclean. I suspect this has to do with a kind of micro-context, or another level of context. In addition to being an American white Protestant, I am also a woman and the adult child of an alcoholic woman. I have seen the nonliberating destruction that obliteration of boundaries can bring, and I lack my own culture's great belief that the loosing of bonds will save us all. The demons and the man are free of their bonds, in this story, before Jesus comes. But their freedom is the man's disintegration, and the man's restored boundaries, his restoration to the ties that bind, mean wholeness and the casting off of oppression.

Part Two

Teachers, Disciples, and Communities

CHAPTER 4

The Misunderstanding of Jesus' Disciples in Mark

An Interpretation from a Community-Centered Perspective

Jin-Young Choi

Life Context

"When I came to have faith in Jesus, I didn't know who he is and what he did." A confession of the first baptized woman in Korea, named Sam-Deok Cheon, begins with this phrase.[1] For the first time, her heart was moved by the story about Jesus, but soon after becoming a Christian she was changed into a Bible woman who walked miles and miles every day to tell people—especially uneducated and wretched women—good news and in some cases to practice exorcism.[2] Their lives were connected to the lives of people and

---

1. She was of noble birth, but like other Korean women at that time her life was confined to home in an oppressive situation in which she was deserted by her husband, who had a concubine. In 1895, she was baptized by missionary W. B. Scranton while sticking her head out of a hole in the curtain because a man and a woman were not allowed to sit together. Deok Joo Rhie, *Pioneer Women in the Korean Church: Struggles for Freedom and Liberation in the Time of Evangelization and Western Civilization* (in Korean; Seoul: Hong Sung Sa, 2007), 24. Most Korean women did not have their own names, could not read, and lived miserable lives under the conditions of the feudal regime and the invasion of Japanese and Western imperialisms.

2. Western missionaries, who arrived in Korea in the end of the nineteenth century, organized and trained Bible women (called *cheondo puin* in Korean) and introduced Western modernized education, teaching them the Bible and English. These Christian women leaders not only were intellectually enlightened but also committed their lives both to evangelizing to people and to bringing emancipation and freedom to the socially, politically, and religiously oppressed Korean women.

the life of the nation in the sense that they sublimated Korean women's *han* into Christian faith.[3] However, Cheon's last words in 1925 reveal how the Western project of mission accompanied by modernization had influenced her life: "I had eyes but didn't see, had ears but didn't hear, and lips but didn't speak; but after knowing of Jesus I became an autonomous woman."[4] For her, being a Christian was concomitant with being an enlightened woman in the modern sense. The first Christian Korean women's commitment to the community brought life back to the people of the nation. On the other hand, Korean women's pathos and passion of religiosity based on a communal sense were gradually replaced by an attempt to search for the autonomy that an individual was able to acquire by being both a Christian and an educated woman.[5]

Today, Korean Christianity has lost the power of influence on the community because of its individualized form of faith, its exclusivist attitude toward other religions, and its expansionist missionary policies and practices in other third-world countries. The Korean church needs to reflect on the ongoing influence of modern rationalism baptized by Western Christianity, and rereading the Gospel of Mark might prove of assistance in this task. I argue that Western readings of Mark based on the pursuit of rationality and its certainty are not very convincing from the community-centered perspective commonly found in Korean contexts, especially as influenced by Confucianism, Buddhism, and shamanism. In order to do justice to my Asian cultural context, I propose here to explore the Markan representations of the disciples' (mis)understanding of Jesus from a community-centered perspective.

---

3. There are a variety of ways to describe Korean *han,* but its significant characteristics include the affliction of the heart of Korean people, a painful gut feeling, or a deep religious disposition, collectively formed throughout the history of the Korean nation, which for centuries was the victim of the rapacity of neighboring countries and endured the trying experience of serving others.

4. Rhie, *Pioneer Women,* 30.

5. Although being a Christian required a Korean woman to radically break with the previous indigenous religions and their practices, the former practices were not totally abandoned, as shown in the case of Lulu Chu, the woman whose mother and grandmother were shamanists. Her non-Christian mother-in-law brought the Bible and a cup of holy water to her, for Chu was often possessed, saying, "Since you are the person who has struggled with spirits, I knew that you would have to believe the *kyo* (religion) of *Cheon-Ju* (Catholic) or *Jesu* (Protestant)." Later, Chu became a Bible woman, driving away evil spirits for the women in horrible circumstances (Rhie, *Pioneer Women,* 75).

The Hermeneutical Perspective
of Western Biblical Scholarship

Since William Wrede formulated the thesis of the "messianic secret" found in the Gospel of Mark, the studies of this Gospel have been dominated by the quest for Jesus' identity.[6] According to Wrede, Jesus teaches in parables in order deliberately to hide his intent from the crowds (4:11-12), while giving private instruction only to his disciples (7:17; 10:10). Despite their privileged position, the disciples in Mark regularly fail to understand Jesus (6:52; 8:17-21). Therefore, somehow discipleship is necessarily related to the disciples' proper understanding of Jesus and his teaching. Although Wrede's specific hypothesis concerning the messianic secret has lost popularity in current scholarship, its influence remains significant in that a proper understanding of who Jesus is constitutes a central concern of many Markan commentators, without taking note that this concern and the subsequent reading are framed by Western rationality and its individualist quest for knowledge. The (messianic) secret should not remain a mystery but rather should become an object of mastery through the reasoning of individuals.

The Western biblical scholars' eagerness to discover truth through the individual exercise of their own reason is present in their expositions of the disciples' failure, which is located mainly in their misunderstanding or lack of knowledge of who Jesus is. Whatever the reason for the disciples' failure and whether they fail or progress, those interpretations describe the disciples as autonomous subjects who should follow Jesus while seeking a proper understanding of who Jesus is and pursuing their individual goals—their autonomous mission.[7] By framing their readings of Mark in this way, Western studies directly or indirectly advocate, indeed mandate, this view of autonomous discipleship based on the individual knowledge of Jesus' identity. For instance, "following" as a technical term denoting discipleship

---

6. William Wrede's *Das Messiasgeheimnis in den Evangelien* was published in 1901; see the English translation by J. C. Greig, *The Messianic Secret* (Cambridge: J. Clarke, 1971).

7. As represented in Theodore J. Weeden's argument that the disciples' failure is devised to correct the theology of glory, many Markan studies are greatly concerned with Christology in relation to discipleship. See Theodore J. Weeden, *Mark: Traditions in Conflict* (Philadelphia: Fortress Press, 1979); Ernest Best contends that the disciples' failure to understand is instructive in that it leads Christians in Mark's day to understand what true discipleship is (*Disciples and Discipleship: Studies in the Gospel according to the Mark* (Edinburgh: T&T Clark, 1986), 128.

often presupposes knowing who Jesus is. Even when "following" is under-stood as adopting the life of the one who is followed so that relationship is in view, it is still regarded as personal relationship.[8] I will argue later that the vertical model of the relationship between Jesus and the disciples as shown in patron–client relations should be replaced by an egalitarian kinship model and that the disciples' "being with" Jesus and his "being with" them is an essential marker of discipleship.

Hermeneutics from a Community-Centered Perspective

In Western culture, individualism, autonomy, and self-sufficiency are highly respected.[9] Yet one might consider that first-century Palestine was different from such an individualist Western climate because the integrity of the group was pivotal in the society, where survival itself was often the issue.[10] Thus, one can read the Gospel as informed by the strong sense of group or community that prevailed in the ancient Mediterranean culture, in which the new community of the Jesus movement arose. The stronger orientation a group has, the more limits the communal code of the group sets.[11] If modern interpreters do not grasp the nature of the communal code operating in a specific sociohistorical context, they will bracket out the dimensions of the text as a product of a communal understanding and a response to sociohistorical circumstances.

Social-scientific criticism in biblical studies has highlighted that the code of honor-shame was the basic value system in the ancient Mediterranean world, including the area of Palestine.[12] Thus, the relationship between Jesus

---

8. John R. Donahue and Daniel J. Harrington, *The Gospel of Mark,* Sacra Pagina 2 (Col-legeville, Minn.: Liturgical, 2002), 29–30.

9. It goes without saying that there are individuals—for instance, Jesus and each disciple—in Mark, and one can read the Gospel focusing on those individuals and on the interactions between the individuals.

10. K. C. Hanson and Douglas E. Oakman, *Palestine in the Time of Jesus: Social Structures and Social Conflicts* (Minneapolis: Fortress Press, 1998), 7.

11. Regarding "communal code," see Brian Blount, *Cultural Interpretation: Reorienting New Testament Criticism* (Minneapolis: Fortress Press, 1995), 62–65, 73. Vernon K. Robbins uses the term "socio-cultural texture" to designate what I call, with Blount, "communal code" (Blount, *The Tapestry of Early Christian Discourse: Rhetoric, Society and Ideology* (London/New York: Routledge, 1996), 1–43.

12. Hanson and Oakman, *Palestine,* 6. In this value system, sustaining honor for oneself, one's family, and larger groups is essential for life. See Bruce J. Malina, *The New Testament*

and the disciples in Mark can be examined in light of the communal code of honor-shame. Additionally, by employing literary criticism, I will see how characters—conceived in and through their relations with other characters and not as individuals—create the dynamics of their relationship in the narrative world.[13] At this point, however, I should note that methodologies themselves as well as the interpretations using them are never neutral, but inculturated. Even when one employs a social-scientific approach for investigating the social system and institutions of the ancient Mediterranean societies, it is not scientifically objective, but affected by the cultural assumptions and prejudices of the researcher.[14]

My use of a community-centered, social-scientific approach along with literary criticism is influenced by my own context, an Asian context comprehending Confucianism, Buddhism, and shamanism. This context is less concerned about individual knowledge than about relationships among people and with the Ultimate. I will not be able to discuss all these traditions in my reading of the Gospel from a community-centered perspective, but will suggest how some of these traditions illuminate the nature of the disciples' understanding in Mark, reading the text with a way of knowing based on relationality and spiritual experience, a way of knowing familiar to many Asian people.

Contextual Interpretation of Mark

Discipleship of Being-With

The relationality of Jesus and his disciples is highlighted when they are described as an alternative family in Mark. Jesus redefines family in 3:31-35:

World: Insights from Cultural Anthropology, rev. ed. (Louisville: Westminster John Knox, 1993), 28–62.

13. Concerning methodologies, I believe that traditional historical-critical approaches have limitations in exploring such communal aspects in and of the text. Despite the attempts of historical-critical interpreters to excavate the historical sites behind the text, their individual motive focuses interpretation in order to see the text or its meaning as an object to be mastered through the interpreter's mental faculty or activity, seeing the social world in which the text is engaged only from the perspective of the roles of individuals in the text, thus excluding the social world as a system and the meanings that work only in the world as a system.

14. For example, L. William Countryman insightfully and vigorously uses the model of honor-shame in his construction of sexual ethics in the New Testament. His approach holds a community-centered perspective, on the one hand, but turns into individualist (capitalist) ethics when he interprets sexuality as property (*Dirt, Greed, and Sex: Sexual Ethics in the New Testament and Their Implications for Today* [Minneapolis: Fortress Press, 2007], esp. 164–77).

whoever does the will of God is his brother, sister, and mother. This is a reorganization or re-creation of kin group. In ancient Mediterranean societies during the first century, kinship was the primary social domain, along with politics.[15] In addition, the patron–client system was a "powerful mechanism in vertical social relationships."[16] Pointing out that many discussions of the Roman patronage system exclude its effect on ordinary people, such as the peasantry and the urban poor, Richard A. Horsley argues that "the personal but asymmetrical (vertical) reciprocal exchange of goods and services in patron–client relations stands diametrically opposed to the horizontal associations and reciprocity embodied in kinship and villages. The vertical bonds of some peasants undermine the solidarity of local peasant communities."[17] In this regard, Jesus' new familial relationship is founded on a different type of reciprocity by comparison with the vertical reciprocity that the patron–client system provides.

This point is significant because it counteracts the temptation to hastily regard the relationship of Jesus and his disciples as that of patron–client or Jesus as broker.[18] Rather, the alternative relationship of family that Jesus advocates is a new kind of reciprocity rooted in equality and solidarity. Moreover, it is a reconstruction of the existing kinship relations, in which genealogy based on patriarchal lineage and sustaining a family's honor play a significant role. Jesus does not seem to appeal to ascribed honor communicated by genealogy.[19]

Yet one may point out that Jesus is revealed as the Son of God and that his authority, manifested in various miracles, is derived from divine paternity, just as Roman emperors such as Augustus were deemed to have divine origins.[20] The Roman emperor placed himself at the top of the

---

15. Hanson and Oakman, *Palestine,* 196.

16. Ibid, 14.

17. Richard A. Horsley, introduction to part 2, in *Paul and Empire: Religion and Power in Roman Imperial Society,* ed. Richard A. Horsley (Harrisburg, Pa.: Trinity Press International, 1997), 90.

18. See Jerome H. Neyrey, S.J., "Miracles, in Other Words: Social Science Perspective on Healings," in *Miracles in Jewish and Christian Antiquity: Imagining Truth,* ed. John C. Cavadini, Notre Dame Studies in Theology 3 (Notre Dame: University of Notre Dame Press, 1999), 26.

19. Unlike Matthew, Mark does not speak about Jesus' genealogy. Additionally, in accounting for his real family, Mark refers to Jesus only as "son of Mary" (6:3). See Hanson and Oakman, *Palestine,* 51–52.

20. Hanson and Oakman, *Palestine,* 55.

pyramidal system by expanding disproportional patron–client relationships throughout the empire. The divine familial lineage of Jesus, however, functions in a way radically different from the imperial patronage. The relationship of Jesus and the disciples as a new model of kinship holds the strong sense of communal solidarity based on the radical experience of God through Jesus. Whoever does the will of God is the brother, sister, or mother of this Son of God.

Thus, patriarchal lineage is replaced with "doing God's will," which is essential for such an alternative form of family. If the foundational value of honor-shame may still work in the new family of Jesus, it is acquired honor that is applied to such kinship ties: "Prophets are not without honor, except in their hometown, and among their own kin, and in their own house" (6:4).[21] According to Stephen C. Barton, Jesus' self-identification as a "prophet" displays not only his sense of belonging to God, that is, as God's son, but also his belonging to those who perceive his prophetic vocation.[22]

What initiates and motivates the relationship of Jesus and the disciples is not the calculating relation of favor and service dominant in the patronage system; it was the intensity of Jesus' calling to profound bonds that made the disciples immediately follow (*euthys . . . ēkolouthēsan*) him, renouncing family and possession (1:16-20). This immediacy of following implies that it is not a goal-oriented action but more like a visceral or gut reaction.[23]

Moreover, "those who are with him" (*hoi met' autou*) as a designation denoting the disciples' relationship with Jesus is no less significant than the term "follow" (1:36; 5:40; cf. 2:19, 25; 3:7; 8:10; 9:2, 8; 11:11; 14:7, 14, 17, 33, 67). It appears that Jesus appointed twelve disciples, above all, in order to be with him (*hina ōsin met' autou,* 3:14). The disciples' being with Jesus or his being with them—the sense of "belonging together"—is fundamental to the relationship between Jesus and his disciples. It represents the relationality of an egalitarian kinship as seen in Jesus' new familial relationship.

---

21. For biblical quotations, I use the text of the New Revised Standard Version (NRSV), unless otherwise specified.
22. Barton maintains that personal identity and honor in traditional societies are related not to the question of "who I am" but to that of "where I belong" (*Discipleship and Family Ties in Mark and Matthew,* Society for New Testament Studies Monograph Series 80 (Cambridge/ New York: Cambridge University Press, 1994), 94–95.
23. On the other hand, the immediacy of Jesus' call (1:20) carries "a sense of the sudden irruption of God's rule and, therefore, of God's new time" (Barton, *Discipleship,* 65).

Faith and Understanding

Despite the significance of this communal tie, what disturbs the reader is that the disciples appear to misunderstand. Regarding this issue, one needs to investigate how understanding is different from knowledge and how faith and understanding are connected in Mark.

Most interpretations of Mark presuppose that one must understand in order to believe, regarding understanding primarily as an intellectual faculty or the activity of reasoning—a Western assumption under the Kantian influence. The relationship between believing and understanding is not always like this.[24] Even when understanding is desired in Mark, this understanding is not confined to having knowledge about something divine. This way of knowing is not the mark of discipleship, because even the unclean spirit knows who Jesus is ("I know who you are [*oida se tis ei*])," 1:24; cf. 3:11). Likewise, the Jewish leaders in Jerusalem appear to "know" (*egnōsan*, 12:12) that Jesus' parable about the wicked tenants was told against them (12:1-12; cf. v. 14), even though Jesus seems to speak in parables in order for "those outside" not to "understand" (4:11-12). It should be noted that the words *ginōskō* and *oida* indicate the "intelligent comprehension of an object or matters" and "knowledge of what really is."[25] Thus, they contain the sense of verification. This is why those words sometimes are associated with the so-called messianic secret (see 5:43; 7:24; 9:30). But the question confronting the disciples is whether they "perceive" (*noeō*, 7:18; 8:17; 13:14) or "understand" (*syniēmi*, 4:12; 6:52; 7:14; 8:17, 21).

The significance of understanding is subtly highlighted in 12:28-34. When a scribe comes to Jesus and asks about the supreme commandment, Jesus answers by first quoting Deut 6:4-5, Josh 22:5, and Lev 19:18. Then, the scribe repeats it while changing the word "mind" (*dianoia*) in Jesus' saying to "understanding" (*synesis*). The two words are not significantly different in meaning, but the word choice in the scribe's saying stresses the significance

---

24. As Augustine puts it, "Believe in order to understand"; one first believes and then may hope to understand (*Crede ut intelligas* in *Sermons* 43.9; see also *Epistula,* 120, I, 2-3). This "faith seeking understanding" is presupposed also by Anselm's definition of theology, *fides quaerens intellectum* (*Cur Deus Homo*).

25. Rudolf Bultmann, *ginōskō, Theological Dictionary of the New Testament*, ed. Gerhard Kittel and Gerhard Friedrich, trans. G. W. Bromiley (Grand Rapids: Eerdmans, 1966–82), 1:689–92.

of "understanding" in Mark.[26] This is seen as a wise answer, so Jesus says, "you are not far from the kingdom of God."[27] In Mark's narrative world, understanding is essential in one's relationship with God.

What, then, is the relationship between understanding and believing? Jesus' questions about faith and understanding may imply their interchangeability in usage and meaning: "Have you still no faith?" (*oupō echete pistin*, 4:40); "Then are you without understanding?" (RSV; *houtōs kai hymeis asynetoi este*, 7:18); "Do you not yet understand?" (*oupō syniete*, 8:21). In these cases, the content to be believed or understood is not expressed.[28]

It is true that Jesus is concerned about the disciples' lack of faith. However, this does not necessitate an interpretation of Jesus using a harsh tone for blaming, as interpreters often assume. When the father of the son who was possessed with the unclean spirit cries out to Jesus, "I believe. Help my unbelief," Jesus positively responds to the father's unbelieving belief (9:24). Faith recognized by Jesus seems to be different from faith, *pistis* (Lat. *fides*), as the core of the ideology of Roman imperialism developed from patron–client relations. The Romans showed their *pistis* by providing faithful protection for their "friends," while the friends of Rome were responsible for their *pistis*, faithful loyalty and submission to Rome.[29] Faith in Mark is also relational, but it is not reciprocity as a social practice based on power relations

---

26. As the Chinese word *sim* indicates both heart and mind, in Greek *kardia* is an equivalent of *nous*, from which *noeō* and *dianoia* are derived (cf. Heb 8:10). The verb *dianoigō* is used once in Mark and translated as "open" (7:34; cf. *anoigō* in v. 35), and it is a symbolic word for "understand." Further, the seat of understanding (*synesis*) is *kardia*. This usage of the words shows that "understanding" and "opening" are matters of the heart. Moreover, the opening of the deaf and mute man's hearing as the consequence of Jesus' healing is described in the passive form. Likewise, in the Old Testament tradition "understanding" is the property and gift of God (1 Kgs 3:9; Dan 2:21). See Behm and Conzelmann in Kittel and Friedrich, *Theological Dictionary of the New Testament*, 4:963–67; and 7:888–96. What is required for the followers of Jesus is this understanding (*synesis*), as given by God, not as human pursuit for knowledge.

27. While some Pharisees and scribes in 7:8 appear to fail to keep the commandment of God so that they are "far from God," the scribe in 12:28-34 seems to perceive what is significant regarding the greatest commandments and thus he is not "far from the kingdom of God."

28. Unlike *ginōskō* and *oida*, grammatically, *syniēmi* does not take a direct object in Mark. In 6:52 it takes a prepositional phrase, *epi tois artois*: "They did not understand about the loaves." In addition, *pistis* ("faith") is used without any modifiers or objects in 2:5; 4:40; 5:34; 10:52; cf. 11:22. Although *pisteuō* ("believe") has an object or an object clause in some cases (1:15; [9:43]; 11:23, 24), in other places the object of "believing" does not appear (5:36; 9:23, 24; cf. 13:21; 15:32).

29. Horsley, introduction to part 2, in *Paul and Empire*, 93.

(patron–client). Rather, faith is absolute dependence on God and a turning toward God. In short, faith is not measured by knowing as rational capacity, but relation-to-God and even gut reaction to God. The disciples' misunderstanding, then, is not a matter of knowledge but a matter of heart. It comes from the hardness of their heart (6:52; 8:17).

Hardness of Heart

As understanding implies an intimate relationship with God rather than the perfect knowledge of God, the heart also is a seat of one's attitude toward God (7:6; 11:23; 12:30, 33).[30] Although it is not clear in Mark whether God causes the hardness of heart or whether human beings generate the symptom, what is apparent is that the term is applied to the disciples as well as to the Pharisees (3:5; 6:52; 8:17; 10:5).[31]

Hardness of the heart is ascribed primarily to the Jewish leaders in Mark's narrative. In addition to direct mention of their hardness of heart (3:1-6; 7:1-6; 10:2-9), in two scenes some scribes question (or discuss or argue, *dialogizomai*) Jesus' authority "in their hearts" (2:6, 8; 11:31). It is surprising, however, that the disciples are not an exception in questioning in their heart. When Jesus speaks about the leaven of the Pharisees and Herod, they "discuss" (RSV; *dielogizonto*) the fact that they have no bread after the miracles of Jesus' feeding the multitude (8:16). Jesus knows of their discussion and relates it to their misunderstanding and the hardness of their hearts (8:17). Again, on the way to Jerusalem right after being told about Jesus' passion (9:33), the disciples argue (*dielogizesthe*) about who is the greatest. These questions or discussions reveal the disciples' double-mindedness, which might be synonymous with doubt—and thus their lack of faith and understanding—and

---

30. It is interesting to see a certain connection between the predominant Greek ideas of the heart as the center of physical life (Aristotle) or the central organ of intellectual life or the seat of reason (Stoicism) and the Western assumption about understanding as an intellectual capacity. But the heart, in the Hebrew Bible tradition, is not only the source of volition as an individual attribute but also the seat of spiritual, moral, and religious life beyond the seat of physiological or mental capacity. See Deut 29:3 (LXX) and Ps 51:10 (LXX 50:12). See J. Behm, "kardia," in *Theological Dictionary of the New Testament*, 3:606.

31. The heart (Gk. *kardia;* Heb. *lēb* or *lēbāb*) is given by God and represents the essence of one's relationship with God (Isa 51:7; Prov 3:5; 7:3; Jer 31:33; 32:40; Neh 9:8; 1 Sam 12:20, 24). On the other hand, the heart as God's creation appears negative and God can even make it hardened (Jer 23:17; Isa 29:13; 46:12; Ezek 3:7 [LXX 3:4]; Deut 29:18; cf. Job 1:5; Pss 5:9; 10:3; 14:1; 17:10; 28:3; 36:1; 53:1). See Donahue and Harrington, *Gospel of Mark,* 95.

problematic in a relationship with God. That those discussions come from the heart—precisely the source of relationship with God—and are evil is proven in Jesus' saying in 7:21-23: "For it is from within, from the human heart, that evil intentions [*hoi dialogismoi hoi kakoi*] come. . . . All these evil things come from within, and they defile a person."

This evidence is suggestive of a similar disposition of "heart" between the disciples and the leaders opposing Jesus. Strikingly enough, the disciples are not saved from Satan's influence on the heart. According to Jesus' explanation of the parable in 4:14-20, one of causes that makes misunderstanding happen is Satan's work.[32] Even Peter is called "Satan" by Jesus and rebuked for his resistance to the idea of Jesus' passion (8:33). Further, the case of the seeds sown upon rocky ground symbolizes people who hear and receive the word but "fall away" (*skandalizō*) because of persecution on account of the word (4:17). In Mark's narrative, this characterization fits the disciples because they "fall away" facing Jesus' passion (14:27, 29; cf. 6:3, 9:42-47).

This *skandalon* is caused by the estrangement of the disciples' hearts from Jesus rather than ignorance of who Jesus is. They lack communal solidarity to be sustained in a new kind of kinship relation and instead pursue the path of their honor (9:33-34; 10:35-37, 41). The latter point contradicts the communal code through which Jesus has tried to communicate with his disciples. If Jesus aims to create a new family and establish the relationship of equality, it is all the more important that they not honor themselves when he takes a position of humiliation.

Facing the challenges of consumerist greed, pride of caste, and nationalism in India, George M. Soares-Prabhu finds a tribal ethos of indigenous peoples' anti-greed and anti-pride in Jesus' teaching in Mark (10:17-27 and 10:35-45, respectively).[33] Anti-greed and anti-pride are community values that the church should pursue by demonstrating its poverty and its humil-

---

32. This parable does not mention the heart but suggests that the hardness of the heart is related to how the word could be sown in the heart. God gives God's word to (the heart of) the people in various ways such as the law, commandments, and words (Isa 51:7; Prov 7:1-3; Jer 31:33 [LXX 38:33]).

33. George M. Soares-Prabhu, "Anti-Greed and Anti-Pride: Mark 10:17-27 and 10:35-45 in the Light of Tribal Values," in *Voices from the Margin: Interpreting the Bible in the Third World*, ed. R. S. Sugirtharajah, new ed. (Maryknoll, N.Y.: Orbis, 1995), 112–28. See also www.kamalakarduvvuru.blogspot.com.

ity (servanthood) as Jesus practiced.[34] Like Prabhu, many readers living in cultures where a communal ethos is predominant give their attention to the communal aspects of the text, such as the relationship between Jesus and the disciples in understanding discipleship. This relationship begins not with knowing who the other is but with feelings of bond and trust. These feelings are fundamentally euphoric. In contrast, double-mindedness at the moment in which one is called to be committed and searching for autonomy in the place of solidarity bring about dysphoria. To be sure, lack of solidarity and loyalty, or betrayal, is shameful. Moreover, it is frightening if the disciples, seemingly the very insiders, could fall away like the people who reject Jesus (6:3) and be treated like the Jewish leaders or even Satan, who drives Jesus to his death, and if they could not be forgiven (4:12).

I argue that the disciples' absence during the passion and their betrayal are shameful, but the relationship between the disciples and Jesus does not easily fail in the Gospel. The renewal of relationship can be sought in communal ways.[35] The reader's identification with the disciples creates anxiety, but their genuine encounter with the mystery can happen by way of communion.

Mystery of Communion

While a paralytic is forgiven as well as healed by Jesus because of his faith and that of his friends (2:5), both the scribes, who question Jesus' authority for forgiveness, and the disciples do not seem to be healed and forgiven because of the hardness of their hearts. Although Mark reveals the disciples' lack of faith and it endangers their relationship with God as well as with Jesus, they can be forgiven when they pray; but this prayer should be accompanied by forgiving others (11:24-25; cf. 9:24, 29). The restoration of relationship comprises both communal and devotional aspects, and it occurs through practicing ritual.

---

34. Soares-Prabhu, "Anti-Greed," 124–25.

35. Some Western scholars conclude that it is an intention of the narrative to help the readers recognize that they could become the outsiders in salvation and, thus, that they should watch out for hardness of heart. Thus, when the disciples return to Galilee and meet the resurrected Jesus, and the reader goes back to the beginning of the Gospel, the reader, as well as the disciples, comes to know who Jesus is and to be restored. Yet this interpretation is still individualist in that the restoration is a personal matter and the relationship is confined to struggling to know who Jesus was and what he did. See Werner Kelber, *The Kingdom in Mark: A New Place and a New Time* (Philadelphia: Fortress Press, 1974).

This holistic experience in ritual is not foreign to Korean culture, especially, in shamanism.

> Shamanism is really about synthesis, about the bringing together of things that might otherwise appear to be disparate: the world of the living and the world of the dead: the past, present, and future; the individual and the community; humans and animals; the persona and the cosmos—and in every case, the synthesis creates a form of healing.[36]

The shaman ceremony causes a community to experience "synchronicity." People are engaged not only "with the shamanic ceremony in which they found themselves, but with each other."[37]

I do not want to confuse Christian ritual with that of shamanism. Yet such an experience of synchronicity in the shaman ceremony may help us perceive the presence of mystery in ritual as represented in Mark. Again, 4:11-12 and 13 are key to grasping Mark's concern with the mystery in terms of understanding and faith. The NRSV translates *to mystērion,* as "the secret," while the NASB, the NJB, the KJV, and others render it as "the mystery." A "secret" is like a knowable unknown thing, while a "mystery" is not necessarily ever uncovered. It often remains hidden.

Whereas in Matt 13:11 Jesus says to the disciples, "To you it has been given *to know the secrets [ta mystēria]* of the kingdom of heaven," in Mark 4:11 Jesus tells them, "To you has been given *the secret [to mystērion]* of the kingdom of God." Thus, in Mark, what is given to the disciples is *the mystery itself,* not the ability to know the mysteries. Luke Timothy Johnson maintains that the mystery is Jesus himself, who is the personification of the kingdom, and the mystery of the kingdom remains alive and fearful, beyond the followers' comprehension.[38]

---

36. Heinz Insu Fenkl, "Reflections on Shamanism," in *New Spiritual Homes: Religion and Asian Americans,* ed. David K. Yoo, Intersections (Honolulu: University of Hawaii Press, 1999), 194.

37. Ibid., 199.

38. Luke Timothy Johnson, *The Writings of the New Testament: An Interpretation,* rev. ed. (Minneapolis: Fortress Press, 1999), 168–69, 172. According to Johnson, parables function like "the coded insider language of apocalyptic." He argues that everything is in parables to those outside, simply because "they do not have the single necessary hermeneutical key: the acceptance of Jesus." Donahue and Harrington (*Gospel of Mark,* 29) also point out that the term *mystery* has "apocalyptic overtones connoting the disclosure by God of a truth hidden until a certain decisive point in the divine plan is reached." But what one can see from their

Many Western scholars maintain that the final revelation has been accomplished and thus everyone can know the mystery; the remaining thing is to accept Jesus Christ and follow him to the cross. Yet many people who suffer from (neo)colonialism, wars, oppression, and poverty in the world cry, "Where is Jesus in our lives?" Is this mere misunderstanding? Actually, these cries come not only from sufferers today; they are expressed in the disciples' desperate sigh, "we have no bread for our journey" (8:16). One typically reads this statement as stressing the disciples' absurdity in that they do not realize who Jesus is even after the feeding miracle. Yet I read this passage as an invitation to ritual, which can help the believer experience the mystery.

They have one loaf (*hena arton*, 8:14) with them in the boat, but they "discuss" with one another that they have no bread (*artous ouk echousin*, 8:16). Unlike in Matthew's parallel passage (16:5-8), they do not recognize the presence of "one loaf" in the boat and their "discussion" implies their hardened heart. Then Jesus sees into their heart, saying, "Do you not yet perceive or understand? Are your hearts hardened? Having eyes do you not see, and having ears do you not hear? And do you not remember?" (RSV, 8:17b-18).[39] On the surface, this saying calls the disciples to remember the event that happened immediately before, the miracle of bread, in which Jesus broke and gave bread to the disciples to distribute it to many (8:1-9; 6:34-44). On a deeper level, however, they are urged to perceive Jesus in or as the miracle of bread, through which he continues to share his body and blood in the Eucharist (14:22-24): ". . . he broke it, gave it to them, and said, 'Take; this is my body.'"

Jesus is the mystery, not given to know, but given to see, hear, touch, and eat. This is what "understanding" means. He is the mystery, the mystery present in the midst of our lives even though we do not realize or grasp that he is here.

---

interpretation is their adherence to "knowing Jesus." "The full unveiling of this secret comes at the cross when the centurion cries out (15:39), and the dramatic challenge of Mark's Gospel is whether the followers of Jesus can accept Jesus' own revelation that he is a Messiah, and whether they are ready to follow him to the cross (8:31-38)."

39. It is interesting to see that the NRSV and the NIV interpret the disciples' inability to see, hear, and remember as "failure," while the RSV, the NASB, the NJB, and the KJV simply state that the disciples do not see, hear, or remember.

Concluding Comments

The communal code in the relationship between Jesus and the disciples is not based on an asymmetrical reciprocal relationship, which is pervasive in the broader culture, but reflects the newly established relationship of bonds and trust between Jesus and the disciples. The radical relationality becomes possible by experiencing the mystery of God's kingdom through Jesus. *Understanding* is the experience of the mystery, not the unraveling or unveiling of its secrets. Understanding is the solid heart and belonging. Knowing cannot make following; but being-with will mean following. Many know who Jesus is. But why does Jesus keep saying to them, "Do you not yet understand?" It is because he is the mystery. If you keep hearing the voice, do not fear, do not feel bad; it is not failure. It is an invitation to communion—communion with the mystery.

CHAPTER 5

The Markan Construction of Jesus as Disciple of the Kingdom

Osvaldo D. Vena

I propose to examine the theme of discipleship in the Gospel of Mark from two different contextual perspectives: my own and that of the author of the Gospel. Even though I feel confident that I can explain my context with a certain degree of accuracy, in the case of the evangelist's it is more complicated, for I have no direct access to the real-life context of the evangelist. Therefore, I have to use the tools provided by the historical and literary methods, in addition to a good deal of informed imagination and creativity. All of this will "create" a context for Mark that needs to be seen as a theoretical construct that will help me relate the message of the Gospel to my own situation. But let me start with my context.

My Context

Context is not necessarily an obvious reality. And that is so because what makes up a person's context is not only his or her present situation but all those things that, from birth, have contributed to it. There is an aspect of context that is hidden and can be made explicit only through a conscious retelling of one's personal history. Therefore, I want to foreground my context in the following way: I am a Latin American *evangélico* by birth and up-bringing, a New Testament scholar, a seminary professor living in the

United States, and a Christian committed to a life of discipleship centered on justice issues.

Latin American Evangélico *by Birth and Upbringing*

Growing up *evangélico* in Argentina, a Roman Catholic country, I knew from the very beginning that I was part of a religious minority. This produced in me feelings of marginalization and inferiority, which the strong apocalyptic element of the particular version of the gospel that I received served to somehow assuage.[1] All of this gave me the first context for reading the biblical text, one that lacked a sociopolitical analysis of society. Concerned only with the final destiny of people's souls, we embarked on an aggressive program of evangelization, which made us feel even more marginal, as we tried to turn the Roman Catholic majority away from their "idolatrous" ways. Feeling the logical rejection that this produced, we took refuge in those passages of Scripture that promised heavenly rewards to those who suffered for the sake of the gospel. During all this time we never, or seldom, used the word *disciple* to describe our predicament. We used rather the word *creyente,* that is, "believer." Our mission was to make believers out of people, not disciples. The difference between these two expressions is important: believers give intellectual assent to doctrines; disciples commit to a certain way of life. One expression is static; the other has movement.

Owing to this lack of social praxis, my denomination never endorsed participation in the political processes of the country. So during the troubled years of the "dirty war,"[2] we lived as if nothing was happening. Unlike other denominations, such as the Methodists or the Anglicans, or even the Roman Catholic Church, there were no *desaparecidos* ("disappeared" persons) among C&MA members.

---

1. I was brought up in the Christian and Missionary Alliance (C&MA), a U.S.A.-based denomination with roots in the Holiness Movements and very closely tied in its beginnings to Pentecostalism. Its main doctrine was what was called the Foursquare Gospel: Christ Our Savior, Sanctifier, Healer, and Coming King. In the early years of the twentieth century, missionaries from the C&MA founded in my hometown a biblical institute which became the ideological base of the denomination. The institute eventually moved to the capital city of Buenos Aires, from where I graduated in 1975 with a bachelor's degree in theology.
2. This is the name given to the years of the military repression in Argentina, between 1976 and 1983, when approximately forty thousand people disappeared.

New Testament Scholar

My training as a New Testament scholar[3] brought about profound changes in the way I read the Bible. One of them was the understanding of the contextual nature of all theology, including biblical theology. This, of course, included apocalyptic thought. It also provided me with tools to understand the societies that produced the text. At the same time, I was learning to "read" my own society. It is here that my apocalyptic vision of the world started to collapse and the historical realities of both the Bible and my own existence began to acquire a relevance they had never had before. But this did not happen overnight. It took several years for everything to materialize.

The process started while I was at Princeton, reading the works of liberation, black, and feminist theologians. In addition, the work of anthropologist Victor Turner, especially *The Ritual Process,* helped me understand concepts such as liminality and marginality.[4] These ideas gave me the tools I would use later on to evaluate my upbringing as a marginal *evangélico.* Back in Argentina, during the Malvinas war,[5] I began to serve a congregation of Scottish Presbyterians who were feeling the social dislocation produced by the war. The church was located in the downtown area of Buenos Aires, where many abandoned buildings were being occupied by squatters and homeless people. My ministry took on a new dimension, as political and social issues became the main focus of my preaching and teaching. At the same time, I started my doctoral work at ISEDET, an institution that had endorsed the work of the Madres de Plaza de Mayo[6] and because of that had endured a bomb attack on its library. When I consider my theological training in all of these institu-

---

3. I received a Master of Divinity degree from Bethel Theological Seminary in Saint Paul, Minnesota, and a Master of Theology degree from Princeton Theological Seminary. My doctoral work is from what used to be called ISEDET (Instituto Superior de Estudios Teológicos), now called Instituto Universitario ISEDET.

4. Victor Turner, *The Ritual Process: Structure and Anti-Structure,* The Lewis Henry Morgan Lectures 1966 (London: Routledge & Kegan Paul, 1969; repr., Chicago: Aldine, 1995).

5. In 1982, Argentina invaded the Falkland Islands, a territory Argentina has claimed as its own since 1833. The short war that ensued ended with the victory of England who regained possession of the islands.

6. The Madres de Plaza de Mayo was a group of courageous mothers who every Thursday afternoon marched around the main square in front of the Casa Rosada, the main government building in Buenos Aires city, demanding information about the whereabouts of their children who had been abducted by the police. This group later became one of the driving forces responsible for the overthrow of the military dictatorship.

tions, I am astonished by the radical nature of the journey it delineates: from a spiritualizing apocalypticism to a radical political engagement in society. The two approaches could not have been more opposed. It was about this time that the word *disciple* entered my theological jargon, due in part to the prominent use of the expression in liberation theology.

Seminary Professor Living in the United States

Teaching in a seminary, I see my work as preparing ministers and scholars for the church. The classroom is my main locus for praxis, and it is here that I encounter students who come to class with a worldview similar to the one I used to have. This worldview is the product of a culture that has been influenced by evangelical and conservative theology, in which concepts such as the victory of good (democracy, Christianity, the Western way of life, capitalism) over evil (socialism, communism, Islam, Islamic societies) and the kingdom of God (globalization, market economy) prevail. In this context I found myself doing a constant work of deconstruction in order to present a strategy of reading that is ethical, liberating, and life-giving. I do this many times by offering my own journey as an example of the kind of epistemological shift that is required to move away from a spiritualizing apocalypticism toward a historical and political praxis.

Christian Committed to a Life of Discipleship Centered on Justice Issues

The church that I serve from my position as a seminary professor is located in the United States of America, a context that has also shaped the way I see the world, and has added some layers to the way I read the Bible. Out of this context, I lift up two sets of issues. One relates to the situation of women and sexual minorities, especially in the life of the church. The other relates to issues of peace and justice, especially those that have been brought to the fore by the 9/11 attacks and the immigration debate of the last years. For me, it is impossible to speak of discipleship without making these two sets of issues a fundamental part of its meaning.

The understanding of discipleship that informs this essay is unapologetically nonapocalyptic[7] and praxis-centered, and it came about in the way I described above: from seeking to prepare people for the imminent end of the

---

7. Apocalyptic, or apocalypticism, is here understood in a traditional, literal, and futuristic manner. It refers to that biblical worldview that sees history as reaching a predetermined

world to seeking social changes inspired by the principles of the gospel. This movement from escape from the world to ministry in and to the world is one that I see also in the Gospel of Mark, and it constitutes the lenses through which I am going to read the text.

Mark's Context

Mark received from the traditions that came from the earliest Jesus movement an apocalyptic worldview and a sense of detachment from the world as its members waited for the *parousia*. Not a small part of this ideology came from the apostle Paul. Discipleship was not even a concept in this worldview. Rather, it came as a de-apocalyptizing concept that was necessitated by and developed during the Jewish revolt of 66–70 c.e. Therefore, I would argue that the whole idea of discipleship is a theological *novum* introduced by Mark and then picked up and developed further by Matthew and Luke using their common source "Q." The apostle Paul, who wrote before Mark, never used the term *disciple* and consequently never conceived of a theology of discipleship.

Discipleship in Mark is a theological development prompted by the situation of his community. When he writes, he constructs a picture of Jesus with the hope of teaching his congregation about the implications of following Jesus in that specific context. Because he was living during a time of heightened apocalyptic expectations that affected the way his community understood its mission in the world, he needed a compelling model for discipleship. So he tells the story of Jesus in which he intentionally portrays the male disciples as complete failures. Naturally, the reader's attention shifts to the female disciples, who, even though they perform better than their male counterparts, in the end seem also to fail to grasp the whole dimension of the resurrection. The reader is then left with only one model to follow: Jesus. He is presented by Mark as the ideal disciple of the kingdom. The kingdom is still an eschatological reality, but, through a reworking of the apocalyptic traditions that he received, Mark manages to shift the focus of attention of the community from heaven to earth. The Son of Man is already present on

---

grand finale that will give way to a new creation to be enjoyed only by the elect, those who remained faithful to God or God's Messiah, Jesus Christ.

earth, and he will never leave it, for the ascension plays no role in Mark's narrative.

I divide this study into two sections. The first will show that Jesus indeed is the model disciple of the kingdom par excellence. The second will analyze the role of Jesus as Son of Man as being a corporate one. This in turn will be read in terms of discipleship: Jesus represents the suffering people of God, that is, his followers, his disciples (but not exclusively the Twelve). I will attempt to prove that it is Mark's context, namely, the Jewish revolt of 66–70 C.E., that prompted this corporate reading of the Danielic and Enochic traditions.

Mark's Rationale

Why was it necessary for Mark to develop an appropriate concept of discipleship and to use Jesus as the supreme example? I suggest two reasons, one external, the other internal.

External

Faced with the dilemma of supporting the revolt, which propelled the Jewish people to rebel against Rome and which ended with the destruction of Jerusalem and the temple, the believers needed to have a model of discipleship that would guide them through those difficult years. The issue at stake was whether being followers of Jesus the Messiah would preclude them from or encourage them to join the uprising. Mark senses the tension, due especially to the mixed nature of his congregation (Gentiles and Jews), and so he embarks on the task of writing the story of Jesus, depicting him as the model disciple of the kingdom of God, one who resisted evil but shunned violent confrontation. Mark is hoping that this will help his congregation make a decision against armed revolution and at the same time encourage them to fix their hope on the kingdom of God, which, in his opinion, was to be brought about not by human efforts but by the power of God through the risen Christ.

Internal

By pointing to Jesus as the model disciple, Mark is trying to counteract a tendency in his community to organize into a more structured group, where issues of power and gender inequality in the leadership were already at work.

Mark is attempting to direct his community, which was showing signs of accommodation to the world, to engage in a countercultural praxis resembling that of the early Jesus movement. Therefore, he describes Jesus as the model disciple, the wandering charismatic par excellence, which serves the purpose of criticizing that authority that is not dependent on the power of the Spirit. In the story, Jesus' disciples, already figures of authority in the early church known by Mark, are portrayed as absolute failures, embodying a type of anti-discipleship.[8] Jesus, then, becomes by default the true disciple, the disciple par excellence. Besides that, Mark sees the Jewish revolt as a sign of the impending end, so he has no desire to foster stable communities but rather is intent on reclaiming an eschatological/apocalyptic ethos similar, though not identical as we will see, to the one that characterized the wandering charismatics of the Jesus movement, in order to offer an alternative to the nationalist messianism of the Zealots. Discipleship and prophetic engagement in society are presented, then, as the true ethos of the group, and Jesus is shown as the one who best incarnates this ethos.

Mark's Portrayal of Jesus as Disciple of the Kingdom

The most obvious place to start with Mark's portrayal of Jesus as disciple of the kingdom is the beginning of Jesus' ministry, his baptism by John.

Baptism (1:9-11)

Jesus appears suddenly in the narrative as coming from Nazareth of Galilee and being baptized by John. The narrator has prepared us to see Jesus as one who is mightier than the Baptist and who will baptize with the Holy Spirit (1:7-8), but even so, Jesus' coming to John can only be interpreted in terms of discipleship.[9] When Jesus finally starts his ministry, he does so by preaching

---

8. I agree here with Richard A. Horsley when he asks the rhetorical question: "Is it possible that Mark's story presses a criticism, within the broader Jesus movement, of what the twelve disciples had become in the course of the first generation, as it summoned the movement back to its roots in the social revolutionary practice and preaching of Jesus?" (*Hearing the Whole Story: The Politics of Plot in Mark's Gospel* [Louisville: Westminster John Knox, 2001], 77).

9. The other Gospels try to qualify this obvious subordination of Jesus to John by adding traditions that depict Jesus as voluntarily adopting a subordinate position which was necessary in God's overall plan. See Matt 3:14; John 1:26-27.

a message that is very similar to the one John, his teacher, preached (1:14-15).[10] He calls people to repentance in view of the approaching kingdom of God. His role is that of one who announces, a prophet, one who has been sent to preach, an apostle, a disciple if you will. He subordinates himself completely to God the Patron and the kingdom. He preaches the gospel of God (*to euangelion tou theou*), not his own gospel. So, whereas for the evangelist Jesus' ministry, passion, death, and resurrection constitute "the gospel of Jesus Christ" (1:1), from the perspective of Jesus' own self-awareness at the beginning of his ministry, the gospel he preaches is all about God and the approaching kingdom. The power he will manifest is God's power, which will signal and illustrate the reign that is about to dawn. This power, the narrator tells us, was unleashed from heaven at the baptism and is now residing in him or, as the Greek suggests, "into him" (*eis auton*). Again, we see how Mark makes an effort to depict Jesus as dependent on John for his vision[11] and on God for his power.

If John the Baptist is not only preparing the way for Jesus' ministry but is also issuing a call to people to get ready for the in-breaking of God's kingdom—which may have been the original sense of Mal 3:1 and Isa 40:3—then Jesus is accepting a call to join forces with all those who heard John's call. The "Lord" of the conflated citation refers not to Jesus—who, interestingly enough, is only once unambiguously called "Lord" in Mark (11:3)—but to the God of Israel.

The Temptation (1:12-13)

Jesus is driven into the wilderness by the Spirit and there he is tempted (*peirazomenon*) by Satan. Like Israel in the Sinai desert, Jesus has to undergo a spiritual preparation for his ministry. He has to get ready for the work ahead, which he will share with his disciples in the same way that John the Baptist

---

10. "The great embarrassment that the Christians faced was that it was well known that John had baptized Jesus—not the other way around! Jesus had come to John and *joined his movement*—which in the context of ancient Judaism meant that Jesus was a disciple of John and John was the rabbi or teacher or Jesus" (James D. Tabor, *The Jesus Dynasty: The Hidden History of Jesus, His Royal Family, and the Birth of Christianity* [New York: Simon & Schuster, 2006], 135).

11. Tabor further suggests that in Luke 11:1-4, when the disciples ask Jesus to teach them to pray "as John taught his disciples," Jesus repeats to them the prayer that he had learned from his teacher, John the Baptist (*Jesus Dynasty*, 137).

shared it with him. But before he can even get started, after having decided to follow John into the Jordan and having received God's word of approval, Jesus has to face the reality of the dangerous path that awaits him. His will be a task of gigantic proportions. Announcing God's kingdom will set him up against human foes and cosmic forces. Satan himself shows up in the wilderness in his traditional role as a tempter, and even though Mark does not tell us, as Matthew and Luke do, about the nature of the temptation, it is safe to assume that Satan is trying to make Jesus abandon his call to be a disciple of the kingdom. Perhaps Satan is trying to convince Jesus that he needs to embrace a triumphal Messiah sort of vocation, but one in which Jesus would first have to pay homage to the tempter (cf. Matt 4:1-11; Luke 4:1-13). This first test of his vocation is met with success, for the text tells us that "the angels waited on him." With this experience, Jesus begins to learn something about the nature of his vocation, namely, that it will entail provoking the very forces of evil. And he will continue to learn throughout his ministry, as he encounters people and calls them into co-discipleship. But this moment remains as a founding moment in Jesus' awareness of his vocation.

The Calling of the First Disciples and the Appointment of the Twelve (1:16-20; 3:13-19)

After calling his first four disciples and inviting them to become fishers of people (1:16-20), Jesus enlarges the group to twelve, a number that seems to point symbolically at a revitalized, renewed Israel. The purpose of the calling was threefold: to be with him, to be sent out to preach, and to have authority to cast out demons. To be with him may imply some kind of training both by example and by teaching. In this regard, Jesus presents himself as a model. He was also sent (9:37) with a mission, which included preaching and casting out demons. His time of preparation must have happened during the time he spent with John the Baptist, his mentor and teacher, from whom he absorbed the passion for God's kingdom. Or perhaps this process had started earlier, when he was growing up in Galilee, studying the Galilean version of the traditions of Israel.

The text of Mark allows for the period prior to Jesus' encounter with John and the period during which Jesus obviously was one of John's disciples as the only time Jesus had to gain a preliminary awareness of what his public activity in Israel was to be. But discipleship is never an overnight occurrence.

It develops through time. So in the case of Jesus, there must have been a developing awareness; that is, a changing sense of what his mission was to be as he encountered people and their reactions to his message. It is now usually accepted by scholars that Jesus' encounter with the Syrophoenician woman in 7:24-30 marks an important stage in Jesus' own consciousness as a prophet/disciple of the kingdom. Here he is being forced by a foreign woman to realize that his ministry should not be limited to the "children" but should also include others, those who up to this point he had considered "dogs." From now on he will see them in a new and different light, namely, as people worthy of God's liberating activity through his ministry (cf. 7:31-37 and 8:1-10: these are all Gentiles). To consider Gentiles part of God's covenant people required an effort beyond anything else Jesus had done to the present. It was a radical change in the way he perceived the God of Israel. All this constitutes part of Jesus' learning what it meant to be a disciple of the kingdom.[12]

Parables of the Kingdom (4:1-20)

All the parables in chapter 4 of the Gospel of Mark are kingdom parables. The first one, the parable of the sower, is important, for it seems to portray Jesus as the proclaimer of God's kingdom. As the sower, Jesus sows the word (*logos*). And what is this word? Judging by what has transpired so far in the narrative, the word is the preaching of the good news of the kingdom of God (1:14-15, 38; 2:2). The clearest correspondence between the sower and Jesus is found in 4:3, which says that the sower "went out to sow." The verb is *exēlthen*, an aorist of *exerchomai*. The same verb is used in 1:38, where Jesus says that he "came out," *exēlthon,* in order that he might preach also in the surrounding towns. Thus, the sower going out to sow is a metaphorical way of referring to Jesus' public activity of proclamation. As the sower, Jesus handles the seed (the good news) and scatters it over different types of terrain, but he is unable to guarantee its growth in the same way that later on he will be unable to guarantee healing in his hometown of Nazareth (6:5-6). It is God who makes the seed grow depending on people's response to the good news. And healing is always God's prerogative. As a disciple of the kingdom,

---

12. "The people of Israel . . . are now undergoing a renewal like their original formation in the exodus and wilderness under Moses' leadership *and* the kingdom of God is now being expanded to include other peoples as well in the renewal led by the new Moses-Elijah" (Horsley, *Hearing the Whole Story,* 89).

Jesus is responsible only to do the will of the one who sent him, namely, to proclaim the word, to sow the seed of the kingdom.

The third parable is that of the growing grain (4:26-29), where again the seed represents the word, the message. Its growth is independent of the person who was given the task of sowing the seed—in this case Jesus, but eventually the disciples also. Jesus is thus presented as being in the service of the kingdom. He is facilitating it as a broker of God's power.

The Sending of the Twelve (6:7-13)

Jesus now sends the disciples on their mission. This had been pre-announced in 3:13-19. They are sent with authority over unclean spirits, to preach repentance and to heal the sick. They are to rely on people's hospitality, as they do not carry anything with them, not even a change of clothes. Jesus is not sending them to do anything he has not already done (with the exception perhaps of the anointing with oil, which is probably a practice of the early church read back into this story), and he tells them not to expect a different treatment from that which he received (cf. 6:1-6a). They should expect their mission to be neither more nor less than what Jesus himself was willing to do in obedience to the one who had sent him, God (cf. 9:37). In so doing, Jesus is modeling true discipleship.

Peter's Confession (8:27-30)

People saw Jesus as a prophet (Elijah or one of the prophets) or even as someone who closely resembled John the Baptist. Peter thinks he is the Messiah. This affirmation does not elicit much enthusiasm on Jesus' part, but rather a prohibition to talk about him. For some reason, Jesus does not want people to know him as the Messiah.[13] Why is that? One answer is that it is still too early in Jesus' career, and such a revelation could have hampered what he wanted to accomplish. Another is that he is not satisfied with the popular expectations concerning the Messiah and therefore he is going to redefine the messianic role radically. I believe this last possibility is closer to the spirit of Mark, especially in the context of the scribal conception of the Messiah as

---

13. In traditional scholarship, this is known as the "messianic secret," first proposed by William Wrede in 1901. But my intention here is to find out how it functions in the narrative, in the story. Whether Jesus or the early church said this is beyond the point for my endeavors in the present work. For a narrative understanding of the messianic secret, see David L. Barr, *New Testament Story: An Introduction,* 3rd ed. (Belmont, Calif.: Wadsworth, 2002), 277–78.

son of David (cf. Mark 12:35-37). I suggest that here Jesus is not even think-ing in messianic terms but more in terms of discipleship. He sees himself as a messenger (1:2), a disciple of the kingdom of God. Notice that right after this passage, Jesus talks about himself using another expression, "Son of Man," and he does so in a context that is clearly about discipleship. I will contend later in this article that the expression *Son of Man* can and perhaps should be interpreted through the lens of discipleship.

Jesus, Apostle of God (9:37)

In this passage Jesus tells his disciples, who had been arguing on the way about greatness, that God has sent him. He also sends his disciples into the mission (3:14; 6:7). In both cases, the verb is the same, *apostellō*. God sends Jesus, and he in turn sends the disciples. This makes them co-participants in the same mission from God. Just as Jesus acts as the broker of God's king-dom, so also the disciples, being sent by Jesus, become themselves brokers, agents of the kingdom of God and co-disciples with Jesus.[14] In 6:30, and perhaps also in 3:14, the disciples are called apostles (*apostoloi*), those being sent. This can only be so because they have been appointed by the one who is himself an apostle of God (". . . and whoever welcomes me welcomes not me but the one who *sent* me [*ton aposteilanta me*], 9:37). Jesus, as an apostle of God, is sending others as his envoys. In the early church, apostleship will have connotations of supreme authority. But here in Mark, it preserves the original meaning: someone being sent to represent the one doing the sending, in this case God or Jesus. It is synonymous with messenger and disciple.

Jesus Calls a Man to Joint Discipleship (10:18)

The story of the rich man provides another illustration of Jesus as disciple of the kingdom. For Jesus, God is clearly the ultimate reality, the only one in whom true goodness resides: "No one is good but God alone," he tells the man. Here Jesus seems to acknowledge his complete subordination to God. He does not see himself as an end but rather as a means to God and to the kingdom. When Jesus calls the man to follow him (10:21), it can be inter-preted as a call to become co-builders of the kingdom, co-disciples. Jesus is not the one who grants entrance into the kingdom. As the context clearly

---

14. Bruce J. Malina says that "they serve as agents of the central broker, Jesus" (*The Social World of Jesus and the Gospels* [London/New York: Routledge, 1996], 152).

shows, it is only God who makes it possible for human beings, including Jesus himself, to access the kingdom (10:27).

The Institution of the Last Supper (14:22-25)

On the occasion of the Last Supper, Jesus again seems to minimize his role, while at the same time maximizing God and the kingdom. His blood is poured out for many, but nothing is said about "the forgiveness of sins," as is the case in Matt 26:28. Nor is the kingdom the "kingdom of my Father," as in Matt 26:29, but "the kingdom of God." A number of things are interesting in this passage. First, there is the idea of a covenant.[15] The figure being used here is that of God's covenant with Israel in the Old Testament (cf. Exod 24:8 and Jer 31:31-34). One possible way of reading this text is that Jesus is presented here as a new Moses who makes it possible for the renewed and revitalized people of Israel represented by the twelve disciples to attain the deliverance foreshadowed in the exodus account. Second, the pouring out of his blood speaks of Jesus' sacrifice, which is done for the benefit of many. This idea was already present in the Old Testament in the righteous sufferer of the Psalms, in the martyrs of the Maccabean period, and especially in the Suffering Servant of Isaiah 53, which had clear atonement connotations. But we do not know if this is what Jesus had in mind. It could very well be that he is thinking about his sacrifice only in exemplary terms. What seems to be clear, though, is that Jesus believed that God would vindicate him—not for being a victim of evil but for being faithful to his prophetic ministry—since he is hoping to drink wine again in the kingdom of God, a classic figure of blessedness taken from the Old Testament (cf. Isa 25:6-8; 49:8-13). This hope for God's vindication is what will inspire believers to endure suffering and even death. If God had vindicated Jesus by raising him from the dead, then God will surely vindicate those who remain faithful as Jesus did. But this hope for vindication is not that of a victim of evil. The disciple is not a voluntary victim. Jesus' death was not voluntary. God's vindication can happen only to those who, like Jesus, find their lives cut short by those who do not want the arrival of a new reality that will irreversibly change the established order of things.

---

15. Luke 22:20 has "new covenant," as does Paul in 1 Cor 11:25. The word "new" is missing in Mark 14:24 and Matt 26:28, but it has been added in some manuscripts in order to harmonize it with the Lukan and Pauline versions of the institution of the supper.

Jesus in Gethsemane (14:32-42)

In the garden of Gethsemane, Jesus is not ready to face his fate, but he is willing to obey the will of God. This, in a nutshell, describes Mark's notion of an ideal disciple: knowing how high the price is for being faithful to God's kingdom; the disciple, personified supremely in Jesus, is willing to pay that price. This may point at the situation of the Markan community, which was probably undergoing strenuous times as the Jewish revolt was forcing people to take sides. Which side was the community going to be on, that of the revolutionaries or that of the priests and aristocrats who favored submission to Rome? Not wanting to endure what seemed unavoidable and yet submitting to the will of God made Jesus the perfect example of how a disciple must behave when confronted with the choice between violent revolt and passive submission. Jesus will endorse neither of the two actions, but rather will propose a third option: nonviolent resistance, thus setting an example that the members of the community could follow.

Mark's Understanding of the Life of Discipleship[16]

Mark's description of true discipleship revolves around the main paradox of 8:34-37, which suggests that life is preserved when given up for Jesus and the message of the gospel.[17] This can be attained only through a total and unconditional allegiance to God the Teacher,[18] the God of the covenant. This allegiance will place the disciple in direct opposition to other authorities such as the temple priests, the Pharisees and scribes, and the Roman Empire. In the Gospel's narrative, Jesus is the only one who embodies this kind of obedience. Therefore, Mark uses Jesus' example to challenge and encourage

---

16. Mark's understanding of discipleship is a theological construct—a novel one—for he seems to be the first New Testament writer to propose this notion. The concept is missing entirely from Paul's writings, which precede Mark's Gospel, and from the rest of the New Testament epistles and Revelation. It appears only in the Synoptic Gospels, the Gospel of John, and Acts.

17. If, as I have argued elsewhere, the whole Gospel has its center precisely at this point, then Mark's description of the life of discipleship, exemplified in Jesus' life, does indeed rotate around this rhetorical axis. See Osvaldo D. Vena, "The Rhetorical and Theological Center of Mark's Gospel," in Guillermo Hansen, ed., *Los caminos inexhauribles de la Palabra*, ed. Guillermo Hansen (Buenos Aires: Lumen/ISEDET, 2000), 343–45.

18. For the concept of God as teacher, see John 6:45; Isa 54:13; Jer 32:33; Hos 11:13; Pss 71:17; 119:102.

his community, for he knows that many of its members, like Jesus, are in danger of losing their lives. We conclude, then, that for Mark discipleship may be seen as an attitude of recommitment to the God of Israel marked by repentance and obedience, a process that goes from having one's life secure and structured within the society of the time to a life that is constantly under threat for the sake of Jesus and the gospel message.

The issue of discipleship, then, lies at the center of Mark's Gospel. Even though recent studies have tried to demonstrate that that is not the case but that, rather, a reorganization of Israel alongside a renewal of covenantal practices is what really transpires in this Gospel,[19] I maintain that discipleship can be constructed as Mark's central theme, for two reasons. First, Mark is the first document in the New Testament to utilize the word *disciple* and to expand on this notion of following Jesus. Paul, who wrote prior to Mark, does not even use the word or the concept. Therefore, the notion of discipleship is well established in the Markan community as a theological expression of the community's obedience to God through Jesus. Second, given the fact that the male disciples are depicted in such a negative light, it is obvious that this is a rhetorical device that attempts to teach the readers of the Gospel a lesson about true discipleship. Thus, Jesus is used as the supreme example. Finally, the leaders of the early movement represented by the close circle of disciples, namely, Peter, John, and James, are depicted as never quite understanding Jesus' actions and pronouncements, whereas women and children and marginal characters are given a place of relevance. Therefore, Mark may be pointing at a local issue as well as one that transcends the boundaries of his community. I would like now to connect this idea of Jesus as disciple of the kingdom with Jesus' role as Son of Man.

Jesus as the Son of Man in Mark

The Markan Jesus, the one constructed by the text, always refers to himself with the title or role of "Son of Man."[20] The question, then, is: Can this

---

19. For this idea, see Horsley, *Hearing the Whole Story*, 99–111.
20. Again, I will bypass the already too familiar debate among scholars about whether Jesus saw himself as the apocalyptic Son of Man or if this is something added by the evangelist. At the level of the narrative, it is clear that Jesus is the Son of man, both the earthly and the heavenly one.

expression be reread through the hermeneutical key of "discipleship"? Can we find justification in the text itself?[21]

Discipleship as Imitatio Jesu/Son of Man (8:31-38)

As I said before, the rhetorical and theological center of the Gospel could be found at 8:34-38, where the call to discipleship seems to be defined in terms of an *imitatio Jesu,* inasmuch as self-denial and the taking up of the cross are characteristics of Jesus' ministry. Since Jesus is identified in the context as the Son of Man, then the disciples are called to participate in the public activity and fate of this figure: to imitate Jesus is to imitate the Son of Man.[22]

This is the third time that the expression Son of Man has appeared in Mark (see 2:10, 28). But there is a new element here: the Son of Man (or Human One) will suffer, die, and be raised on the third day. All of this provides the backdrop against which one has to read the call to discipleship in 8:34-38. The disciple is someone who renounces a life lived according to the social expectations of the time and joins the group of Jesus' followers who are willing to die, if necessary, for the sake of the gospel. Paradoxically, being willing to risk and even lose one's life will actually save it, the idea here being one of vindication in the new age. Therefore, the disciple shares in the fate of the Son of Man, both in his sufferings and death and in his vindication through resurrection.[23]

But the text says something else about this Son of Man: he will come in the glory of his Father with the holy angels (8:38). This idea is taken from Dan 7:13-14, where the prophet sees one like a Son of Man, or a human being,

---

21. In this section, I use Gerd Theissen's *Sociology of Early Palestinian Christianity*, trans. John Bowden (Philadelphia: Fortress Press, 1978). But whereas his work concentrates on discovering the sociological realities of the community behind the text, I attempt to find a model of discipleship that uses the text as its basis. My presupposition is that Mark, as an author, is rereading the traditions concerning the Son of Man and is offering his community a new model for a specific reason.

22. "The figure of the Son of Man was central for the Jesus movement. His situation corresponded to their situation. Here belief and practice formed an indissoluble whole. The unity of this whole was deliberate. It formed the focal point of the idea of discipleship" (Theissen, *Sociology,* 30).

23. Theissen reminds us that the disciples participate also in the more positive aspects of the Son of Man's role, namely, forgiving sins (Mark 2:11; cf. Matt16:19; 18:18), and having authority over the Sabbath day (Mark 2:23-28) and the regulations of fasting (Matt 11:18-19; cf. Mark 2:18-19) (*Sociology,* 26).

coming to the Ancient of Days and receiving from him power, honor, and the kingdom. An analysis of the context would show that this angelic figure is acting on behalf of the people of Israel, who are suffering under the tyrannical power of Antiochus IV Epiphanes. The Son of Man in Daniel is really a corporate figure, a collective symbol representing the suffering people of God who would soon be vindicated.[24] Would it not be logical, then, to see the Markan Jesus in the same way; that is, as the representative of his co-disciples, those who were not afraid of giving their own lives for the gospel? The problem with this interpretation is that we know that by the first century C.E., Dan 7:13-14 was being read through the lens of the book of *1 Enoch,* especially the section called the Parables of Enoch (chapters 37–71), where the Son of Man is an individual figure, an agent of God's activity, not a corporate symbol for the people.[25] But what if Mark intentionally is ignoring the more prevalent Enochic interpretation and is going back to the traditional Danielic reading of the Son of Man as a collective figure? What would preclude him from doing so? We will try to demonstrate that the evangelist, prompted by the specific situation of his community, may have done precisely that.

Discipleship and Eschatological Glory (10:35-40)

A problem for this way of reasoning may be presented by Mark 10:35-40, where James and John seem to hold to the traditional apocalyptic belief of the Son of Man as an individual figure who will come at the end of time, for they ask Jesus to make them participants in his eschatological glory. But if we take the position outlined above, namely, that Jesus as the Son of Man represents the new people of God, a renewed and revitalized Israel, then Jesus is telling them that to ask for special privileges is to misunderstand the nature of the eschatological kingdom. There are no positions of privilege in the kingdom, only the sharing of power among God's redeemed humanity. In the same way that in 8:35 to lose one's life on behalf of Jesus and the gospel means to save it, so also here the disciples have to be ready to make

---

24. Thomas Kazen, "Son of Man as Kingdom Imagery: Jesus between Corporate Symbol and Individual Redeemer Figure," in *Jesus from Judaism to Christianity: Continuum Approaches to the Historical Jesus,* ed. Tom Holmén, Library of New Testament Studies 352 (London/New York: T.&T. Clark, 2007), 94.

25. George W. E. Nickelsburg, *Ancient Judaism and Christian Origins: Diversity, Continuity, and Transformation* (Minneapolis: Fortress Press, 2003), 110.

the supreme sacrifice for the kingdom if they want to be part of that people whom the Son of Man represents. If this is so, then the exaltation of the Son of Man in Daniel and of Jesus/Son of Man in Mark is something in which the disciples, as members of the new people of God, will eventually participate. Notice that the context does not suggest a coming of the Son of Man from heaven but simply the realization on the part of the two disciples that Jesus is going to be glorified ("in your glory").

In Mark 10:33-34, Jesus had announced for the third time his sufferings, death, and resurrection, utilizing again the image of the Son of Man. In Jesus' hands, this apocalyptic figure has been transformed into a symbol of his own ministry and that of his disciples. Consequently, the first readers of the Gospel—but also contemporary readers—begin to read this symbol with the hermeneutical key of discipleship: any time that the expression "Son of Man" appears, they suspect that it has something to do with their own praxis.[26] In the case of the Markan community, sharing in the sufferings of the Son of Man would come from being faithful to a nonviolent understanding of the kingdom in the midst of the Jewish revolutionaries' vision of an armed revolt against Rome. But their suffering would give way, as in Daniel 7, to their vindication, which was anticipated in Jesus' resurrection.

The Final Coming of the Son of Man in(to) Glory

The doctrine of the victorious return of Christ to earth to reward the faithful and to exercise judgment upon those who do not believe in him is firmly established in the New Testament. It was most probably developed by the early church, following ideas found in *1 Enoch* and *4 Ezra,* in order to explain to the world Jesus' shameful death and to bring consolation to those who were suffering for their faith. This is especially prominent in the eschatological passages of the Synoptic Gospels, in the book of Revelation, in 1 Thess 4:13—5:11, and in 1 Cor 15:20-28. The apostle Paul had no small role to play in the shaping of this doctrine. But what would happen if one were to regard the coming in clouds of the Son of Man not so much as the appearance of Christ at the *parousia* but as a metaphor, or a symbol, for that moment when

---

26. Again, Theissen says: "Above all in the figure of the Son of Man, early Christian wandering charismatics were able to interpret and come to terms with their own social situation" (*Sociology,* 27).

God gives the kingdom to God's people, doing justice to those who suffered for their obedience to Jesus and the gospel?

I propose that those passages in which the Son of Man is coming in clouds (see Mark 13:24-27; 14:62) point to the vindication of the suffering people of God and not so much to Christ's *parousia*. From a narrative point of view, Jesus does not have to come back in victory from heaven, because he never went there in the first place. He is *already* present among the disciples as the risen one who will meet them in Galilee.

The Son of Man Comes in *and* with *Clouds:* Parousia *Redefined*

In 13:24-27, Mark includes a tradition, based on Dan 7:13-14, that seems to point to the coming of the Son of Man, Jesus Christ, to earth in the end-times. As we said before, this tradition was already being reinterpreted through the lens of the book of Enoch, where the Son of man is portrayed as an individual who comes to earth to establish the messianic kingdom. Mark, or the tradition he utilizes, changes the Danielic quotation to make it read as if the Son of Man comes down to earth "in clouds" (*en*) instead of "with" (*meta*) clouds, as is the case in Daniel, where the idea seems to be that the Son of Man goes *to* the Ancient of Days.[27] But the problem is that Mark's narrative strategy deconstructs this reading. What is missing in his Gospel is that moment that makes it possible for Jesus to return to earth; namely, the ascension. So the coming of the Son of Man is announced, but this coming does not necessarily mean to earth. Rather, as in Daniel, the Son of Man is coming to God (this is described in visionary fashion at the transfiguration), to receive the kingdom. I suggest that it is plausible that Mark understood this as happening at the resurrection. By virtue of his resurrection and glorification, Jesus as the Son of Man is given power and authority in a representative way, but the kingdom is not yet given to the people of the Son of Man until he meets them in Galilee, after the resurrection.

In 14:62, Jesus answers the high priest's question: "Are you the Messiah, the Son of the Blessed One?" with "You said that I am."[28] And he quickly

---

27. See my discussion of Norman Perrin's treatment of this idea in Osvaldo D. Vena, *The Parousia and Its Rereadings: The Development of the Eschatological Consciousness in the Writings of the New Testament,* Studies in Biblical Literature 27 (New York: Peter Lang, 2001), 180–81.

28. The manuscript evidence for this reading is as follows: Θ *f*13 565 700.

adds: "And you will see the Son of Man seated at the right hand of Power, and coming with the clouds of heaven." This is the same quotation from Dan 7:13-14 that was used in 13:26, except that this time the Son of Man is seated at the right hand of God (cf. Ps 110:1) and comes "with" (*meta*) the clouds of heaven! From his use of Old Testament passages, it is obvious that Mark is trying not only to preserve some authentic oral traditions about Jesus but also to construct a Christology suitable to his audience, the gist of which is as follows: Jesus is affirming his role as Son of Man, the Human One, the representative of God's suffering people. He anticipates his own vindication as well as that of the disciples, his followers. This is described as being seated at the right hand of the Power to whom he will come with the clouds, that is, through his glorification at the resurrection. The historical moment in which Mark's congregation is living would point to this understanding of the kingdom. His community should disregard the messianic claims of the revolutionaries, who are trying to establish God's reign by force, and look forward to the day when Jesus, the risen Son of Man, will receive from God the power to rule and will share it with his co-disciples. At that moment the disciples who lost their lives for the sake of Jesus and the gospel (the message of the kingdom) will save their lives. At that moment their vindication will take place. To say more than this would be to import insights from other Gospels or from other authors, like Paul. We contend that this reading is especially warranted by Mark, though there are elements for a similar reading in the other Gospels.

The Son of Man Goes to God (the Transfiguration)

As in the text of Daniel, so also in Mark the Son of Man does not come down to earth but goes to God and receives the kingdom. And when does such a thing happen in Mark? It does not. Jesus never goes to God in a visible way as he does in Luke-Acts. But in Mark 9:1-8, we have a glimpse of it in visionary fashion. Here, at the transfiguration, the disciples have a preview of the Son of Man's future glory, to which he will have access through the resurrection. And the whole scene is preceded by the affirmation that this is a vision of the kingdom of God coming with power. Notice the words in the Greek: see (*horaō*), power (*dynamis*), God (*theos*), Son of Man (*huios tou anthrōpou*), glory (*doxa*), cloud (*nephelē*). Compare that with the LXX of Dan 7:13-14: I saw (*theōreō*), power (*exousia*), clouds (*nephelōn*), Son of Man (*huios anthrōpou*). Like Daniel in the past, Peter, James, and John have a vision of the future triumph of the Son of Man. As in Dan 7:13, here Jesus is presented to God, for it is God's voice that testifies to his special status as beloved son. The voice utters from God's throne in heaven, and Jesus is standing in front of it. Elijah and Moses, two prophets of the past who were transposed to heaven without tasting death, are with him. The setting is a high mountain, a traditional place for epiphanies, but the idea here is not that heaven has come down to earth but rather that the disciples are given a glimpse of heaven at the moment when the Son of Man receives the kingdom from God. It is a vision of heavenly things which assures the disciples that things on earth will be affected by this vision. Therefore, even though the coming of the kingdom with power, which implies the giving of dominion and authority to the people of the Son of Man, does not happen in the narrative, it is announced through the vision as something that will happen in the near future. The resurrection will enable this power and authority to be bestowed on Jesus, the Son of Man, and the kingdom will follow shortly. In Galilee, according to the evangelist's belief, the disciples will see the kingdom's actualization on earth. This is particularly warranted by the lack of an ascension narrative in Mark. It is very plausible that Mark thought that this was going to happen during his lifetime (cf. Mark 9:1).

Mark's Rereading of the Danielic Tradition

I believe that what we have in Mark is a rereading of Daniel 7 done from a similar political context: Antioch IV Epiphanes equals the Roman Caesar (cf. Mark 13:14, where the desolating sacrilege, which in Dan 9:27; 11:31; 12:11 seems to refer to Antiochus's profanation of the Jerusalem temple, may point at the Roman presence in the temple). The saints of the Most High of Dan 7:18, 21-22, 27 find their parallel in the faithful followers of Jesus, in this case the Markan community; and the Son of Man of Daniel 7:13 becomes, likewise, a corporate figure who represents God's suffering people. Jesus' resurrection as the Son of Man anticipates the vindication of God's people, since he is their representative. His resurrection means that the righteous one has been vindicated; God has been faithful to God's promises. The disciples now know that by meeting the risen one in the Galilean mission front they will continue a project of liberation that was set in motion by Jesus' resurrection and will culminate with the actualization on earth of the kingdom of God. They are co-disciples with Jesus, who now, having been raised, is going ahead of them to Galilee. With no ascension narrative in the short ending of Mark, which we take as the original one, the only way of explaining such a meeting is that Mark thinks that God is about to bring the kingdom. The moment of vindication for the suffering people of God is about to happen.

The advantage of this interpretation is that, while maintaining the eschatological nature of God's kingdom, at the same time it also de-apocalypticizes it, for this reading does not necessitate the coming of Jesus at the *parousia* to gather the elect, understood as those who believed in Christ. But if Jesus is the representative of God's suffering people on earth, that is, all those who suffer under the oppressive forces that oppose God's kingdom, and if his resurrection announces beforehand the final vindication of the faithful, that vindication will happen when God brings the kingdom and the new age begins. Mark may have thought that this was about to happen, and so in his Gospel he does not include the ascension of Jesus. Jesus is still around, as the risen one who symbolizes the vindication of the disciples of the kingdom, the ones who suffered for the sake of the gospel. His presence in Galilee (by the way, "presence" is another meaning for *parousia*), points to a moment of truth, which, according to the evangelist, is about to unfold. But he is still on earth as a presence (*parousia*) that testifies to God's final liberating act. Given the suffering that the community is probably facing, this idea constitutes a true theodicy.

A Fusion of Horizons

In the light of what has been proposed above, how can an understanding of Jesus as disciple of the kingdom and as the community's representative be an answer to the problems facing Mark's audience? And how can it be an answer to the issues raised by my own context in the United States? In other words, how can these two horizons merge? How can these two contexts be brought into dialogue?

Mark's Context

Mark's context was marked by several factors: a heightened apocalyptic fervor (Jewish revolt), ethnic enmities (Jews and Gentiles in his community), gender issues (leadership in his community was becoming increasingly male and hierarchical), and imperial harassment (Rome blamed the Christian communities for collaboration with the rebels). In this section, we will examine how the Gospel deals with each of these factors in turn.

The apocalyptic fervor was mitigated in the Gospel by relocating the place where the kingdom was going to be manifested (not in Jerusalem but in Galilee) and by redefining who the agents of this kingdom were going to be. Certainly not the self-appointed messiahs mentioned in Mark 13:21-22 but the Son of Man and his persecuted and suffering community, the company of faithful co-disciples who were going to receive the vindication that their suffering deserved. And all of this was going to be accomplished through nonviolent means, through the overcoming of suffering, not through inflicting suffering on others. This concept itself destabilized the revolutionaries' apocalyptic dreams of vengeance and helped the congregation to focus on its primary function, that of preaching the gospel to the nations (13:10).[29]

Mark deals with the ethnic rivalries by portraying the Son of Man as representing all of God's people, both Jews and Gentiles. The call to discipleship is for everyone, as 8:34 clearly suggests: Jesus calls "the crowds with the disciples" to follow him in risking their lives. Other examples in the narrative also point out the important role Gentiles played in Jesus ministry. For example: the Syrophenician woman in 7:24-30, the demon-possessed man in the country of the Gerasenes in 5:1-20, the mostly Gentile multitude who are fed in 8:1-10, the centurion at the foot of the cross in 15:39—to mention the most obvious ones. This can be seen as Mark's narrative strategy to mend ethnic rivalries in his community, a situation aggravated by the Jewish revolt. Jesus' example as the model disciple of God's kingdom would have sent a clear message to Mark's community about what their attitude toward those of different ethnic backgrounds should be.

In addressing gender issues, the Gospel has women play an important role in the narrative, outshining the male disciples on many occasions, such as during Jesus' passion, death, and resurrection, where the absence of the male disciples is contrasted to the faithful presence of the women throughout

---

29. Here, *gospel* should be understood in Markan terms, not Pauline terms. It refers to the preaching of the good news of the kingdom illustrated by the story Mark is telling.

the ordeal. The message to the Markan community is clear: women are as qualified to be disciples as men, sometimes even more qualified, as the emphasis on the need for *diakonia* (service) among the disciples seems to show (Mark 10:42-45). This may be addressing a growing problem in the early church between what was rightly perceived as an open attitude toward the leadership of women, manifested by Jesus and Paul, and a desire to concentrate power in the hands of the adult males of the community, which became the norm in the church from the second century onward. Here, at the beginning of the second half of the first century, the problem is beginning to surface. Mark tries to deal with it by means of a story that privileges women over men as disciples and followers of Jesus.

The harassment by the Roman authorities was expected any time a revolt was in full swing, as was the case in the Jewish–Roman war of 66–70 c.e. The small congregations of Jesus' followers must have felt the pressure from the government to remain faithful to the emperor in the midst of the extensive recruitment done by the rebels. Those of Jewish ethnicity would automatically be suspected of collaboration with the Zealots, while being a Gentile would make a person more likely to favor the Roman retaliation. This would pit believers against each other, as the congregation was in all probability a mixed one. Mark's message in this context is quite clear: the community will have nothing to do either with the Roman military machine (5:1-20) or with the royal-political messianism of the revolutionaries (the Messiah is not the son of David, 12:35-37!). They are to remain unaligned, waiting for the manifestation of God's kingdom in Galilee, ironically the bedrock of the Jewish revolt.

My Context

My own context in the United States of America is marked by analogous, though not identical, issues: apocalyptic rhetoric and worldview emanating from both official and nonofficial sources, ethnic/racial prejudices and misunderstandings both in society and in the church, gender-related issues, especially when it comes to leadership roles in the church, and imperial harassment represented by the vociferous pro-war and anti-immigration rhetoric emanating from the White House during the years of the Bush administration. And this "objective" context is filtered through my "subjective" context; that is, the way I described myself in the opening section of this essay: a Latin

American Christian who moved from a spiritualizing and apocalyptic world-view that demanded detachment from society to a political praxis driven by a new way of reading both culture and the Bible.

The need to see Jesus as the example of true discipleship grows directly out of my own journey in the Christian faith. I got to a point where theories of atonement and heavenly rewards became totally irrelevant for my life. Only discipleship, understood as the construction of a new order, a new society, made any sense.[30] I find ample justification for this new understanding in the Markan story of Jesus. The metaphor that I like to use is that of Jacob wrestling with the man at Peniel in Gen 32:26. When the man (angel?) wanted to leave, Jacob said: "I will not let you go, unless you bless me." My hermeneutical struggle with the text resulted, in the end, in blessing.

I am constructing Mark's construction of Jesus as disciple and by so doing I am trying to overcome an overspiritualization, by the church in which I grew up, of what it means to be a follower of Jesus. That overspiritualization was also a "construction" done for the purpose of advancing the missionary agenda.[31] When relieved of its traditional apocalyptic and spiritualizing clothing, discipleship becomes a model for engaging reality in liberating and ethical ways, rather than being an excuse for making people disregard their responsibilities to a hurting world. In other words, discipleship becomes something concrete, something political.

The Markan construct of Jesus as disciple of the kingdom is helpful in a number of ways. First, by denying the relevance of the apocalyptic rhetoric of the Jewish revolutionaries and by subscribing to a nonviolent agenda of non-alignment, the Markan model helps us to combat the apocalyptically imbued discourse of the conservative, which was well represented in the Bush administration; being disciples of Jesus Christ will always be at odds with that kind of mentality. This discourse included the justification of war in the name of our "manifest destiny" to be representatives of what is good and just (democracy, Christianity, the Western way of life, capitalism) over against what is evil and unjust (totalitarian regimes, Islam, Islamic societies, communism

---

30. For this idea, I am deeply indebted to Ched Myers and his seminal work *Binding the Strong Man: A Political Reading of Mark's Story of Jesus* (Maryknoll, N.Y.: Orbis, 1988).

31. This agenda was perhaps unconscious, but the ultimate goal was to make people "a-political" so they would not interfere with the military governments that were aligned ideologically with the North.

and/or socialism). When the real test for true discipleship becomes not so much how faithful one is to a supposedly spiritual gospel of deliverance from earthly things, but rather how faithful one is to resisting a rhetoric that invokes divine sanction while at the same time hiding a clear political and expansionist agenda (this was the case of both the Roman Empire and the Jewish revolutionaries), then Mark's depiction of Jesus as the disciple of the kingdom and the representative of God's faithful, and thus suffering, people is absolutely crucial for our present praxis.

Second, despite the acknowledgment that we live in a highly pluralistic and diverse society, the latest anti-immigration rhetoric coming from both official and nonofficial sources is proof that ethnic and racial prejudice and misunderstanding are commonplace in American life. The proliferation of studies and resources of all types that treat the reality of the multiethnic nature of our society is met with an incredible lack of awareness and/or sensitivity by the general public. Theory and practice do not seem to go hand in hand, as more and more often ethnicity and race become stumbling blocks for people's interactions. When transferred to the church, this attitude is seen in the existence of segregated communities and/or segregated worship services. Jesus as disciple of the kingdom of God models the right attitude toward diversity: he was willing to learn from a Syrophoenician woman in the region of Tyre; he ministered among those who were not ethnic Israelites (chapter 5); he fed four thousand people in a largely Gentile area of Palestine (chapter 8)—thus making it clear that his ministry was inclusive. The rhetorical centrality of some of these incidents, especially those in chapters 7 and 8, seems to point to Mark's own agenda of emphasizing the importance of Gentiles in his community. The general call to discipleship of 8:34-38, delivered in the highly hellenized area of Caesarea Philippi, serves to reinforce the inclusive and multiethnic nature of discipleship, as Jesus calls "the crowds with the disciples" to a cruciform discipleship (8:34).

Third, when faced with the current issues of women, gays, and lesbians in roles of leadership in the church, the model provided by Mark of a Jesus who described himself in terms of the service that only women and slaves were supposed to provide in that society (Mark 10:45) is crucial for our present praxis. This model of Jesus as disciple does away with gender and class distinctions, for here a disempowered male peasant from Galilee is presented as the example of one who leads through service, thus debunking the cultural assumptions of the time which expected the leadership roles in the church to be assigned to aristocratic males (cf. Luke-Acts, Pastoral Epistles).

Finally, my having experienced cultural and religious marginality because of growing up as an *evangélico* in Argentina brings an important ingredient into the picture, as it relates directly to Jesus' own marginality. He was not a Judean but a Galilean Jew, and his views of the Torah, God, and Israel as God's people betrayed this marginal origin. He adhered to the "Little Tradition," a version of the Torah that developed independent of the control of Jerusalem and its leadership, who represented the "Great Tradition" (Jesus calls it "the tradition of the elders").[32] The "Little Tradition" preserved the memory of prophets such as Elijah and Elisha and served the Galileans well in their criticism of Jerusalem and its ruling classes. In my case, being an *evangélico* in Argentina placed me in a branch of Christianity that was seen as marginal at best and heretical at worst. In many ways, the Roman Catholic Church represented the "Great Tradition," which emanated from that religious center par excellence that is Rome. We, on the other hand, subscribed to the "Little Tradition," the Protestant tradition, which was, for Catholics, a deviant and alternative version of Christianity. This marginal self-understanding informed everything I did—and to some extent it still does—even though in the United States I now belong to the mainline (Great Tradition?) church.

But there is still more to Jesus' marginality. He was suspected of having been born illicitly. He was criticized for pretending to have a right to lead when in reality he was the son of a carpenter. He inhabited a liminal space. So did his disciples, for Jesus' call to follow him separated them from their kin, from their villages, and from a life of submission to the control of the Roman Empire. Jesus and the disciples carried on a ministry that was geared toward those on the periphery, those who found themselves in between realities because they were deemed deviant, impure, or countercultural. I grew up marginal, too, not only because of my religious affiliation but also because of my class. My father was a cobbler, and this profession, though noble and necessary to society, was regarded as low class. My father repaired the shoes

---

32. See William R. Herzog's discussion of this topic in *Prophet and Teacher: An Introduction to the Historical Jesus* (Louisville: Westminster John Knox, 2005), 175–90.

of the lawyers and doctors of our town, and sometimes he asked me to help him. Knowing that I had handled their shoes[33] made me feel inferior and an outsider to that circle of professionals whose sons and daughters were my classmates at school. For many of them I was just *el hijo del zapatero* (the son of the cobbler). This classism could be seen everywhere in my hometown. While the upper and aristocratic strata of society were defined by land, religion, and profession, we *evangélicos* had none of these: we did not own any land, we practiced the wrong religion, and we belonged to the working and lower class.

Conclusion

Even though I was born and raised in Argentina under the conditions described above, I have lived in the United States of America for a total of twenty-four years. Naturally, I preserve some of my Argentine traditions and ways of thinking, of feeling, of sensing the world, but these are all intertwined now with my adopted culture. These two cultures coexist, sometimes harmoniously, sometimes at war with each other. I am split between them and I do not completely identify with either of the two. All of this has naturally come to shape my understanding of discipleship.

These two contexts come to fruition in the classroom, my primary place for praxis. There, I encounter people with whom I share a similar "objective" context, namely, living in the United States. But each one of them filters that context through their own social location, informed by their personal stories (what I call the "subjective" context). Some of these stories interconnect, so the classroom becomes a reading community with similar assumptions and expectations. Even those students who are in a different place hermeneutically and theologically contribute to the dialogue as dissident voices and dialogue partners. The *eisegesis* that ensues brings about changes in both my students

---

33. There is something fundamentally degrading about terminology related to feet. It is the part of the body that is farthest removed from the head, the center of a person's honor. It is also the part of the body we use to express disdain and rejection. Kicking somebody, throwing shoes at somebody (at George W. Bush, for example!) or treading on somebody's private property, be this land or his/her own body, is seen as the ultimate insult. Handling someone's shoes connotes, then, submission and servility, if not shame. These are powerful images that deeply affect a person, especially a young one as I was, producing feelings of resentment and inadequacy.

and me, forcing us to try out new hypotheses and to reconsider old conclusions, as we continue to journey into a life of discipleship that lies ahead
and which is susceptible to new hypotheses and conclusions, that is, to new
re-contextualizations. Jesus as disciple of the kingdom provides a model that
privileges social transformation through political praxis over escape from the
world, which is how I have come to understand the task of the church.

CHAPTER 6

The Conflict in Mark

A Reading from the Armed Conflict in Colombia

Elsa Tamez
Translated by Leticia Guardiola-Sáenz

Colombia, like many Latin American countries, is beautiful. Life is lived with intensity in the towns, and everywhere you go you can hear music and run into popular festivals, cultural or sport events, or educational and religious activities. But there is a difference between Columbia and other countries: the police and the army are visible in every corner, and in some cities, where guerrilla and paramilitary activity is common, there are many roadblocks. The news programs will not stop talking about events related to armed conflict, the paramilitary, and drug trafficking.

In Colombia, people are afraid of talking in private and in public. There are peace demonstrations and marches against kidnappings, but people are very afraid to denounce the violent deaths that often occur because of guerrilla attacks, paramilitary genocides, official military rescues and crimes of army officials against poor civilians,[1] combat between factions, the execution of drug dealers, kidnappings, and criminal assaults or vendettas. The people are also afraid to formulate alternatives that differ from those officially proposed by the government, which has insisted on eliminating "terrorism" with blood and fire. The situation is complex; drug trafficking is intertwined

---

1. We are talking about the "false positives," a term assigned to the murder of supposed guerrilla members, motivated by rewards or the urgency to show the government positive results.

with all factions, including guerrillas, paramilitaries, the national army, and certain politicians. The foreign interference via transnational companies in search of natural resources only intensifies the conflict. The same applies to external military support.

Many of the deaths or kidnappings are motivated by rewards or payoffs. Informing on others for money or other rewards, known as *sapeo,* or "frogging," is common, as are more regularly employed informants. Hence, the people fear speaking even in front of neighbors, because they cannot be sure to whom they are speaking—a paramilitary, a guerrilla from the Revolutionary Armed Forces of Colombia (FARC) or the National Liberation Army (ELN), a drug dealer, a military agent dressed like a civilian, an unscrupulous criminal, a "frog" or informant from any faction. There is a self-imposed silence or censorship among both Colombians who live in Colombia and those who live abroad.[2]

The Gospel of Mark was written during a time of war and persecution of Christians. From beginning to end, we can notice that the themes of silence and fear are fundamental. There is a strategic silence advised by Jesus himself and a self-imposed silence motivated by fear. The shadow of betrayal, even within the Jesus movement, is ever present in the Gospel. The price of thirty silver coins on Jesus' head reminds us of the price on the heads of guerrillas, drug traffickers, and paramilitaries. What does Mark have to say regarding such a conflicted reality, dominated by fear? What does Mark say to the Christians of today who dare not speak, out of fear, like the women followers of Jesus who, paralyzed by fear, did not communicate the message of the risen one? How can we be good followers of the risen one in times of war?

Analysis of the Contexts

When we read the Gospel of Mark from the situation of armed conflict, we can perceive three contexts: that of Jesus, that of the author (Mark), and that of the present reader. Each context is different, but certain elements recur: persecution, fear of betrayal, corruption, silence, and confusion. The origin of the conflict is similar in all three contexts: a poor and oppressed people,

---

2. According to United Nations statistics, there are more than sixty thousand exiled and sheltered Colombians abroad. In reality, there are many more thousands, the majority unregistered for fear of the informant networks.

the hoarding of land by a few privileged families, and the abandonment of people's basic needs by their religious or political leaders. Moreover, there is external interference that intensifies the conflict: the Roman Empire in the first century and the transnational corporations and the Pentagon in the present century. Finally, people are confused regarding which option they should take, given the current events. I will concentrate briefly on the context in which the Gospel of Mark was written and on the Colombian context in relation to the armed conflict. Mark rereads the Jesus event in light of his context of the Jewish rebellion against Rome. We will reread this Gospel, taking into consideration its context and the context of the armed conflict active today in Colombia.

The Context of Mark: The War and the Armed Conflict in Palestine

Mark was written between 66 and 70 C.E., during the revolt against the Roman occupation forces and the capture of Jerusalem by Titus's troops. Beginning in 66, riots in Judea and elsewhere in Palestine intensified, but the real struggle against the Roman forces began in Judea. Some of the factors leading up to this war were these: dissatisfaction with the appropriation of land by the religious and political elite, exploitation of the peasants, the burden of various taxes, the marginalization of those most impoverished, religious disrespect, and the presence of the occupying forces. According to Ched Myers, the last straw was when the clergy leaders, led by Ezekiel, son of Ananias, and supported by the popular rebel leaders, decided to reject the offerings of the Gentiles, among them the sacrifices in honor of the emperor and the Empire.[3] Josephus says: "This was the true beginning of our war with the Romans; for they rejected the sacrifice of Caesar on this account" (Josephus, *Jewish War* 2.17.2 §409). Several factions of the insurgent movements gathered in Jerusalem and overthrew the Roman garrison and the high priests whom Florus the Procurator had left in command, and captured the city.[4] Flavius Josephus was sent by this provisional government to lead the

---

3. Ched Myers, *O Evangelho de Sao Marcos* (Sao Paulo: Paulinas, 1992), 97.
4. Richard A. Horsely and John S. Hanson (*Bandits, Prophets and Messiahs: Popular Movements in the Time of Jesus* [Minneapolis: Winston, 1985]) and Myers (*O Evangelho,* 87–95), rereading Josephus, find a variety of movements: messianic movements, zealots, social bandits

fight against the Romans in Galilee, but he ended up getting in trouble with the popular leaders because he allied himself with the dignitaries of Galilee and had, as his strategy, to persuade the dissidents to negotiate with the Romans. In the year 67, when Vespasian's troops crushed the insurrection in Galilee, Josephus deserted his post and allied with the Romans. The war was disastrous for the Galilean farmers. The consequences were devastating, not only in terms of the food shortages and permanent insecurity that follow any war but, according to Myers, because the farmers were recruited by the rebels to defend the city of Jerusalem and the temple, the center of the religious, economic, and political power of the Jews.[5]

Josephus speaks of the existing hatred against the Jews and how the non-Jews took advantage of the war to attack them (Josephus, *Jewish War* 2.19–22 §§513–654). Mark's community was probably experiencing a similar situation. It is uncertain whether this community was based in Galilee or in Rome. For one living in Galilee, being a Christian Jew could have drawn persecution from three fronts: the religious elite, the Romans, and the leaders of the armed front against the Romans, since not supporting this last group in defending Jerusalem could have been grounds for persecution. If Mark is writing from Rome, the same insecurity was felt. First, as people coming from a province that has risen up against the empire, they would be despised by the inhabitants of the city, and could even be lynched at the news of the failed attempts of the Roman troops to defeat Jerusalem in the first two assaults.[6] Besides, not long ago they had suffered an atrocious genocide at the hands of Nero.[7] On the other hand, living in neighborhoods alongside their fellow Jews, the Jewish Christians would be confused as to what action to take and would not have much freedom to act against the armed struggle to defend Jerusalem and the temple, or to take a stand on some of the issues that were at the forefront of the fight. Their situation was not only uncomfortable

---

(these benefited the farmers by giving them some of the goods they robbed from the rich), of *sicarii* (these selectively assassinated urban collaborators; they kidnapped children to request ransom; and, like the social bandits, also robbed from the powerful ones). Josephus, when writing from the point of view of the winners, describes these groups as terrorists.

5. Myers, *O Evangelho,* 120ff.

6. According to Josephus, the city was taken after the third siege.

7. Tacitus mentions in detail the way in which Emperor Nero blamed them for the fire of Rome and tortured them (*Annals* 10.256).

but unsafe: Jerusalem, with its temple-state, had been the center from which the persecution of the founder of their faith and his disciples had come; Rome and Jerusalem had been allies for a little more than thirty years against Jesus, the risen one whom they followed. According to Myers, Mark's community suffered persecution for its nonaligned position.[8]

During all the years that the war lasted, fear was all they breathed and there was an imposing silence. There were too many deaths, too much confusion, corruption, and betrayal on all sides. Greed was present in every aspect of the war; on both sides, the Roman troops and the armed groups—and even among ordinary people—would take advantage of the circumstances. Josephus, referring to the massacre of Jewish civilians in Caesarea and Syria, says:

> Greediness of gain was a provocation to kill the opposite party, even to such as had of old appeared very mild and gentle towards them; for they without fear plundered the effects of the slain, and carried off the spoils of those whom they slew to their own houses, as if they had been gained in a set battle; and he was esteemed a man of honor who got the greatest share, as having prevailed over the greatest number of his enemies. (Josephus, *Jewish War* 2.18.2 §464)

In this situation of war and conflict, the victims were the poorest families, women, and children. Josephus himself repeats again and again how sometimes the only ones who could flee from Jerusalem, where the different factions were fighting and at the same time resisting the Roman army, were the wealthy people; poor people, in contrast, were killed. But ambition does not have barriers. When rumors spread that those who were able to escape from Jerusalem carried gold pieces inside their bodies, people in the Roman army, driven by greed, ruthlessly opened the bowels of as many people as escaped. According to Josephus, in one night they opened the bowels of two thousand people. Because of greed, the soldiers would not stop opening bellies even at the threat of the death penalty declared by their commander, Titus. For as Josephus says: "and there is neither adversity nor damage so great that it can be compared with greed and the desire for more, because every other has an end, and fear restrains it" (*Jewish War* 5.13.5 §§558–59).

---

8. Myers, *O Evangelho*, 495.

Mark's community had to be very frightened, like everyone else, even more so for their delicate position of following a messiah who had been crucified by the Roman Empire, whose position was contrary to the state authorities of the temple-state in Jerusalem. The risen one had come to show a new order in favor of humanity, starting with the most marginalized of society. His audience had to be very careful and not trust anyone or they could be handed over. For in those contexts there is much deception and betrayal; we see this as even our privileged source on the war, Flavius Josephus, was himself a traitor.

The Context of This Reading: Current Armed Conflict in Colombia [9]

The conflict stems from the "periphery"; that is, the rural regions, less populated, with no political power and often discriminated against and exploited by the "center." In those marginalized places non-state armed movements emerged. Today, the war has spread in all cities and the countryside. The FARC and ELN guerrilla movements, due to their marginal geographical and political situation, have not been able to assume power, and the state, with its fragmented leadership, has not been able to resolve the conflict. For this and other reasons, including the degradation of war, the UN report states that the war is a failure, an impasse in which the only exit is human development.[10]

The high rates of poverty in the countryside are a fundamental problem. In the last thirty years, poverty has increased from 40 percent to 87 percent, and urban unemployment is growing at a rate between 13 percent and 21 percent, in addition to the informal moonlighting in which two of every three workers participate.[11] Moreover, analysts have also perceived the motivation

---

9. In order to analyze the conflict, I take as a basis the report from the United Nations Development Program (UNDP), *El conflicto, callejón con salida: Entender para cambiar las raíces locales del conflicto,* Informe Nacional del Desarrollo Humano para Colombia, 2003 (Bogota: UNDP, 2003). This is a collective work, in which the participation of serious intellectual personalities, external and internal, offers an objective frame and a proposed solution oriented to human development. Although the report was written in 2003, it is still applicable today, since the diagnoses could be verified by observation.

10. United States Development Program, *El conflicto,* 99f.

11. Ibid., 42.

of revenge in the origins of armed groups, usually revenge for the murder of a family member. At the time that the guerrillas were born, they embodied the aspirations of farmers with respect to social security, compensation for displaced farmers, land reform to eliminate large estates, and attention to government investment in the field. However, after many fruitless years of war, the guerrillas lost their horizon. Kidnappings, murders, extortions, forced displacement, and bombings, which occur in rural areas as well as in the city, have made people experience war as a criminal threat or insecurity, not as confrontation or hope. Dissatisfaction with the reality of injustice, poverty, and violence is expressed by many Colombians not aligned with either the guerrillas, paramilitaries, or the government. They do not feel free to express their position, given the context of insecurity and fear in which they live today. On the one hand, they do not approve of the methods of the guerrillas, such as abduction and drug trafficking, and, on the other, people are afraid to risk any expression of sympathy with groups that have been stigmatized as terrorists, for fear of reprisal from the government or the paramilitaries.

The paramilitaries arose in response to the actions of guerrillas in the rural areas. It is "an extension of private armies, which are a necessity of the illegal industries" such as drug trafficking and the emerald trade.[12] The report emphasizes that the paramilitaries arise mainly from greed or desperation. It is greed that emerges from the emerald trade or when the guerilla seeks wealth through the drug trade; or out of despair, when the owners or the traffickers do not want to pay more "vaccinations" or extortion. Later on, the paramilitaries were supported by other owners, such as miners, landowners, political leaders, and some members of the public forces.[13] But the guerrillas and the paramilitaries are not the only groups that have caused fear in rural and urban populations. With the rise of drug-trafficking, the war escalated. There was a time in Medellín, for example, when "there were combats of all against all."[14]

Today, according to the United Nations report, the armed conflict has a high degree of degradation on all sides, including the national army. Mili-

---

12. Ibid., 29.
13. Ibid., 56.
14. For example, Bolivian Militia, FARC, ELN, armed militias from the people, Revolutionary Front of Popular Action, "Self-defense of the Metro Blockage," and "Front Cacique Nutibara," and sixty more criminal leagues. See United Nations Development Program, *El conflicto*, 64.

tarism is part of the logic of degradation. The political has been put aside in the guerrillas to give way to militarization, and the state, in order to quell the conflict, has also turned increasingly toward the military. Paramilitary groups themselves do not even have a political platform. With the scale weighted in favor of the military, irregular and regular military forces grow exorbitantly. In this situation, the civilian is seen in a very simplistic way, either as a "collaborator" or as an "enemy." Therefore, every citizen must be careful what he or she says and does. Another part of the logic by which the agents of war guide themselves is "profitability." Illegal trade and crime are crucial means of sustaining the war, and in many cases the war has become a pretext for profit. Extortion, kidnapping, and unofficial tolls are common in the guerrilla movement, while the appropriation of the land from the displaced farmers is common in the paramilitaries. Insecurity and fear are in the air, for when the different groups fight for territory and then become established, they form a kind of parallel state with its rules and laws. This situation gradually produces terror. For example, paramilitaries begin with what they call "cleaning"; that is, removing the robbers and gang members. But then they look for other "undesirables" among the population, and that is where homosexuals, prostitutes, and people who think differently are included. The population is closely monitored, since other territories are governed by other armed groups. The civilians at any moment can be seen as enemies. So the United Nations report concludes that most Colombians are against the conflict and feel themselves to be victims of it.[15]

Criminalization is another level of war's degradation. The abuse of military weapons for purposes of personal revenge, robbery, and sexual abuse is common. Members of the armed forces of the state are not exempt from these degrading acts.

One of the worst things that causes fear and limits freedom of expression is the *sapeo,* literally "frogging." This is the betrayal of someone for profit, or the act of being a longtime paid informant, obtaining information from any side. All groups have their informants, particularly the public force. For several years now, the current president has allocated millions from the national budget destined to pay rewards to those who turn in a guerrilla, a paramilitary, or a drug trafficker. The armed forces, for their part, have a

---

15. United Nations Development Program, *El conflicto,* 90.

bonus program for military actions in which the soldiers manage to defeat guerrillas. This greed for money has made groups betray one another,[16] and even members of the army to claim that they have fought guerrillas when in truth they have abducted poor youths and murdered them in war games.[17] When atrocities like these occur, motivated by money and perpetrated by the armies themselves, and by highly trusted officials, what is perceived is extreme human degradation. The big losers in this conflict are none other than the civilian population and the poorest of the poor. A solution other than armed struggle is needed, one along the lines of human development, as proposed by the United Nations report.

We have taken a brief look at the two contexts. As we have seen, they differ: in Mark's community the conflict was armed resistance against the Roman troops and internal conflict between the rebel forces, while in Colombia the conflict is an internal one, exacerbated by external economic and military interference. However, fear and silence emerge in both contexts, a reality to which we refer in the following analysis of the text.

Rereading the Gospel of Mark

Mark titles his book "The good news of Jesus the Messiah and Son of God." However, the end of the book is not what we expect. Women trembling with fear do not say anything to anyone (16:8). This enigmatic ending is in line with the entire atmosphere that is breathed in the narrative: conflict, persecution, fear, and silence. The behavior of Jesus in favor of humanity unleashes a conflict that will lead him to death, and his identity as Messiah and Son of God, faithfully reflected in his practice, will be the target of controversy, misunderstanding, and his death sentence. Jesus wants it to be kept secret for as long as possible, but the demons expose him, identifying him by his name; and those he has cured cannot stop talking about the wonders, attracting attention to him. The Gospel is truncated; Mark does not want to include the story of the spreading news of the resurrection, so the community will

---

16. In March 2008, an ex-serviceman of the FARC killed its commander to receive a reward of 1.15 million dollars. The ex-guerrilla came to the military with the hand of Commander Ivan Rios to prove his action.

17. In October 2008, twenty-four members of the armed forces were terminated from the military service for presenting young civilians as guerrillas ("false positives"); among those terminated were several officials of high rank.

not have to see itself facing the dilemma of escaping persecution or going to Galilee to pursue the cause of Jesus.[18]

The introduction of the book (1:1-13) condenses the plot to be developed throughout the sixteen chapters. Here we see Jesus identified as Messiah and Son of God (1:1), and we hear this identification confirmed by a prophet, John the Baptist (1:7) and by God (1:8). Immediately, Satan's opposition emerges, the enemy interfering with Jesus so that the project of the kingdom will not become a reality. Both Satan (the enemy) and the demons, (the evil spirits) symbolize the war that degrades the human being.

I consider two themes in this rereading: war and conflict, on the one hand (Mark 13), and fear and silence, on the other (several texts on silence and treason). In the conclusion, I will attempt to answer the question how to follow Jesus in times of war. To do this, I will offer some hints extracted from the lessons woven into the three passion announcements (8:31-45).

Mark 13: War and Conflict

Chapter 13 is like a crystal ball through which we can observe a war and all the horrors war entails: destruction, violence, persecution, betrayal, terror, and internal conflict. It is a discourse of Jesus mainly of a paraenetic type,[19] couched in eschatological and apocalyptic language. The apocalyptic language, we know, is typical of critical situations with no end and much suffering. Chapter 13 is a call to the Markan community to stand firm and to endure the horrors of war and especially to remain vigilant and not succumb. The speech appears between the end of Jesus' practice (13:1-12) and the end of his life here on earth (15:1—16:8). More specifically, after the announcements of the passion of Jesus (8:32—10:52) and prior to the passion, we read the passion of the community of his followers (chapter 13). In this analysis, I focus on war and conflict, keeping in mind the situation of the recipients of Mark.

Chapter 13 is divided into two parts: an introduction and the speech of Jesus. In the introduction, the disciples admire the magnificent stones of the temple, but Jesus announces its inevitable destruction (vv. 1-2). The speech itself is divided into three parts and also has an introduction. In this

---

18. Carlos Bravo Gallardo, *Jesús, hombre en conflicto: El relato de Marcos en América Latina* (Santander: Sal Terrae, 1986), 241.
19. Camille Focant, *L'evangile selon Marc* (Paris: Cerf, 2004), 478.

introduction, the disciples ask when these things will happen and what will be the signal indicating the fulfillment of these things (vv. 3-4). Jesus replies with a vague, uninterrupted speech. The first part of the discourse speaks of wars, persecutions, and deceivers (vv. 5-23). The second announces the arrival of the Son of the Human Being[20] after the great suffering (vv. 24-27) and the third part deals with two comparisons (vv. 28-37).

The chapter begins by saying, "After leaving the temple." This expression is not only an expression of trivial movement but an indication of separation from the church-state institution, whence emerges the greatest hostility against Jesus. Jesus had overturned the money-changers' tables recently and had called the temple a "den of robbers" (11:15-17). From this time on Jesus will not enter the temple anymore. As usual in Mark, Jesus and his followers see the world differently. The disciples admire the grandeur of the buildings; Jesus announces their destruction. The use of two different verbs with the meaning of "seeing" is interesting. In 13:1, the disciples use the imperative *ide* (from the verb *eidon,* the aorist of the verb *horaō*). This verb is used also by deceivers when they say "look [*ide*], the messiah is here! Look [*ide*] there!" (v. 21). This imperative is used to attract attention. Jesus uses the verb *blepō,* "look, see," without the connotation of admiring, to indicate that the stones will be destroyed. In fact, the chapter uses *blepō,* "see," in the words of Jesus five times, four of the instances in the sense of "be careful," "be vigilant" (vv. 6, 9, 23, 33). Jesus uses the verb *horaō,* "to see" or "perceive," precisely when he announces that they will see the Son of the Human Being descending (v. 26). It is over there, toward the future new humanity, where they must look carefully. Meanwhile, what they must see (*horaō*) in the present are the fatal events and their soon approaching end (v. 29).

The first part of the speech (vv. 5-23), according to its content, follows a concentric structure.[21] The subject moves from wars and deceivers (vv. 5-8), to persecutions (vv. 9 -13) to wars and deceivers again (vv. 14-23), in that chiastic order. This is precisely the situation in which the community to which Mark writes is living, whether in Galilee or in Rome.

---

20. The term in Greek is *huios tou anthropou,* and it is traditionally translated "Son of Man."

21. Jan Lambrecht, *Die Redaktion der Markus-Apokalypse* (Päpstliches Bibelinstitut, 1967), quoted by Juan Mateos, *Marcos 13: El grupo cristiano en la historia* (Madrid: Chistiandad, 1987), 174ff.

The center of the chapter (vv. 9-13) refers directly to those who are causing the persecution. There are three kinds of hostile forces: the local authorities of courts and synagogues, which correspond to the Jewish elite; the authorities of the Roman occupation, such as the governors and kings assigned by the emperor; and our own family, with conflict among siblings and between parents and children. Interestingly enough, we find the most to fear from the last section; while the local authorities only whip, the children kill their parents. The text refers to the overall degradation of the war.

The framework of this first part consists of the deceivers, who pose as the true leaders. Probably this is a reference to messianic movements. The leaders will say, "I am," usurping the name of the true Messiah (v. 6), and at the end of this section we see false messiahs and prophets (vv. 21-22) who are probably looking for people to join their movements.[22] Mark wants to remind his readers that Jesus was against the government of Jerusalem and especially the way the temple was administered at the expense of the poor. Jesus was interested in the project of the kingdom of God and not the oppressive institutions. Jesus has no sympathy with the Roman Empire, but does not declare himself in defense of Jerusalem. It is likely that he even shared the feelings of the rebels against Rome, because, as Myers points out, Jesus himself will suffer the same death penalty imposed on the "social bandits" when he is crucified in their midst (15:27). But Jesus is not in favor of the defense of the temple. That is why, when Jesus gives this speech, he is sitting on the Mount of Olives facing, that is, opposite (*katenanti*) the temple. His speech, obviously because of the danger, must be given privately (*kat' idian*) to those closest to him—Peter, James, John, and Andrew. These were the ones who always walked with Jesus, as safeguards in this situation of persecution.

Our text refers to a fratricidal conflict. In this middle section of this first part, the text stresses the word "surrender" (*paradidōmi*), repeating the word three times. The teacher had already announced several times that the Son of the Human Being was to be handed over both to the local authorities and to the authorities of the occupation (9:31; 10:33). This will happen immediately after this speech, when Jesus will be betrayed by one whom he trusts (14:10). His followers will be delivered by the people to the authorities to be whipped and by his family to be murdered.

---

22. Myers, *O Evangelho*, 120–21.

The first (vv. 5-8) and last sections (vv. 14-23) of this first part of the discourse talk about the war between peoples and its horrors. Verses 5-8 introduce the atmosphere of war that existed at the time this Gospel was written. Indeed, Rome was at war not only in Judea but also with the Germans and Gauls (Josephus, *Jewish War* 7.4.2 §§75–94). While hunger and earthquakes are typically apocalyptic terms, they are not unrealistic in times of war. The assaults we read about in Josephus, especially Jerusalem's last defense (68–69 c.e.), reveal the extreme calamity that happens when the water and food supply run out. The severity of the situation is such that in most cases betrayal becomes widespread, while others end in the self-extermination of the population, as in the Roman siege of Masada. All this destruction happens as the result of a horrifying fidelity to the ideals. The earthquakes embody total impotence; for those of us who have experienced them, we know the terror they cause because before them nothing can be done, and depending on how long they last, it is only expected that everything will collapse. In vv. 14-23, the issue of war is addressed again, but in a very close way—at home. "The abomination of desolation," an apocalyptic term borrowed from Daniel, is reread by Mark as the desecrating presence of the Romans in Jerusalem, especially in the temple, as the straw that breaks the back of tolerance. In Josephus, we read that many conflicts and massacres erupted on account of disrespect toward the Jewish religion and culture on the part of Roman soldiers. The statue of himself that Caligula ordered set up in the temple and the desecration of the Torah by a soldier caused riots, which were ruthlessly crushed by the Roman troops. Ultimately, this section of the chapter speaks of the horror in Judea that causes the invasion of Jerusalem by the Roman army. The advice is to flee, to leave the city and run to the mountains, and not take a step back to collect belongings. Those who will suffer the most are the most vulnerable, including pregnant women or women with small children, because they will not be able to escape easily. This suffering is depicted as the worst in history.

The second part of the speech (vv. 24-27) announces the fall of the oppressive powers through the use of apocalyptic language, such as the falling of the sun, moon, stars, and astral powers[23] and the arrival of the Son of the Human Being, which marks the end of the great suffering. The arrival

---

23. Mateos, *Marcos 13*, 471.

of the Son of the Human Being, although taken from Dan 7:13, has a different meaning. He is coming not to judge and face up to the evildoers nor to announce the end of the world. Instead, he comes to join the elected ones (v. 27), those who represent the community. He is not arriving by himself, but with his disciples, who are the angels. The Son of the Human Being has different meanings in Mark.[24] In the case of Mark 13, there is a certain consensus in seeing the meaning not only in its individual but also in its broader, collective sense, including the human community in its fullness, "where the kingdom of God is exercised,"[25] which has been the project of Jesus since the beginning of his movement. This means that, when the community follows the Son of God (the identity of Jesus), it is geared toward human fulfillment. Mark counters the war of the armed messiahs against the empire with the coming of the Son of the Human Being, a figure that refers to a new humanity, of which Jesus is the prototype and inaugurator.[26]

The third part of the speech is devoted to paraenesis (vv. 28-37), where "be vigilant" and "pay attention" to what is happening is the fundamental advice. It includes two short parables. The one about the fig tree refers to time; it teaches that there are indications of when the predicted things will happen, but that nobody really knows the time (vv. 28-32). That lack of precise knowledge is why, following the second parable, we must be attentive, dutiful, and vigilant, like keepers of a house who do not know when the owner will come (vv. 33-37).

The purpose of this message in Mark is not to scare readers with the announcement of war or internal conflicts; they are already living the persecution. Rather, the purpose is to tell them that Jesus also suffered persecution during his own time, and for a time kept his identity secret, so they can also be quiet without feeling guilty.[27] Mark wants to warn them to take care of themselves and be ever vigilant against deceptions and betrayals. Thus, we find not only the middle section on the coming of the Son of the Human Being as a sign of the end of suffering, but also signs of hope and inspiration interspersed throughout the speech. In v. 8, the image of "birthing sorrows"

---

24. Ibid., 500–501.
25. Ibid., 512–13.
26. Ibid.
27. Gerd Theissen, *La redacción de los evangelios y la política eclesial* (Estella: Verbo Divino, 2002), 36.

is a figure that expects a new being. When you have been arrested and taken to court for thinking differently and for testifying about the good news of the kingdom, you should not worry because the Holy Spirit will help you to defend yourselves (v. 11). Verse 13 says that the person who manages to hold on (*hypomenō*) will be saved; when speaking of the most intense suffering ever, he adds that the Lord is going to shorten it for the love of his chosen ones, who will be invited from everywhere when the Son of the Human Being returns (v. 27).

Mark: Fear and Silence

In times of war or armed conflict, what prevails among the people is fear, and hence silence. No one wants to say anything to anyone. So we should not be surprised by the end of the first account that came from the hands of Mark.[28] Trembling with fear, the women said nothing to anyone (16:8). The whole Gospel is like a mirror placed in front of Mark's community, which lives out the war in fear. Perhaps that is why Mark draws the last events of Jesus' movement against a background of horror: the movement's leader has been imprisoned, tortured, and crucified. One of their own betrayed him (14:10-11, 43-45). When Jesus is caught, the disciples flee (14:50). When Jesus is condemned by the Jewish authorities and slapped by their servants (14:64-65), Peter, accused of belonging to Jesus' movement, denies it three times. When Jesus is tortured and crucified, he is all alone and feels abandoned even by God (15:34). The women see him only from afar. The women cannot erase this disastrous end from their minds; against the evidence of the empty tomb, they fear the unknown man wearing white and do not announce the good news of the resurrection or the plan of restarting in Galilee (16:7). Just like the women of Jesus' movement, Mark's community is not saying anything to anybody because it is terrified and paralyzed by the events of the war and the internal armed conflict.

One of the reasons for fear is the possible accusation of treason, the fear of being denounced. In the case of Jesus, his fear is that information considered subversive would reach the local Jewish authorities, represented by the high

---

28. There is consensus in accepting that the manuscripts translated in our Bibles present other endings added at a later time. The earliest manuscript of this Gospel ends at 16:8.

priest, the teachers of the law, the Herodians, and the Pharisees; and that it would get to the hands of occupation forces, represented by the Roman governor and the troops. *Paradidōmi* has several meanings: "to deliver," "to transmit," "to trust," "to permit." The meaning that Mark usually employs is "to deliver" to the authorities; Mark is the Gospel that uses this term the most, and in that sense.[29] Of the nineteen times the term appears, only twice does it have a neutral meaning: "to permit" (4:29) and "to transmit" (7:13). In all the other occurrences, the meaning is negative in the sense of "to deliver up" or to hand over to authorities. Mark also dedicates various passages to Judas Iscariot, as the disciple who delivers Jesus up, who betrays him; in this case we are able equate "to deliver" with "to betray." Mark announces the betrayal very early, in 3:19, when Judas is chosen by Jesus as one of his right-hand men.

The atmosphere of fear shows right from the start of the Gospel. It is not by chance that Jesus' ministry begins when John the Baptist is delivered up (*paradothēnai*), that is to say, imprisoned (1:14). We are therefore in a situation of complete insecurity. Even before we arrive at the second chapter before Jesus is already unable to walk freely in the towns but has to remain on the outskirts, in solitary places (1:45). Already in 3:6, the internal forces, that is, the Pharisees, and the external ones, the Herodians, are planning to kill Jesus. As the narrative advances, the local authorities lie in wait to accuse him (3:2); they set traps to get him (8:11; 10:2; 12:13; 14:1); they try to arrest him (12:12; 14:1) and to kill him (3:6; 11:18; 14:1). In Jerusalem, where the opposition is concentrated, Jesus dares to walk only during the day. At night he leaves the city (11:19). Jesus should be cautious, so we may perhaps suspect that Jesus had his contacts in adjacent villages and even in Jerusalem. These contacts are not known, not even by the people close to him. On two occasions, two of his disciples are sent on an errand without knowing the person whom Jesus wants them to contact. In 11:1-6, on the Mount of Olives, Jesus tells these disciples to go to the village (Bethphage or Bethany), where they will find tied a colt; this colt had already been prepared beforehand. And for the celebration of Passover, Jesus sends two disciples to the city. His contact

---

29. Matthew uses *paradidōmi* thirty-one times; Mark nineteen times; Luke sixteen times; and John fifteen times. Mark is the shortest Gospel, so proportionally, this Gospel's use of the word is higher.

is a man and the sign of identification is a pitcher (14:13-16); this man was the only one who knew where they were going to meet for the Passover, and he had everything ready, as Jesus had asked him to do. Mark does not say who those contacts were. Perhaps they were some poor people whom Jesus had healed or some women whom he trusted. Thus, therefore, Jesus' ministry in favor of the excluded occurs in an atmosphere of insecurity for both Jesus and his followers (13:9-13).

When there is fear, silence is a must, because one has to be very cautious. But there are strategic silences and others that are self-censorship out of fear. This last kind should be reviewed. Let us now examine the recommendation to keep silence.

Jesus, during his practice in favor of the kingdom of God, decides not to go public for safety reasons. Apparently, his identity as Messiah and Son of God (1:1) was going to stir up serious conflicts between the foreign and local authorities. The traditional understanding of Messiah, allegedly, was the one who would free the people of Israel from the dominion of the oppressors, in this case the Roman Empire. The Messiah would triumph over the powers of occupation and would force them out. Such an understanding is extremely dangerous, particularly during the time the Gospel was written, when the rebels of different tendencies were fighting against the Roman troops in Jerusalem. Politically speaking, being the Son of God is an imperial title. From the perspective of the Jewish authorities, it is blasphemy. What we do not know until the second part of the Gospel is that Jesus understands both titles differently, as we will see further on. Since the identity of Jesus and the armed conflict go hand in hand, Jesus prefers not to call attention to himself; he keeps the revelation of his identity a secret. When the time comes to face the local and imperial courts to say who he is, he will be condemned to death by the Jewish (14:62) and Roman law (15:2, 15). For now, while he spreads the good news of the kingdom of God through his acts and teachings, he must hide his identity to avoid premature repression. Traditionally, this has been called "the messianic secret," but when we locate the text in a situation of armed conflict, we can see it as a strategy of survival.

It is very interesting that the first to be asked by Jesus to be silent are the demons. In 1:24, in his first act of healing a human being, while he casts a demon out of a man from Capernaum, the demon recognizes him and in a loud voice shouts: "I know who you are, the Holy One of God" (1:24). Jesus orders him to be silent and to leave the victim. The demons (unclean spirits) know that Jesus has come to destroy them. That same day, at dusk, the people bring him those who are sick and possessed by demons. The summary ends: "And he cured many who were sick with various diseases, and cast out many demons; and he would not permit the demons to speak, because they knew him" (1:34). The same thing occurs in the summary of 3:7-12; by then, Jesus' fame had spread in Galilee, Judea, Idumea, Tyre, and Sidon. We are told that many who had diseases came to be cured, and whenever the unclean spirits saw him they shouted: "You are the Son of God!" but Jesus sternly ordered them not to make him known (3:11-12). The evil spirits are the first ones to betray Jesus. They know him and they denounce him. They are the "frogs," as we would say in Colombia. They do not call on him to praise him, like the healed people who cannot stop speaking about their new condition; rather, they shout his identity to betray him. The last encounter with a possessed person, and the worst of all, was in Gerasa (5:1-20). It is believed that the story alludes symbolically to the Roman troops. The name "Legion" seems to allude to the Roman occupation.[30] This legion of demons recognizes Jesus' authority; they throw themselves at his feet and denounce him: Jesus, Son of the Highest God![31] These events take place in a Gentile region; in this place, Jesus does not order the demons or the man freed from them to be silent. Rather, he tells the man to go and tell everyone what the Lord has done for him. Apparently, there is not much danger in this space. Here we have the two titles used by the emperor, Son of God (5:9) and Lord (5:7), used of Jesus. Jesus takes these titles because he, not the emperor, is the true Son of God and Lord. That is why, at the end, right after Jesus dies on the cross, a centurion—that is, a leader of one of the Roman legions—gives the proper recognition of Jesus as the Son of God (15:39) and not to the emperor.

But Jesus cannot hide his identity for much longer. The disciples, through Peter, will discover it halfway through the narrative, when Jesus asks them

---

30. A Roman legion was usually divided into ten cohorts of six centuries, which was equivalent to a legion of six thousand men (G. R. Watson, *The Roman Soldier* [Ithaca, N.Y.: Cornell University Press, 1969], 22).

31. Jesus throws the legion of demons into the sea, incarnated in the pigs. For Myers (*O Evangelho*, 502), this recalls the moment of liberation in Exodus when the Egyptians, who were persecuting the Hebrews, fell into the sea and drowned, like the pigs.

about it (8:29). Jesus asks his disciples not to tell anyone a word about him (8:30); he asks the same thing from them after they experience the presence of Elijah and Moses on the mount and hear the voice of God that confirms Jesus' identity as the Son of God (9:7-8).

But even earlier in the narrative, Jesus asks the people coming to him who receive healing not to say a word about it. In 1:43, after healing a leper, Jesus sternly orders him: "See that you say nothing to anyone" (1:44). The problem is that such moving news as the healing of a leper is impossible to hide. Renewed people cannot stop sharing their testimony; and even if they did not proclaim it, their healed bodies will announce, or denounce, Jesus as the expected savior. Thus, this person, as soon as he leaves, begins to proclaim openly what had happened; the news spreads, and Jesus loses the liberty to walk in populated areas (1:45). Later on, his popularity is such that not even in Tyre, a Gentile region, would he be able to walk unnoticed (7:24). Because the more he ordered people to tell no one, the more zealously they would proclaim the news; like those who were present when he cured a deaf person and gave him back his ability to speak (7:36). But these people are not like the demons who betrayed Jesus by shouting his name; they simply share the news about the wonders of what has happened to them. These facts create different reactions. While some people seek Jesus to be healed or cleansed of demons, the authorities are looking for him to arrest him. Jesus' actions, more than his words, speak of his identity. That is why, just before his identity as Messiah is revealed within his movement and he announces his passion, when a blind peasant is brought to him in Bethsaida, Jesus takes him out of the village and cures him, and then instructs him to go to his home, avoiding the village (8:26).

Why the hostility set against someone who only does good to others? This is because Jesus disagrees with the way the authorities and the elites, especially those of the temple-state in Jerusalem, administer the power, how they oppress and take advantage of the poorest. Their religious laws marginalize the poor—hence the controversies with teachers of the law, hypocrites, and Herodians. Jesus wants a deep renewal of his people, beginning with those most disadvantaged. Jesus' actions, even without trying, are provocative: to heal the sick and to harvest wheat on the Sabbath, to disregard purity laws, to seek the company of people with bad reputations. Jesus calls hypocritical those who pursue a religiosity completely disconnected from the practical, and in fact to the detriment of the widows (12:40) and the family (7:11-12). The issue seems to have its root in money. Jesus loses his patience in Jerusalem and openly overturns the tables of the brokers (11:15-19). The source of wealth for the temple has been taken from the pilgrims. They come to change money in order to buy the animals to offer sacrifices. Jesus takes this action because his fate has already been set; he knows that he can be imprisoned at any moment now. Perhaps he already suspected the treason of one of his own, who, also for money—a reward of thirty pieces of silver—will deliver Jesus with the sign of a kiss. This is one of the saddest human tragedies; endangering the life of innocent people by passing information about them just because of money, greed, or revenge.

However, there are things that cannot be silenced. The fact that the one who was crucified and buried is no longer in the tomb but is now alive and waits in Galilee for his people, those who have resisted the wave of repression—this fact cannot be silenced. The community of Mark needs to know that the risen one expects them to go back to the road with every confidence and without fear. The community cannot remain quiet with crossed arms. The community, as opposed to the women who have just witnessed the crucifixion, knows the complete story of Jesus, knows that the message of the resurrection has been proclaimed in many communities of faith in Palestine and in many provinces of the empire.

Conclusion: Following Jesus in Times of War and Conflict

Through the rereading of the Jesus event, Mark shows that war between nations and internal armed conflicts can only bring human degradation. At least in these contexts, the Gospel tells us to avoid being absolutists. These extreme situations are fertile ground to awaken even more the hunger for power, money, and revenge. Wars are born out of the sin of injustices committed by the strongest and most powerful against the most vulnerable. The armed reaction in the struggle for justice can easily fall victim to the same vices when it makes use of the logic of militarism and the need to kill others. Violence against violence generates more violence and more victims. That is why Jesus in Mark rejects war and armed conflict and proposes an alternative of human renewal through the practice of justice, of healing wounds, and cleansing evil spirits. The Gospel, through the practice of Jesus, shows us actions that help the diversity in humanity relate to itself. If the discontent among the peasants, unions, students, and others, generated by the injustices committed against them, raises conflicts, what is needed is respect for these sectors. This respect can happen only by paying attention to the claims of the marginalized and limiting the avarice of the powerful. There is a big difference between the camps of the Roman legions set against their commanders and the "camps" of those who are hungry for bread and hope who sit before Jesus. The first receive coins by killing; the second receive pieces of bread and fish to survive (6:33-44; 8:1-10).

The report of the United Nations and the Gospel of Mark coincide in those two conclusions, that war is degradation and that human development is an alternative solution. In Mark, we observe the rejection of war through Jesus' option of choosing the way of the cross. This may sound pathetic because of its injustice, but it entails at its core a deep revolution, where forgiveness and radical change in human practice and attitude are capable of putting an end to the spiral of violence. Or, as Myers says, "In a world governed by the logic of militarism, armed conflict becomes counterrevolutionary."[32]

We can get instructions on how to live in the midst of war. The Markan Jesus offers several proposals as he clarifies his mission as the suffering Son of the Human Being to his followers. They are like orders that one must assume in the midst of the persecution and fear produced by the conflict. Fundamentally, he recommends not fleeing, that is, not turning their backs on the conflict as if did not exist. One must protect life, certainly, by going into exile, or moving to another place, but one cannot ignore the concrete reality. To do so creates a trivialization of the horrors of the armed conflict that has lasted for more than forty years. Jesus recommends that we be attentive and vigilant, adopt a strategic silence, not expose life in front of the "frogs" or informants. But there are times when is not possible to be silent; otherwise, impunity becomes the norm. For a while, Jesus hid his identity, but at the same time he behaved coherently when the need arose; for example, healing someone even when prohibited by the law. There are times when it is impossible to be silent, such as when we face genocides perpetrated by paramilitary, kidnappings executed by the guerrillas, false subversives murdered by members of the official army, or lies spread by the government. In the same

---

32. Myers, *Binding the Strong Man* (Maryknoll, N.Y.: Orbis, 1989), 453.

way that Jesus was troubled by the presence of the brokers in the temple, we should be troubled by the atrocities of the conflict. The recommendation is to be alert, not to flee out of fear but to resist without being crushed, protesting through a practice in favor of a new humanity where there will be no more discontent caused by injustices. For Mark, this means going in search of the risen one in Galilee (16:6-7) and starting over again. The hope behind all of this is that the crucified one was raised by God.

To continue the road that Jesus opened for the sake of a new way of being community, there are three fundamental principles that should be in place: (1) those who win are the ones who lose; (2) the last are the first; and (3) those who lead are the ones who serve others. Each of these statements comes after an announcement of the passion.

1. Those Who Win Are the Ones Who Lose

When Jesus affirms that seeking to save our lives is to lose them, he means that one cannot win when one kills. The person is degraded and loses the quality of humanity, because upon killing another, one kills oneself. A war or an armed conflict is a collective suicide.[33]

To forget ourselves means to forget our personal interests and to adopt the cause of the reign of God. In the context of Colombia, this implies likewise not to betray or to deliver the neighbor or friend or any other innocent person, for the sake of saving our lives or to get benefits or rewards. The soldiers who killed civilians to present positive results in battle, will they be able to live in peace? If they can, they have lost their life. Mark says: "For what will it profit them to gain the whole world and forfeit their life? Indeed, what can they give in return for their life?" (8:36-37). What Jesus is saying is that life is priceless. It is a valuable gift of God that should be preserved like a treasure, for nothing can buy it. No reward received for treason will be worth the life of the one who has been delivered. In a degraded war, everyone loses their life in trying to save it. Those who win using weapons or dirty actions lose. Jesus, we insist, shows us another way, that of humanizing humanity by

---

33. On this point, see Franz Hinkelammert, "El asesinato es un suicidio: De la utilitidad de la limitación del cálculo de utilitidad," *Pasos,* no. 74 (San José, Costa Rica: Departamento Ecuménico de Investigaciones, 1997).

healing the social and physical wounds and exorcising the demons of militarism and of those who betray.

2. The Last Are the First

That the last will be first is asserted at the beginning and at the end of the second announcement of the passion. In the society of the first century and in ours, those who are first are the important ones, the ones who have power, prestige, nobility and, in military conditions, more and better arms. These are the ones who occupy the first positions. The disciples or Christian communities are not exempt from this way of thinking. In fact, twice the disciples talk among themselves about seeking power and being important (9:34; 10:35-37) even within the reign of God. Jesus teaches them another way of thinking and acting, opposed to the established one: those who seek the first positions have to give themselves the last position and seek not to be served but to serve (9:35; 10:43-45).

Jesus illustrates this point with the most marginalized and vulnerable members of society, the children (9:36-37; 10:13-16). He takes them in his arms and identifies with them. To receive a child is not only to receive Jesus but to receive God. This is one of the guidelines of following Jesus: to serve the last, the most helpless. In times of war, the most helpless are the children, the women, the elderly, the disabled ones, and the poor, those who suffer the consequences. To protect them is the natural way of serving God.

Between these two allusions to the last position that appear at the beginning and at the end of the second announcement, we find two very important teachings that we should take into consideration: to reject the exclusive protagonists (9:38-41) and to condemn those who induce innocent people to sin (9:42-50).

For Jesus, those who follow him should understand that there can be other groups that follow the same values of the kingdom even when they do not belong to the movement. In the narrative, the disciples are upset because other groups expel demons in the name of Jesus. They want to be the only ones. Jesus teaches them that they are mistaken and tells them: "Whoever is not against us is for us" (9:40). From this, we understand that the Christian community should be open and happy when other communities share in the same practice and vision. If to cast out demons means to reject war and to expel the evil spirits of the "frogs" and informants, all people who suffer violence should be happy when such demons are expelled, regardless of what group does the exorcism.

Jesus comes down hard on those who induce the little ones to sin or to stumble; he announces a horrendous end for them. In a situation of war, there are many things that induce one to sin; for example, hunger, produced by the social injustices, or the avarice of contaminated hearts. In military terms, those who induce others to sin are the leaders of the armed forces, be it officials or irregulars; the illiterate peasants are induced to kill for causes they do not even know. The promise of rewards also causes people to sin, for they denounce people for money. That is why in this section of the second announcement Jesus speaks of the need for deep purification[34] and to seek peace: "Have salt in yourselves, and be at peace with one another!"

In the end, Mark mentions the theme of the rewards. The disciples left it all, as opposed to a rich young man who was very good in religious matters but was unable to give his wealth to the poor (10:17-22). The disciples will have their reward for leaving everything behind to follow Jesus' cause. With this, Mark wants to show that those who give their entire life for the cause of the kingdom will have true rewards from God. Not rewards for killing, or betraying, but rewards for giving their life to the cause of the kingdom. These, who are the last, will be the first (10:29-31).

3. Those Who Lead Are the Ones Who Serve Others (10:32-45)

In this third announcement, Jesus explains how the Son of the Human Being will be delivered to the local authorities and to the forces of occupation, and how they will torture him, but how he will be raised on the third day. The intervention of two of Jesus' disciples, very close to him, is not connected with the announcement of the sufferings; on the contrary, it is located on the opposite side, in the struggle for power (vv. 35-37). Once again, in this third announcement, Mark gives the guidelines of how the Christian community should behave. James and John seek honor and power next to Jesus in the *parousia*. Jesus instead helps them go back to the road of painful resistance and teaches them another way of understanding power.

The power of the rulers and the "great ones" is described by Jesus as tyranny and despotism (10:42). The two Greek words (*katakyrieuousin* and

---

34. Guillermo Cook and Ricardo Foulkes, *Marcos,* Comentario bíblico Hispanoamericano (Miami: Caribe, 1990), 243.

katexousiazousin) allude to this excessive control. This is the type of power that we are experiencing today in many societies, including Colombia. They speak of democracy, but in reality there is an evident authoritarianism. Jesus condemns this form of government because it does not fit the standards on how leadership is done in the reign of God. [35] "But it is not so among you" (10:43) is a forceful phrase. If there is someone who wants to be great and important, the only way to do it is to serve others (10:43-44). This is the way in which the new humanity inaugurated by the Son of Human Being is manifested. Jesus' example was that of serving to the point of giving his own life; he did not come to be served but to pay with his life for the freedom of all, to pay for the freedom of both those kidnapped by the sin of war and those enslaved by the sin of greed.

All in all, Mark advocates for human life against violence and treason, because the meaningless and degrading war, which kills and seeks personal interests, goes against the very nature of the human being. Here there is a chance for the full humanity that, when it is lived under the horizon of the reign of God, guided by the three principles above, will not give rise to the injustices, the exploitations, and the disrespect of cultures that cause discontent against responsible leaders.

---

35. When he talks about these types of governors, he uses the participle *hoi dokoũntes,* "those that seem to govern," that is to say, those who believe they are governing. In this way, he is condemning this traditional concept, which does not go well with the form of governing in the reign of God.

CHAPTER 7

Children in Mark

A Lens for Reading Mark's Gospel

Teresa Okure, SHCJ

Reading as Contextual Reception

Reading as a concept draws attention to the activity of the receiver in his or her sociocultural context. Culture forms the inescapable lens for receiving the gospel message even as it formed that of the Evangelists and other biblical authors. This receptive soil (or soils) is particular and general, local and global. Its influence on the reader's understanding of the message is taken for granted. At the same time, the cultural and contextual lenses give new insights into the text.

A key global issue today is that of children and their rights. Contemporary society is very much concerned with children and their plight and rights in an adult world. The media lays much emphasis on children's rights; laws are enacted against child labor; global efforts are made to combat trafficking in children and women (in the ancient world as today, especially in African contexts, women and children always seem to go together and suffer the same fate from church and society).

The struggle for children's rights can in some cases be a reversed form of child exploitation, as when children are encouraged to report their parents to the police and have them arraigned for the least offence. Such measures indirectly teach children to flout God's law, which counsels respect for parents as the commandment that has a special blessing attached to it. "Honor your father and mother so that you may live long in the land that the Lord your God is giving you" (Exod 20:12). Because of an excessive exaggeration of the child's rights, parents are literally scared stiff and rendered powerless to correct their children in love, knowing that God has entrusted those children to them to bring up as people created in God's image and likeness and as heirs of the kingdom along with themselves. The people who push this distorted agenda of the child's rights are themselves human beings, as are the parents who through fear of reprisals leave their children to grow wild. Oppressive supervision of one's child and a totally laissez-faire attitude toward them are both inimical to the child.

On the sociopolitical level, it is often said that children are the heirs or leaders of tomorrow, so they should be treated well now so that they may play their role correctly tomorrow. Yet how many children today will live to be leaders of tomorrow? Whom will they lead and how? What of the great masses of children who will never grow to become leaders, just as today the adult masses (who were once children) have no opportunity to lead but are rather exploited, abused, and lorded over by their few leaders? For the most part, they may have no power to prevent a dictator from staying on indefinitely, as is currently the case in Zimbabwe. The best they can do is to conduct protest marches en masse, but in the last analysis, they still depend on the goodwill or the ability of their minority leaders to effect the needed changes. Even if their protests bring down a regime, the people have no power to control how the new regime will function.

From the gospel and the divine perspective, do children exist only for tomorrow (when they will become adults), or do they have an intrinsic worth and right of their own as children in God's kingdom? What if they never live to see tomorrow? Will they be thereby deprived of sharing in the blessings of the good news? Do they in Jesus' gospel have an intrinsic worth and role here and now in their capacity as children?

Many, if not all, cultures value children, not for themselves, but for their usefulness to the adult world. In the African context, marriages can break up because of lack of issue, especially the male issue. Such cultures value children not for their own intrinsic worth, but as sources of wealth or, for the boy child, as a prospective "permanent resident" (one who will inherit the father's property, look after the parents in their old age and continue the family name and line), in contrast to the girl child, who is viewed as a "temporary resident" (since she will be married off and will change her name to that of her husband). The search for the male child "permanent resident" often leads to irregular marriages and the begetting of more girl children until the much-sought permanent resident arrives. Girl children born under this condition come into existence as by chance, because the family was looking for the one that matters. In India, the woman's family pays a dowry to the husband's family, not only once (for herself) but continuously for every girl child she gives birth to in the marriage.

In Nigeria, as in many developing countries, children parade the streets in the midst of heavy traffic, breathing in the vehicle fumes, exposed to scourging sun and other inclement weather conditions, hawking for their masters/mistresses or their own street parents. At the end of the day, they are likely in addition to receive harsh treatment from their "owners" or be denied food, should they happen to miscalculate what they sold, or if they sold nothing at all, or if they allowed any of the commodities given them for sale to get spoiled or lost.

Elsewhere, children are sometimes aborted because the would-be mother, backed by societal approval (legalized abortion), claims the right to do what she likes with her body (forgetting that she herself would not have had a body to do what she liked with had her own mother exercised the same right over her body when she was conceived). Children are conscripted into crime at home and in society by what the media, the entertainment industry, and the Internet display daily before them (all warnings of the need for parental control notwithstanding).

Concerning the Gospels and the New Testament generally, the overall feeling is that children have little or no place in them, especially since the good news of the kingdom was originally preached to adults, from whom it required the response of conversion or belief. In Mark's Gospel, John the Baptist proclaimed "a baptism of repentance for the forgiveness of sins" (Mark 1:4). After him, Jesus continued in the same vein with the clarion call: "The time is fulfilled and the kingdom of God is at hand, repent, and believe in the good news" (1:15). Appropriate response to these invitations belongs to adults, who alone can exercise the faith and personal decision required.

Based on this, critics of the Catholic Church and of other churches who practice infant baptism opine that the practice is not founded on the Gospels. Children should be allowed to grow up first and then to decide for themselves what religion to choose. Baptizing them as infants is allegedly infringing on their right to religious freedom, which includes denominational freedom. Ironically, while many who hold this view allow children the right to choose life spiritually, they give no thought to allowing them to choose life naturally; in the case of abortion, those who abort the children decide for them that they do not want to, or have no right to live. But if the child has no say in coming to natural existence, why should it be allowed to decide to come to birth in the spiritual existence?[1]

Second, it is noted that children were not listed among the followers of Jesus. At best, children, like most women, were to be seen and not heard—maybe not even seen, but certainly not counted, since culturally they were not regarded as legal persons. In the Jewish culture in which the gospel was first preached, the boy child at least had a legal sense of belonging to the covenanted community. His circumcision on the eighth day gave him direct entry into, and made him an heir of, the covenant. The girl child had no such legal provision for belonging to the covenant community. She could only belong indirectly through her father and, later, her husband. As an unmarried daughter, she could take part in the family celebrations but not as an independent heir of the covenant. When the gospel later spread into the wider Greco-Roman world, the situation it met was not radically different. The girl child's and the woman's worth still depended largely on that of the father or husband, especially in the era of Augustan reforms. Thus, both in Judaism (ancient and contemporary to Mark) and in the wider Hellenistic world, the girl child remained the most marginalized and excluded in society.

In contrast to the global and local scenario (ancient and modern) sketched above, Mark comprehensively views his Gospel as "the good news of Jesus Christ, the Son of God" (1:1); that is, the good news that is Jesus Christ (subjective genitive), as Paul would put it (Rom 1:1, 16), or the good news that belongs to or is from Jesus Christ (objective genitive). Common sense would

---

1. This is not the place to address this issue at length. Suffice it to say that the view under discussion fails to understand the significance of baptism in the New Testament. If baptism is allowing the child to receive new birth in and from God, just as conception allowed it to receive natural life from God through the same parents, then it makes little sense to ask the child to wait to grow up before making that decision. No more than one waits on a child to decide whether or not it wants to become a human being, that is, be given natural birth and life through conception and birth into a human family.

lead one to understand this designation in both its subjective and objective senses. The New Testament tradition declares unequivocally that "God has no favorites" or "shows no partiality" (see Rom 2:11; Gal 2:6; Col 3:25; Eph 6:9; Acts 10:34; 1 Pet 1:17; see also Jas 2:1, where the brethren are exhorted to make impartiality an integral part of their belief in the Lord Jesus Christ). If this is true, can God's good news and its proclamation leave out *a priori* any stage or sector of humanity? Has the gospel any good news for children, as for their societies and cultures?

This study reads Mark's Gospel against the background of the status, rating, and experience of children in our multicultural local and global contexts as well as in Mark's world. What new insights do the individual and common experiences of children across the globe give into Mark's Gospel? In particular, how are children featured in Mark's Gospel itself (especially the girl child) and for what purpose? Does the Markan Jesus offer anything new, countercultural, and liberative for children as an essential aspect of his proclaiming and being God's gospel, which, according to Luke, is God's general amnesty for the entire creation ("the Lord's year of favor"; Luke 4:19)?

Children in Mark's Gospel fall basically into two categories, designated by the Greek words *paidion* (little child) and *teknon* (child or offspring, emphasizing the fact of being begotten by somebody regardless of age). Mark focuses predominantly on the first category, little child (*paidion*) or little children (*paidia*), as being the most vulnerable group. In a few other instances, children appear without being designated by either of the two terms, as in the case of the daughter of Herodias. This current reading examines the relevant passages in which children are treated under these categories, bearing in mind the set of questions raised above. But first, what is the status of Mark's Gospel itself as a genre in relation to the other three Gospels? Can it be seen as a baby/child Gospel, thus having relevance for the question at issue?

Mark, the "Baby" Gospel

Scholars hold—rightly or wrongly—that Mark invented the gospel genre (aside from the *Gospel of Thomas* or the hypothetical Q). If so, it can be described as a baby gospel, the least theologically and christologically developed of the four Gospels. Mark's Greek is basic *koinē*; his style anything but polished. Mark speaks like a child for whom the present is what counts. His most cherished and overused phrase is "immediately" or "there and then" (*euthys*). As a little child would do, Mark says it as it is. His portrait of Jesus is in some instances "crude" (for instance, when his relatives go in search of him, convinced that "he was out of his mind" (*existē*; 3:21) or when he "experiments" with healing the deaf and dumb in private, using mud and spittle (7:32); or cures the blind man at Bethsaida whom he leads outside the village and spits on his eyes such that he first sees people as if they were trees but walking, before he receives full sight (8:22-26).[2]

Most often, Mark reports that Jesus teaches the people in their synagogues, towns, and villages without actually specifying the content of his teaching (cf. 1:21-22, 39; 2:1-2, 13; 6:1-2, 6b, 34). An outstanding exception is his parabolic teaching in 4:1-34, in which Jesus gives the content with explanations to his disciples in private. In the resurrection account, the shorter ending of Mark (16:1-8, considered the original ending) has no actual appearance of the risen Christ. The women who see the messenger in the tomb run away frightened and say nothing to anyone.

An interesting question is whether these "primitive" features of the Gospel go back to Jesus himself or reflect Mark's own status as an inexperienced, untrained theologian and narrator. Whatever the case, his Gospel stands apart in every way as the most undeveloped, though not the least sophisticated, of the four Gospels.[3]

Mark himself has been identified as "John whose other name was Mark" (Acts 12:12), the cousin of Barnabas, and the young man who ran naked in the garden during the arrest of Jesus, leaving his sole loincloth with the guards who sought to arrest him as well (14:51-52). If this identity is correct (and there is no way of saying with certainty who he was), he hailed from Syria; his mother had a house in Jerusalem, which was most probably the venue of the Last Supper. Mark himself could thus have been the man carrying a

---

2. There are of course other possible explanations for these events than that Mark's Jesus is an inexperienced healer. If this were the first miracle of healing in the Gospel, the charge of experimentation would stand, but that is certainly not the case. These are interesting questions, which need not delay us here.

3. On this sophistication, see the commentary on Mark by Hisako Kinukawa in the *Global Bible Commentary*, ed. Daniel Patte et al. (Nashville: Abingdon, 2004), 367–78, where the author shows that behind the apparently innocent stories of the miracles is a sophisticated critique of the power relations and structures (Roman, Tyrean, and Judean) operative against Galilee at the time.

pitcher of water (14:13), something men did not normally do in the culture. That Jesus uses him as a sign for the venue of his Last Supper, a climactic event of his ministry, is itself indicative of the countercultural nature of his mission. Water carrying in Palestine then, as in Africa today, was girls' and women's work. The upper room where the disciples gathered in preparation for Pentecost, where the primitive church on mission was subsequently born and which served as its first center in Jerusalem (Acts 1:13-14; 2:1; 12:12-17), would have been his mother's house.

Mark's audience was likely not all Jews; many scholars would say they were predominantly Gentiles, if the Gospel was written in Rome or Egypt. Scholars have noted that Mark translates Aramaic words for the addressees (3:17; 4:41; 7:11; 15:22, 34), not so Latin ones (5:9; 6:37; 12:14-15; 15:15-16, 39). This evidence could lead one to conclude in favor of a Gentile, Roman audience. If the situation of children was almost the same globally as sketched earlier, what would this audience have heard concerning the status of children in the Gospel? What would Mark, himself a youth, have heard as he received, interpreted, and transmitted the contents of his Gospel? Jesus himself, said to be about thirty to thirty-four years old when he began his public ministry, would have been a youth. He and John Mark are identified as women's sons in the tradition. In Mark 6:4, Jesus is derogatorily called "the son of Mary." In Acts 12:12, John Mark is identified with his mother, not his father. Did children and the youth feature among his intended audience? We may not be able to say with certainty who the audience was or what it heard, but we have a responsibility to hear what the Gospel says about children in its own context and in our local and global contexts.

Children in the Gospel

We proceed in three stages, first a consideration of children with emphasis on their being little child/children (*paidion/paidia*); then child/children with focus on their being begotten, irrespective of their age (*teknon/tekna*); and finally a daughter (presumably a little one) who features outside the two terminologies and is abused by adults for their own selfish purposes. The term *child* covers from infancy to the age of twelve. In Jewish and Roman contexts, girls were said to reach maturity (marriageable age) at twelve. For a boy, it was eighteen.

1. *Little Child/Children* (paidion/paidia)

Of the fifty-two occurrences of the term *paidion* (in singular or plural) in the New Testament, twelve occurrences are in Mark (sixteen in Matthew, thirteen in Luke, and two in John). This is remarkable, given the relatively short character of Mark's Gospel. These passages are examined one by one below to discern their ancient and contemporary significance.

MARK 5:39-41

The first occurrence of *paidion* in the Gospel (here four times) is in the episode of the little daughter of Jairus. *Paidion* is neuter and applies to either a boy or a girl. In raising her from the dead, Jesus addresses the girl as *talitha* (literally, "lamb," perhaps expressing her childish innocence but also as a term of endearment, though most translations render it as "little girl"). In the complexity of this story, the fate of the little girl (twelve years old) is linked with that of the woman with the hemorrhage, ill for twelve years. I have argued elsewhere that the ages of these two women are symbolic of that of the nation. Until both are cured, integrated into the community or raised to life to live their own life independently, the nation as a whole cannot be healed. Moreover, in a culture where theologians interpreted the Aaronic blessing of Num 6:22-27 to mean "May the Lord bless thee with sons and keep thee from daughters" or Abraham's being "blessed in all things" to mean that he was "blessed with sons not with daughters," it was still better to have an only child alive, even if that child was a girl, than to be childless. The father evidently loves this little girl. When Jesus orders her to rise (from the dead), the little girl gets up and walks. He then orders the parents to give her something to eat and thus sustain her own life on its own merit.

MARK 7:24-30

This passage recounts the episode of Jesus' encounter with the Syrophoenician woman in the district of Tyre and Sidon. The evangelist is careful to emphasize her Gentile status: she is "a Greek, a Syrophoenician by birth." Here a woman, a foreigner, asks Jesus to drive out a demon from her little daughter (*thygatrion*). Jesus replies that she should let the children (*tekna*) eat first, since it is not right to take the children's (*tekna*) food and throw it to dogs (*kynes*). The woman retorts that, true as this may be, little dogs or house dogs (*kynaria*, as opposed to scavengers implied by Jesus when he uses "throw") do eat of the crumbs that fall from the table of little children (*paidia*). Or, more specifically, little children love to feed house dogs from their own ration.

Thus, while Jesus, by using *tekna*, focuses on the issue of race—the disparity between the rich people of Tyre and the poor Galileans (a region out of which, even for the Judean Jews, prophets are not to arise [John 7:52])—the woman underscores that not all in rich Tyre and Sidon belong to the same rich class. She (apparently a single mother, likely to be a widow), and the deprived Jewish little children in Galilee share the same lot (*kynaria* and *paidia*, respectively), namely, that of being the rejects of society and victims of unjust societal structures. Accordingly, both stand in need of being helped in their diverse needs by Jesus. Children call the adult world to this reality by their nondiscriminatory attitude toward little house dogs. Both have something in common, their littleness. The demon possession of the girl could have been as a result of her low social status in a rich urban city. Impressed by the woman's wisdom and social awareness, Jesus assures her that her word, her own unyielding stand, has driven the demon out of her daughter: "For saying this [or because of your word, *logos*] the demon has already left your daughter." The verb tense is the pluperfect (*exelēlythen*).

In Africa, women are the persons most frequently accused of being witches, especially if they are of lower class. The demons of hunger and disease caused by oppression, unjust social order, and marginalization in an otherwise rich nation (such as oil-rich Nigeria) stand equally in need of being cast out through the proclamation of the gospel. Today, when the economic crisis has hit the world, sparing almost nobody, the gospel needs to be proclaimed anew so that the economic base and strength of every nation will be located in the welfare or well-being of the masses, not in fictitious bank accounts and bogus profits that have no relation to the reality on the ground. Little girls and their lower-class mothers are hardest hit, especially in Africa. In the towns, villages, and refugee camps (both internal and external) dotted across the continent, evangelists are challenged to empower the mothers to seek the kind of help that will liberate both the oppressors and the oppressed. Faith is needed here, because even if faith is not specifically mentioned in the passage, the woman would not have gone to Jesus for help had she not been convinced that he had the power and would actually rid her daughter of the demon that possessed her. Her unyielding stance made Jesus also change his attitude toward her and see the relationship between the Galileans and the Judeans in a new light.

MARK 9:17-29

In the account of the father and the epileptic child, this time a little boy is possessed by a demon. The father brings the boy to Jesus' disciples, who are unable to cast out the demon. The disciples in question may be a mixture of men and women. What is important is that the demon has proved beyond their power to cast out. Is their discipleship in question? Do they have the faith to do it? Do they see themselves as those who possess the power, thus turning stewardship to ownership? Mark notes that Jesus, coming down from the mountain of the transfiguration, is disappointed with the faithlessness and unbearable attitude of "this generation" when he meets his disciples arguing with the crowds. The disciples were part of that generation. Later, Jesus will tell them that they needed prayer, a dependent attitude, to be able to cast out that type of demon.

The father of the boy, also in desperation, pleads with Jesus to do something if he possibly can. The issue is not whether or not Jesus can but whether both those seeking help for the demons that possess our children from birth and those from whom help is sought can muster up the necessary faith backed by prayer and action to get rid of these demons. Until the social and spiritual demons are eliminated through selfless service rooted in love, the little boys and girls in our communities will not enjoy even in their youthful age the liberation that the gospel offers them free of charge. Quite the contrary, their vulnerability and helplessness make them greater victims of the unjust and exploitative social, political, and economic systems. Adults are major players and contributors to the plight of the children and youth in our society. Today, many would-be disciples indulge in power seeking and prestige in the name of being miracle workers. The gullible masses fall victim to their self-aggrandizement.

MARK 9:36-37; 10:13-16

I have decided to look at these two passages together, for they move Mark's concern with children from their being people in need, vulnerable people who are to be given their share in the goodies of the kingdom, to their being unique models of Jesus and the kingdom itself. In the first passage (9:36-37),

Jesus counteracts his male disciples' dispute about who among them is the greatest by calling and setting in their midst "a little child" (which could be a boy or girl). "Embracing" the child, Jesus tells his disciples that whoever receives one such little child in his name receives him. In a culture where children were not legal entities, the disciples would have been shocked at this gospel revolution: that Jesus, their master and teacher, identified himself with such little children (*toioutōn paidiōn*). Jesus here emphasizes the intrinsic worth of little children for their own sake, not for their function in the adult world, whether present or future. While grownups seek to touch Jesus (for example, the woman with the hemorrhage), Jesus on his own seeks out children, embraces them, and roots his gospel proclamation (in the objective and subjective senses) in them.

Mark 10:13-16 narrates that "they were bringing little children to" Jesus "so that he might touch them" (*hapsētai,* purposeful touch as in 5:28—the woman with the hemorrhage—perhaps even a hug, as in 9:36). But the disciples "rebuked" them (*epetimēsan*); that is, the disciples rebuked those who brought the children. These would most probably (if not certainly) have been women, the mothers or nannies of those little children, since men did not normally carry children in private or in public—then as now in Africa and elsewhere—though this may be gradually changing. Luke (18:15) calls them "infants" (*brephē*). In the Gospels, men are fond of rebuking or reproaching women who approach Jesus, as in the case of the woman who anointed Jesus (Mark 14:4-5) and Mary of Bethany (John 12:3-5). This is a reflection of the cultural mind-set. Women and children are two undesirables in the patriarchal cultural setup, but not in Jesus' gospel economy. Moreover, these women would have been emboldened in their action by Jesus' attitude toward children, whom shortly before he had dramatically set before his disciples as representing him (Mark the narrator is aware of this). The disciples seem not to have heard him. Had they done so, they would not have rebuked or scolded or prevented the women who brought the children to Jesus.

In turn, Jesus is also typically "indignant" (*ēganaktēsen*) with the disciples and orders them to "allow" (not to prevent) little children to come to him. Interestingly, Jesus sees beyond those who are bringing the children, to the children themselves. "Let the children come to me, do not prevent them; for of such is the kingdom of God." This time Jesus expands the child model beyond himself to God's own kingdom: "of such is [not 'to such belongs' as some translations put it], the kingdom of heaven." This is as social a revolution as any. From not being legal persons culturally worthy of being counted, little children become living models of what God's own reign is like. The Markan Jesus presses this model further by extending it to the level of reception of the kingdom: "One who does not receive/welcome God's kingdom like a little child (*hōs paidion*) will not enter into it" (10:15). The disciples apparently lack this spirit of receptiveness; otherwise they would not have rebuked those who came to receive the blessing from Jesus.

One's imagination here is as good as another's concerning the nature of this modeling of both God's kingdom and the condition for its reception. In a world where one gets on in life through sheer prowess and one's hard-earned money and achievement, it becomes difficult, if not nearly impossible, to think of receiving God's kingdom like a little child. Little children have absolute trust in their parents and depend on them for everything as a matter of course. Their very helplessness, innocence, straightforwardness, nondiscriminatory attitude and ability to transcend boundaries (or, better still, their being boundary-less) endears them to all. Good parents, too, see it as their natural duty to provide for their children all they need, no matter the cost to themselves.

In this double imaging (of the nature of the kingdom and its reception), Mark captures what other New Testament authors call grace. God's gift of salvation is totally free of charge, not dependent on any human considerations and nondiscriminatory. The sole condition for receiving or entering into it is to believe God and open oneself up to receive its immense blessings, not because of anything one might have done or will do or because of one's works or worth, but solely because of God's immeasurable, incomprehensible, and incredible love (see, for instance, Eph 1:3-14; 2:4-10; Titus 3:4-7, and parallels). Mark hereby not only reverses the status and dignity of little children in the culture. In his gospel view, the adult world needs to recapture the spirit and attitude of little children if it is truly to enjoy God's blessings and have the freedom and resources it needs to overcome and get out of its current economic depression (for instance) brought about by a long-standing and long-neglected (even promoted) moral depression. In this gospel sense, the little children function in the adult world not so that they may serve their interests but so that, from them, the adult world itself might learn how to receive, enter, and in turn model the kingdom.

2. *Children as Begotten* (teknon/tekna; *Hebrew* bēn)

Occurrences of children under this category are not many. Mark has nine out of the ninety-nine occurrences in the New Testament: 2:5; 7:27 (twice); 10:24, 29, 30; 12:19; and 13:12 (twice). The usage in 7:27 has already been discussed above in the episode of the Syrophoenician woman and her little daughter. All these occurrences reveal one or another aspect of God's reign.

MARK 2:3-5

Jesus responds to the sagacity of the faith of those who stop at nothing, even destroying somebody's roof, in their determination to draw his attention to heal the paralytic. In response to their faith, Jesus addresses the root cause of the problem, by forgiving the paralytic his sins ("Child [*teknon*], your sins are forgiven you"), to the indignation of the religious authorities present. Forgiveness of sins is integral to the proclamation and reception of the kingdom. The passage does not say for how long the person had been a paralytic. What is clear is that he would have been a burden on his relatives or friends, who were determined to get him cured. One may think of the different terminal diseases that people's relatives suffer today. Some of these diseases, such as malaria and even HIV and AIDS, spread because the human family is not really determined to get rid of them or to allow God's gospel to penetrate, expose, and destroy their root causes. Sin in biblical thought is essentially a missing of the mark, a getting out of orbit. Personal interests and superficial approaches to human suffering keep the diseases going, especially when racial, economic, and gender factors come into play.

Where today is the concerted will to rid our societies of their social, moral, human, and other paralyses? Would it make a difference if people saw one another as members of the same family, begotten anew by God in Christ? The African Synod of 1994 adopted the concept of church-as-family-of-God to be the model that best explains its self-understanding as church, universal and local. To what extent has this concept, now fifteen years later, translated into reality in concrete life relationships across the African continent and globally?

MARK 10:24-30

The occurrences of *teknon* in Mark 10:24-30 are in the context of the rich person (the text does not specify whether he was young or old, man or woman) who is sad and finds it hard to sell his riches, give the proceeds to the poor, and follow Jesus. Commenting on the sad response of the person, Jesus addresses his disciples as children (*tekna;* this too is gender neutral). The disciples are surprised to hear that, contrary to their cultural belief (that wealth is a sure sign of God's favor), the rich, by virtue of being rich, may find it hard to enter into God's kingdom. Jesus was not inviting the person to be poor for poverty's sake but radically to share wealth with the poor. Go, sell all, and give to the poor; then come and be my disciple and experience the blessing of spending your life to enrich others even as God and Jesus do (cf. Phil 2:6-11; 2 Cor 8:9). Experience the joy of being Godlike or of having your treasure in heaven.

As usual, the disciples pay little attention to or miss out on what is at stake in this gospel demand. Peter, speaking for others, wants to know what they would gain, having left all things to follow Jesus. Jesus in turn solemnly assures them that they will receive a hundredfold in this world: children, houses, property, and in the next world eternal life. But for that to happen, one must be prepared to stick to the values of the kingdom, especially in times of persecution. In other words, to be begotten (*teknon*) in the kingdom, one must be prepared to endure its birth pangs (cf. John 16:21-22).

MARK 12:19

Mark 12:19 deals with the provision for levirate marriage. The Sadducees who question Jesus are not really interested in finding out the truth about the situation of marriage after death. Their interest is in disproving or at best rendering ridiculous the belief in the resurrection. That apart, the provision whereby a woman can be married by as many as seven brothers in order to beget children for the first brother who died without issue shows no consideration either for the woman or the child who is sought. As was said at the beginning, the quest for a male child (which is the one presupposed in this passage, since female children would not normally continue the man's name) can lead in modern contexts to broken marriages. In most of these cases, the woman and her girl children are the ones who suffer. Other women who enter into the marriage to spite the first forget that they in turn can be dumped or set aside by their husbands for another, in search of a male child. The girl children in this arrangement are personae non grata.

In some Nigerian cultures, as said earlier, girls are multiplied as an appendix until the boy child appears. Even here the boy child is not valued for his own sake, though this appears to be the case, but for his destiny to continue the family name and assume the father's role and responsibility toward the family after the father's death. Jesus counters this practice by pointing out that, in the resurrection or in God's reign, social arrangements whereby the woman finds meaning in life only by being a "Mrs. Somebody" or the "mother of Somebody" do not exist. In Africa, Jesus' position would be a major sociocultural revolution. One's ability to contribute to the continuance of the clan by begetting children is a criterion for admission to the abode and rank of the ancestors, which in the African traditional setting is the afterlife, what the Sadducees tag the resurrection.

Jesus neutralizes such criteria. By the same token, he reinstates the equal dignity between husband and wife, between the boy child and the girl child. In the future of the kingdom, the end-time, all—parents, boys, and girls—enjoy the same status, dignity, and freedom as God's children on their own ticket. According to Heb 12:18-24, one's status as a child in the kingdom transcends what it was in the old dispensation, where people needed middle persons or mediators like Moses. In the new dispensation, all are citizens on equal footing, all have the dignity of the firstborn, because by their new birth at baptism, when they are begotten by God in Christ, all possess or are endowed with the dignity of Christ, the firstborn members of whose body they are since the assembly is that of the firstborns (*ekklēsia prōtotokōn*, Heb 12:23).

MARK 13:12

The final passage, Mark 13:12, occurs in the eschatological description, in which Jesus predicts that fathers will betray children and children their fathers; that children will arise and kill their parents (those who begot them) because essentially they have failed to heed the clarion call of the gospel, to "repent and believe/receive, to accept and live by the good news." That this is happening even today, in many developed countries perhaps more so than in developing ones, indicates that we live in the eschatological times. Even here, too, children are victims of a world that has lost the sense of life and that makes them think they can take lives anyhow, even the lives of their parents, to settle one score or another.

Today, we would add to the Marcan list that children will kill other children, their teachers, and other adults as a way of addressing their grievances, big or small, and parents will kill their children. Here, as in previous cases, children are victims of a sinful world order, a world order that refuses to heed Jesus' gospel call to repent, turn around, and believe the good news, assured that God's kingdom has come through Jesus' own life, ministry, passion, death, and resurrection, assured that one's true worth and dignity lie in entering into and becoming a child of God, living in God's reign (kingdom).

3. The Daughter of Herodias (Mark 6:14-29) and the Sons of Zebedee (Mark 10:35-54)

Our final passages deal with parent–child relationships: the daughter of Herodias and the sons of Zebedee. Both reveal the kind of intrigue whereby parents use their children for their aims or children hide behind their parents to get what they want.

The daughter of Herodias on Herod's birthday dances so well that the king promises her anything she asks for, even half of his kingdom (6:14-29). One would have expected her to ask for something that is life-generating, in keeping with her gifts as a dancer and as a child. Instead, she becomes the victim of her vindictive mother and perhaps an equally vindictive stepfather, Herod (though he is unconvincingly projected as having great respect for the Baptist). Both lure her into doing their dirty work for them. The mother asks her to request the head of John the Baptist. On her own, she adds that she wants it there and then in a dish; the irresponsible stepfather gives it to her because he does not want to break his promise to her. Herod's weakness here recalls Pilate in the trial of Jesus.

Our concern is not to analyze the dubious characters of these people but to highlight how children can be morally affected through the false life of their parents. It is reported that in a secondary school, teachers counseled children against telling lies and practicing corruption. The children retorted that the teachers should speak rather to their parents, not to them on the matter. Mark does not say how old Herodias's daughter was; but that she had to run (perhaps in her childlike innocence) to ask the mother, implies the youthful trust she had in the mother. Both the stepfather and the mother failed her. The head of the Baptist in a dish would have relieved the parents (especially the mother according to the story, in a culture where women were always stereotyped as the guilty ones) of their guilty conscience that the Baptist pricked. But what did it do to or for their daughter? In beheading the Baptist through a family plot in which the daughter was a central figure, the parents probably dealt an even more fatal blow to their own consciences and initiated their daughter into the path of taking life for flimsy reasons. Such practices are with us today in real life as reported frequently in the media.

Whereas Herod and Herodias use their daughter to achieve their personal aims, the Sons of Zebedee (10:35-54) use their mother to achieve theirs. Trusting perhaps in Jesus' love for and attention to women, they put their mother forward to ask for powerful positions for themselves in the kingdom, though if they had listened to Jesus at all, they would have learned that the kingdom is not about power but about selfless service. Characteristically, Jesus in response addresses not the mother but the children. Whether they can live up to their boast that they can drink the cup of Jesus remains to be seen. Of interest here is that today parents allow themselves to be used to seek for their children things that are not good for them. In some contexts, parents buy examination results for their children. In other words, they fall into the trap of wanting for their children powers, positions, and qualifications that do not go with their actual acquired skills. This type of false love is equally an abuse of children. Even if children want to manipulate their parents, parents should have the adult wisdom not to allow themselves to be used in this way.

Toward a Conclusion

As I said at the beginning, the aim of this commentary that focused on children in Mark's Gospel was to raise an issue that is little touched on in the study of the Gospels, the New Testament, and the Bible generally. Commentaries on the Gospels rarely discuss the relevant passages on children. What is at issue here is to see children not just as foils for proclaiming the kingdom but as people who in their own right are presented by the Jesus of the Gospels as having a place in the kingdom as children.

What has emerged is a complex picture of the exploitation and rejection of children at the macro level, by culture and society, but their acceptance and cherishing by their parents, especially the mothers, in the cases of little children (*paidion/paidia*). Jesus goes further to identify with these vulnerable children, the rejects of society, and proclaims them as visibly modeling the kingdom and its reception. On the level of *teknon/tekna,* children are still essentially victims of a society that is turned in upon itself instead of on God. Jesus uses the parent–child relationship to warn his hearers to stay alert to ensure that they are in deed and in truth children of the kingdom, those begotten by God, who know God and live like God.

The outcome of this study raises great challenges, invitations, and graces for our current world structures and its crises in child upbringing and treatment of children generally. The issues surfaced need to be studied more in depth than is possible in this current context. An interesting dimension would be to explore how the children passages are interwoven in the Gospel with those of the related themes of divorce and marriage (10:1-2) and the rich aristocrat (10:17-31). In brief, focus on how the children passages function in the Gospel can give greater insights into the surrounding passages themselves.

Because of the global yet local nature of the issue of children, the context of study is equally local and global. The single most important recommendation of this study, perhaps, is for each reader to receive the gospel from the lens of the actual plight of children in her or his own context, and thereby to rediscover the graces of the gospel as offered to us through Jesus' attitude toward and reception of children in deed and word. Another all-embracing outcome of this study is the need to conduct more studies on children in the New Testament and the Bible generally. Such studies are necessary for providing a sound scriptural and theological foundation for the contemporary efforts to protect the rights of children. They will help to ensure that those noble efforts do not actually do more harm than good to the children. Here, too, local and global approaches are needed, even as the child issue today is both local and global in our globalized world.

Part Three

Putting Other Readings in Context

CHAPTER 8

Sexuality and Household
When "Cultural Reading" Supersedes and Skews the Meaning of Texts

Hisako Kinukawa

Patriarchies in Contexts

I say "patriarchies in contexts" to emphasize my idea that patriarchy is different in each context. Patiarchy/kyriarchy has been a heuristic key for scholars who are doing feminist theology and biblical exegeses. In the summer of 2008, I was at San Francisco Theological Seminary summer school teaching Feminist Hermeneutics of the Gospels. In my class were sixteen women with diverse social locations and backgrounds. They represented nine countries: Nigeria, Kenya, Guyana, Mexico, Tonga, the Philippines, Malaysia, Myanmar, and the United States of America. Including myself, we had an enormously diverse group with various ethnic, economic, political, and social backgrounds. I also found a variety of configurations in our households; some were single, some married/remarried, some in the process of divorce, some divorced, and some lesbians. Some had young or adolescent children, and some did not. As I listened to the sharing of their social locations, I was made aware that though each of us unanimously used the concept "patriarchy/kyriarchy" to explain our oppressed or marginalized situations, it has different connotations, content, or meaning in each society, and it appears in a variety of ways in daily life. Though the concept certainly plays a very important role in every society, I began asking each one to describe where and how she could experience patriarchy/kyriarchy, since it is very important to describe it in our own words.

Even among those from Asia and the Pacific Islands, there were quite different experiences of patriarchy/kyriarchy. Ting Jin Yong from Malaysia, who lives in a mixed society of multiethnic, multireligious, and multicultural complexities, talked about women internalizing their marginalization, having lost their identity and groping to become subjects. Htoo Htoo from Myanmar told us that she feels a strong need for the consciousness-raising of both men and women so that they may realize that women and men are created equal. Margaret Lacson from the Philippines, currently working in Japan, said that in her society nobody mentions contraception because of their faith tradition and therefore women easily get pregnant. Lo from Tonga pointed out that the power of the national religion, the Methodist Christian Church, has been strongly owned and controlled by males. She points to the need of emptying the power from the church system to make it truly egalitarian as well as Christian. In Japan, my country, patriarchy has also been a big issue for those who do feminist theology or practice feminist biblical exegesis, and this is where I would now like to turn.

Definitions or descriptions of patriarchy/kyriarchy have to be changed in different places and times as social, political, economic, and religious situations change.[1] I once wrote, "I use it as a major basis on which to observe, describe, and analyze male-dominant structures of society and to locate all kinds of oppressive forms of marginalization, dehumanization, and exploitation in

---

1. For example, Elisabeth Schüssler Fiorenza began with the definition "a socio-cultural system in which a few men have power over other men, women, children, slaves and colonized people" (*In Memory of Her: A Feminist Theological Reconstruction of Christian Origins* [New York: Crossroad, 1983], 29). Later she produced a new definition: "I use patriarchy 'in the narrow sense' to signify the domination of *elite* Western man over his gendered, raced, classed, and colonized 'others' whom Gustavo Gutierrez calls the 'nonpersons'" ("Text and Reality—Reality as Text: The Problem of a Feminist Historical and Social Reconstruction Based on Texts," *Studia Theologica* 43 [1989]: 19–20). Then recently she started using patriarchy/kyriarchy. She writes in her book published in 2007, "Kyriarchy articulates a more comprehensive systemic analysis of empire, in order to underscore the complex inter-structuring of dominations, and to locate sexism and misogyny in the political matrix—or better, 'patrix'—of a broader range of dominations . . . to comprehend the complex multiplicative interstructuring of gender, race, class, age, national, and colonial dominations and their imbrication with each other" (*The Power of the Word: Scripture and the Rhetoric of Empire* [Minneapolis: Fortress Press, 2007], 14).

different spheres of life in society."[2] As a basic definition, I do not feel I need to change what I wrote, but I would like to make more explicit in the following pages how I see patriarchy/kyriarchy related to the understanding of sexuality and the family/household in Japan.

The Intention of This Article

For the purpose of making patriarchy explicit as we Japanese women currently experience it, I would like first to reflect on the foundational traditions or views that have affected the minds and behaviors of the Japanese and colored their perceptions. I will then focus my work on reading the texts in Mark that seem to talk about the concepts of sexuality and family/household. My study is motivated by my awareness that Jesus' words recorded by Mark in the Greek are not necessarily translated accurately or interpreted appropriately by Japanese scholars, who are mainly male, nor are they transmitted properly by the leaders of our male-centered churches. I suspect that the traditionally nurtured and supported ideas on sexuality and family/household in Japan have deeply and decisively affected the translation and interpretation of Jesus' words recorded in Mark. I would like to pursue my suspicion that Japanese churches have a strong tendency to practice an implicitly cultural reading of the texts concerned with sexuality and family/household. I am, of course, aware of the fact that the original words were written from certain vantage points that also were nurtured by the patriarchally biased society of first-century Palestine.

Traditionally Nurtured and Culturally Conditioned Views on Sexuality and Family/Household in Japan

Traditionally nurtured and culturally conditioned views include multifaceted elements that have worked together and intertwined with each other. I place particular attention on patriarchy in Japan through considering: (1) the family registration system started under the influence of Buddhism, (2) the emperor system and state Shinto, (3) Confucian teachings. All of these

---

2. Hisako Kinukawa, *Women and Jesus in Mark: A Japanese Feminist Perspective,* Bible and Liberation Series (Maryknoll, N.Y.: Orbis, 1994), 9.

elements, together with the tradition of gender roles and the division of labor, have contributed to creating the meaning of family in our society. In Japan, the family is quite private and closed. The household has been a basic unit of the society. As a result, only heterosexual marriages have been legitimated. Thus, other sexual orientations and gender identities have been ignored or suppressed until very recently.

Family Registration

The history of the system of family registration goes back to ancient China, from which it was imported to countries in northeast Asia (Japan, Korea, and Taiwan), as China was formally a political, cultural, and social model for the formation of these countries. It is said that a form of family registration existed in Japan before 600 C.E., but 1638 C.E. marks a new era, when the Shogunate established the *danka seido* (a system of household registration incorporated with a Buddhist temple). This set up a system in which every Japanese household was obliged to register with a local Buddhist temple and to support it financially. This occurred shortly after Christianity came to Japan. In 1662, the government added the *terauke seido,* a "system of temple certification attesting innocence of association with subversive religion, namely Christianity,"[3] and asked every adult to get an annual certificate from the Buddhist temple in order to prove her or his noninvolvement in Christianity. Thus, people were under a mandate to relate to Buddhism, and Buddhist temples became the only institutions authorized to conduct funerals. The tradition of having Buddhist temples take care of the dead has long been kept alive among the people.[4]

State Shinto and the Emperor's One Big Family

After the Meiji Restoration, in 1868, when the court took over power from the Shogunate, this legal system of family registration became part of the emperor system. The emperor system was the politico-legal institution recognized by the Meiji constitution and supported spiritually by Kokka (State) Shinto. Kokka Shinto is said to be a new branch of traditional Shintoism,

---

3. David Reid, *New Wine: The Cultural Shaping of Japanese Christianity* (Berkeley: Asian Humanity Press, 1991), 9–10.
4. Ibid.

which has its origin in the prehistoric indigenous religion of the Japanese people, animism. However, the Kokka Shinto begun in 1868 by the Meiji imperial government was a distinctively politico-religious institution that lasted until the end of the Second World War, in 1945. It was used for the purpose of uniting all the people under one living god, the emperor. The philosophy of the emperor system, which was closely tied to State Shinto, emphasized the concept of one household with the claim that the nation of Japan consists of one big family. Shinto shrines took over the role that had belonged to Buddhist temples. The father of the nation-family was the emperor, and each family member was required to obey him as the absolute authority. The original meaning of patriarchy, "the rule of the father," was literally practiced by the emperor, who claimed the whole nation as his family. When the government worked toward national unity, State Shinto played a very important role by heightening the spirit of loyalty and patriotic sentiment through honoring the emperor as a living god.

This system of national patriarchy naturally contributed to strengthening the patriarchy in each family. Nationally, the emperor was absolute as the father of the nation; domestically, fathers had absolute authority over their households. Wives and children were to be subordinate to the lords of their families. Thus, the discrimination against women and girls became even more clear-cut. Women were valued only when they gave birth to male heirs. Until recently, marriage was a matter not of two individuals but of two families. Social classes and family lineages have been the two important elements to be considered when one decides one's partner, though there have been more conscientized women and men who have rejected the traditional ways and chosen their partners freely. Patriarchy in Japan thus engendered the gender role system and legitimated the division of labor between women and men by casting men as breadwinners and women as housewives and mothers.

Japan was forced to abolish the emperor system in 1945 as a result of Japan's defeat in the Second World War. The emperor now declared his humanness and became a symbol of the people. However, patriarchy remains as a norm for living, influencing, and forming the frame of reference for thinking, morals, and beliefs: in other words, it shapes people's consciousness. Despite the new constitution guaranteeing equal rights between wife and husband/woman and man, and abolishing the paterfamilias system, the traditional manners and habitual customs have remained and survive in subtle ways to this day. The family registration system has never been abolished and continues to discriminate against illegitimate children and make it difficult for immigrants to set up their families legally. It must be admitted that laws cannot transform human consciousness so easily.

Confucian Teachings, Family Ties, and Genealogy

Another element we need to take into consideration when we talk about the mentality that reveres close family ties and honors ancestral connections is brought in by the Confucian teachings that influenced these same countries in Northeast Asia. The way it influenced each culture varies. Filial duty to one's family has been taught as the core of Confucian teachings in Japan. It has buttressed the patriarchal family system by offering various spiritual rites and ethical bases of behavior. It kept the idea of a personal identity as a member of a family, and so it became very important for a person to speak and behave with the awareness that they might bring either honor or shame to the family.

As I dig into the meaning of patriarchy/kyriarchy in my own context, I face a vortex of multifaceted spiritual and religious backgrounds, all of which have contributed to the creation of patriarchal/kyriarchal mind-sets. The residue of the historical systems that were based on patriarchal religions is more seriously and explicitly observed in our family system. It still remains intact through the continuation of family registration as the basis of the current political system of Japan.

My Focus

I would like to find a way for us in the Christian churches of Japan to cope with and overcome this mentality, which can be observed even now. Reading texts in Mark, especially those that talk about family, household, and family ties, with this lens is common practice. I must admit that in our Japanese churches, voices that seek to legitimate only traditional heterosexual marriages are still very strong. This attitude is deeply related to and influenced by the traditional concepts of family I have described above. On the other hand, we cannot deny that a more liberating voice that is trying to recognize diverse expressions of sexuality and relationships has often been heard, yet suppressed.

In what follows, we will look at the texts with the question in mind of what we can trace in the life of Jesus and his followers of their thoughts about sexuality and sexual relationships, particularly about the household or family.

Overview of Women in Mark and Jesus' Sexuality

Peculiarity of Women in Mark

We hardly meet a couple in Mark's Gospel who is actually married. As far as women are concerned, almost all of them are either single, divorced, or widowed. In other words, they have no male person to protect or represent them in the patriarchal society of the time. Many examples come to mind: the hemorrhaging woman (5:21-43); the Syrophoenician woman with her daughter (7:24-30); widows who lost all they had because of shrewd scribes (12:40); the poor widow who donated her last two *lepta*s (12:41-44); the woman who anointed Jesus (14:3-9); the servant girl of the high priest who challenged Peter (14:66-72); Mary of Magdala; Mary the mother of Jacob; Salome; and other women who were at the cross and the empty tomb (15:40-41, 47; 16:1-8); Peter's mother-in-law, who became the first female disciple of Jesus and kept serving (1:29-31); and Mary, who gave birth to an illegitimate son, Jesus (3:20-21, 31-35; 6:3; [15:40-41, 47]; 16:1-8]). Among the many female characters found in the Gospel, only the wife of Jairus, the leader of the synagogue, is part of a couple recorded as being legitimately married (5:21-24, 35-43). It is uncertain whether Herodias, whom Herod remarried, is legitimately divorced (6:14-29). The women to whom Mark pays much attention are mostly unmarried. In the Hellenistic-Roman world, where most women were married, the women mentioned above belonged to the marginalized among the marginalized. We can clearly see one of the outstanding characteristics of the followers of Jesus' movement in this statistic.

Did Jesus Marry?

There is no evidence that Jesus was married. However, this fact does not mean that Jesus had no sexuality or was celibate. It may be incidental; in the Hellenistic-Roman world, men did not marry until they reached thirty or older. If we say that, when Jesus began his movement he was about thirty (see Luke 3:23), there is a high possibility that marriage was still just beyond his interest.[5]

Despite this fact, in the history of the church, Jesus has been considered a model for an unmarried man and has become a symbol of those without sexuality. This interpretation of Jesus has reinforced the separation of sexuality from the body, an asceticism that did away with sexuality as an expression of love, and a theology that permits sexuality only for reproduction.[6]

In the second century, Clement of Alexandria noted,

> There are those who say openly that marriage is fornication. They lay it down as a dogma that it was instituted by the devil. . . . Next, they do not know the reason why the Lord did not marry. In the first place, he had his own bride, the Church. Secondly, *he was not a common man* to need a physical partner. Further, he did not have an obligation to produce children; he was born God's only Son and survives eternally. It is this very Lord who says, "Let no human being part that which God has joined together."[7]

What did the author mean by saying that Jesus was not a common man? It seems that Clement needed to keep Jesus without sexuality for the sake of becoming Christ.

On the other hand, Augustine of Hippo, who was active in the fourth and the fifth centuries, wrote,

> Human nature, then, is without *doubt ashamed of this lust; and justly so,* for the insubordination of these members, and *their defiance of the will,* are the clear testimony of the punishment of *man's* first *sin.* And it was fitting that this should appear specially in those parts by which is generated that nature which has been altered for the worse by that *first and great sin—that sin from whose evil connection no one can escape,* unless God's grace expiate in him individually that which was perpetrated to

---

5. Dale B. Martin, *Sex and the Single Savior: Gender and Sexuality in Biblical Interpretation* (Louisville: Westminster John Knox, 2006), 104; Antoinette Clark Wire, *The Corinthian Women Prophets: A Reconstruction through Paul's Rhetoric* (Minneapolis: Fortress Press, 1990), 75.
6. Robert E. Goss, *Queering Christ: Beyond Jesus Acted Up* (Cleveland: Pilgrim, 2002), 115–16.
7. Clement of Alexandria, *Stromata* 3.49 (emphasis added), http://www.ccg.org/English/s/b3.html. Also partly quoted in Goss, *Queering Christ,* 115.

the destruction of all in common, when all were in one man, and which was avenged by God's justice. (*City of God* 14.22)[8]

It is not clear if Augustine wrote this in order to emphasize Jesus' unusual nature or in order to lay bare his own lamenting heart as he realized how much discipline he needed to become like Jesus. In either case, he seems to have understood sexuality as something to be overcome rather than to be accepted it as it is.

Robert E. Goss writes that in the twelfth century, "Thomas Aquinas maintained that Jesus assumed all the bodily defects due to sin. He was subject to death, hunger, thirst, and all such human needs. Aquinas argues that although Christ assumed the bodily defects due to sin, he possessed all the grace and the virtues most perfectly, controlling any taint of concupiscent appetite or sexual drives."[9]

As we have seen, it may be plausible to say that the history of the Christian church shows the way believers understood Jesus' celibacy as his sexual self-denial and invented steps for a self-disciplined secluded life in hopes of coming closer to Jesus' holiness.

Sexuality Negated in Church History

Following the quotation above, Augustine advances his argument as follows:

And therefore that marriage, worthy of the happiness of Paradise, *should have had desirable fruit without the shame of lust,* had there been no sin. But how that could be, there is now no example to teach us. Nevertheless, it ought not to seem incredible that one member might serve the will without lust then, since so many serve it now. Do we now move our feet and hands when we will to do the things we would by means of these members?" (*City of God* 14.23)

Augustine legitimates heterosexual intercourse only and limits it for procreation. Thus, heterosexual marriage has been recognized as the ideal for the concept of "family" and has expanded its function as a basic unit for a society/nation. The concept has gained significant value and has been used

---

8. Emphasis added; translation http://www.newadvent.org/fathers/.
9. Quoted in Goss, *Queering Christ,* 116.

rhetorically in many ways to protect the status quo. Needless to say, the concept of "family" has been widely used by those in power in the church.[10]

Thus, sexuality and procreation have become separated. Procreation is legitimated while other sexual behaviors are ignored. If procreation is valued, women are valued only for their reproductive function. Then freedom of choice concerning the issues of pregnancy and the dignity of controlling one's own body may be withdrawn. This marriage system is nothing other than a patriarchally controlled relationship between women and men. Here we can see how power can control a relationship.

As a result, the system has excluded many: sexual minorities, gender minorities, single parents, singles, illegitimate children, barren women, unmarried women, and remarried women. The overwhelming power of heterosexual marriage has, through the centuries, degraded many persons to second-class citizenship.

Thus, procreation has become a political doctrine that supports the value of the traditional family system. Since the doctrine has been accepted by most of the Christian churches in Japan, they have had to face a more serious issue if they want to welcome homosexuals and transgendered persons to their faith communities, even if they are "generous" enough to accept the couples who cannot give birth to babies or those who decided not to have babies.

Ideally, sexuality is in tune with reciprocity, love, sympathy, intimacy, community, friendship. It has no concern about the power relationship of dominance and subjugation. Therefore, such violent relationships as rape, forced intercourse, sexual abuse, sex as weapon, addictive relationships, and intercourse without affection cannot be included as a part of sexuality.[11]

According to Michel Foucault, "Sexuality is part of our behavior. It's part of our world freedom. Sexuality is something we create. It is our own creation. . . . We have to understand that with our desires go new forms of relationships, new forms of love, new forms of creation. Sex is not a fatality;

---

10. On relationship of family with society in Japan, see Kazue Yano, "Re-reading Ruth through Marriage and the Family," *News Letter* 14 (Center for Feminist Theology and Ministry in Japan, 2002); idem, "The 'Problems' in Contemporary Marriage: What TFR 1.29 Tells Us," *News Letter* 29 (Center for Feminist Theology and Ministry in Japan, 2006).
11. On sexual abuse and violence, see reports on a summer intensive seminar in *News Letter* 40 and 46 (Center for Feminist Theology and Ministry in Japan, 2007, 2008).

it's a possibility for creative life."[12] His statement seems critical about the situation that sexuality has been hidden under the surface of the water and been suppressed in silence, even though it is a part of God's creation and we cannot evade it as long as it is within us. It is true that all sorts of prohibitions, limitations, and rules have been added to sexual activities by churches. As a whole, we have had a long period of time of legitimizing only heterosexuality as well as limiting marriage to heterosexuals.

There are some who think that the love relationship based on justice, which is rooted in the metaphor of covenant described in the Scriptures, can provide the energy to overcome patriarchy and misogyny, as well as the hatred of homosexuality and transgendered persons that is rooted in patriarchy.[13] If we take sexuality as being furnished by God and as creating a just relationship with a partner to whom one devotes her/his love, we must say that it is too narrow-minded to insist that only those in a heterosexual marriage can practice such a relationship. If we define sexuality as being fully open to one's partner and accepting her/him as she/he is, it is not limited only to heterosexual persons. Vulnerability to expose one's body and mind to another person is not the monopoly of heterosexuals. If we gain a wider perspective on sexuality as stated above, it makes it possible to see more diverse and richer relationships.

Jesus' View of Sexuality

For Jesus, was sexuality not an urgent issue? It is difficult to find his teaching on sexuality. We cannot imagine that he was without sexuality as a human being. Did he intentionally keep silent on the issue? For Mark, silence might be the only solution, the only way to limit sexual intercourse to procreation through heterosexual marriage so that Jesus' sexuality might not be a source of scandal, as he was the son of God.[14]

There is no text that witnesses that Jesus left any teaching that directly talked about sexuality, but there are valuable texts in which we can read Jesus' very critical statements about the traditional family system, including marriage. I would like to see what we can learn from them, and I would like

---

12. Quoted in Goss, *Queering Christ,* 88.
13. Ibid., 97.
14. Cf. Martin, *Sex and the Single Savior,* 104.

to show how far church history strayed from the original way that Jesus and his followers might have exercised their sexuality.

Jesus' Concept of the Family

Contrast between Behaviors of Jesus' Family and the Scribes

What did Jesus think about the family as it was given birth through marriage? Mark wrote in an early chapter, "His family went out to restrain him" (3:21). The reason his family came to retrieve him is that they heard people saying, "He has gone out of his mind" (3:21). There was also a rumor frequently heard that said, "He has an unclean spirit" (3:30). His family did not think this reputation was desirable and viewed it as a shame on the family. They were apparently concerned about their appearances as members of his "family." Mark continues the story by describing in much detail how his family tried to contact him (3:31-35). It is then that Mark includes Jesus' ideas on family. When his mother and brothers came to fetch him, none of them dared talk to Jesus directly. They instead waited outside and sent a messenger to him. They might have stayed outside because they did not want to make their family trouble public, or they might have been concerned about the social reputation they might get as a shamed family. The behavior of Jesus' family shows a pattern typical of a culture in which people think it a very important norm to bring the family honor. It is no wonder that his father never appeared in this scene. This episode concerning Jesus' family is divided into two scenes, which sandwich a dispute between Jesus and the scribes. Intercalation is one of Mark's literary tools. In the dispute, the scribes are also afraid their pride might be hurt by Jesus. In this sense, his family and the scribes have the same level of concern not to lose face and to keep their honor. Nevertheless, the scribes openly challenge Jesus by saying, "He has Beelzebul," and "By the ruler of the demons he casts out demons" (3:22). They try to get public recognition by challenging Jesus in public, and in this sense they behave quite differently from Jesus' biological family.

They sound as though they are insisting that Jesus is a social pollution by declaring that he has Beelzebul and labeling him as unclean. The scribes try to lead the people by attempting to sink Jesus into oblivion, creating a situation in which they assert that nobody can take Jesus seriously. This is a very bad situation for Jesus' family, so it is natural for them to try to retrieve him and hide him from the public eye.

Unexpected Response Given by Jesus

Jesus, however, surprised everyone by throwing a remarkable response to both his embarrassed family and the socially and religiously powerful scribes. Mark writes that Jesus said, "Who are my mother and my brothers? Here are my mother and my brothers! Whoever does the will of God is my brother and sister and mother" (3:34-35). According to Jesus' definition, the focus of a community as a family lies in "doing the will of God."

What is distinctive in this definition can be found in the following points: (1) Jesus' faith community implies not only that it is open to everybody but also that it breaks down the traditional barrier of family as blood-related or lineage-connected. (2) It also implies liberating women from their obligation to give birth to heirs of the family. (3) In addition, the traditional concept of family that is signaled by a marriage between a man and a woman is over-written. It is very valuable to observe here that neither sexual orientation nor gender identities are questioned in living under such a concept of family.[15]

Separation from the Idea of Blood-related Ties

Mark recounts a story that happens just before Jesus goes up to Jerusalem (10:17-30), in which he tells how difficult it is for the rich to get into the reign of God. In the story, Jesus speaks to his disciples, calling them "Children," which alerts us that the calling may reflect a patriarchal hierarchy between Jesus and his followers. Yet at the end, he says, "Truly I tell you, there is no one who has left house or brothers or sisters or mother or father or children or fields, for my sake and for the sake of the good news, who will not receive a hundredfold now in this age—houses, brothers and sisters,

---

15. For more detail, see my *Women and Jesus in Mark,* 49–50. On Jesus' concept of family, Matthew records as follows: "whoever does the will of my Father in heaven is my brother and sister and mother" (12:46-50); and Luke also writes in the same sense, "My mother and my brothers are those who hear the word of God and do it" (8:19-21). We can say that both Luke and Matthew show the same understanding as Mark. The people who are from the same village as Jesus cannot grasp the meaning of family beyond being a blood-related community. They ask, "Is not this the carpenter, the son of Mary and brother of James and Joses and Judas and Simon, and are not his sisters here with us?" (6:3)

mothers and children, and fields with persecutions—and in the age to come eternal life" (Mark 10:29-30). Jesus calls his disciples children, members of his family with a new concept of doing the will of God. Therefore, the story may imply that doing the will of God means specifically to leave one's blood relatives, as well as one's house and fields, which have shaped a shared territorial bond. It should be noted here also that Jesus does not deny a blood-related family, but widens its concept and borders. It is also remarkable to see in Jesus' speech that the word *father*, which is included in the subjects or nouns to leave behind, is left out in the phrase about receiving a hundredfold of houses, brothers and sisters, mother and children, and fields. We may see here Jesus denying patriarchal fathers who have maintained the power over their families.

In another case, when Jesus prayed in Gethsemane, he said, according to Mark, "Abba, Father, for you all things are possible; remove this cup from me; yet, not what I want, but what you want" (14:36). Mark may think that Jesus considered God to be the only father of us all. If it is so, it becomes very plausible for us to take Mark and probably Jesus, too, as having an image of a household that is limitlessly open to everybody.

The reason Jesus not only initiated being unmarried and leaving his family, but also urged his disciples to do the same, may have been to teach them to look for an alternative, eschatological fellowship, family, community, and state. We may conclude that it is the very traditional family system that has functioned as an important part of the world order that Jesus is challenging.

Jesus' View of Marriage Seen through the Story in Mark 10:1-12

Interpretation of Japanese Scholars Affected by Traditional Culture

Family or household has been considered one of the main teachings of the Christian faith in Japanese churches, and in the minds of believers as well. Nevertheless, the concept of family or household seems to have been based on the traditionally nurtured concept in relation to family registration born of the mixture of Buddhism and State Shinto, and the Confucian teachings on family. Confucian thinking teaches that life is continuous from the deceased to the ones to be born in the future. It emphasizes the genealogical connection of the blood-related family. Given those emphases, it is natural that marriage based on heterosexual relationships has been predominant over other sexual relationships.

Most theological scholars in Japan have agreed that Jesus offered teachings about divorce. Therefore, the teaching implies remarriage, because the discourse would not have happened if remarriage was not an issue. In addition, many insist that heterosexual marriage is the only legitimate form of family. Based on this argument, could we say that Jesus supported only heterosexual marriage? It seems too quick to conclude so. I would like to scrutinize the text concerning "divorce, remarriage and adultery" recorded in Mark 10:1-12. But first I would like to begin with Jesus' saying which is found at the end of the story (vv. 11-12).

Discourse on Marriage, Divorce, Remarriage, and Adultery

Jesus' saying: "Whoever divorces his wife and marries another commits adultery against her; and if she divorces her husband and marries another, she commits adultery" (Mark 10:11-12 NRSV) is found as an addition to the discourse with the Pharisees. It is his reply to a further question raised by his disciples. First of all, Mark surprises us by drawing our attention to the fact that Jesus refers to a woman's initiative on divorce as well as a man's. The expression puts women and men on an equal footing, while the Pharisees refer to men only when they ask Jesus: "Is it lawful for a man to divorce his wife?" They ask the question based on the Deuteronomic law, which is written in Deut 24:1: "Suppose a man enters into marriage with a woman, but she does not please him because he finds *something objectionable about her,* and so he writes her a certificate of divorce, puts it in her hand, and sends her out of his house" (NRSV). Scholars assume that this is the foundation of the discourse in Mark. According to the law, "divorce" can take place at the will of the husband any time he likes. It is a patriarchal biased law, which demotes wives to a very subordinate position.

In all the Japanese translations of the saying, we notice that the man "takes a wife," while the woman "is taken to a husband." The Greek uses in both cases the same word *gameō,* meaning "to marry." The translations reflect the Japanese traditional patriarchal view of marriage, in which women are always dealt with as passive and as possessions. The translations result in not only supporting the old traditional marriage, but also erasing the egalitarian expression that Jesus uses. This surely reveals that translation is none other than interpretation.

Migaku Sato, who is a distinguished translator/exegete of the Gospels in Japan, comments on "adultery," referring to Jesus' saying in Matt 5:32: "anyone who divorces his wife, except on the ground of unchastity, causes her to commit adultery," as follows:

> Once a wife is divorced, she becomes almost a non-person in Jesus' time in Judea. The only way left for her to survive is to be remarried. However, in this text, it is said that if she is remarried, the previous marriage is definitely broken. It is so, because the husband is never considered to commit adultery even when he breaks the marriage, while the wife is convicted of adultery when she breaks the marriage.[16]

In addition, he makes another comment on Matt 5:27, "In the male-centered Judaism of the time, 'adultery' is the sin committed by a wife against her husband."[17] His comments remind us of the traditional marriage relationship in which men are always exempt from sexual guilt while women always receive blame for sexual transgressions.

In other words, we can infer that Sato interprets Jesus' saying on adultery as follows: (1) When a husband divorces his wife, he does not commit adultery. (2) A wife, when divorced, has only one choice; that is, to be remarried. According to his interpretation, adultery comes into existence when a woman remarries another man after her husband divorces her. Thus, she is convicted of adultery. Reading his interpretation makes me ask anew how adultery comes into existence in the Hebrew Scripture and to check if his comments are true or not.

According to the Deuteronomic laws, adultery occurs when a man victimizes a woman who is married or unmarried. In other words, adultery is committed when a man infringes on the wife of another man or the virgin daughter of a father whose property she is. Therefore, the man is first of all considered a criminal, and then the wife, who has now been labeled his accomplice, is accused of sin (see Deut 22:22-29). Certainly, Sato's comment is true in saying that a husband who divorces his wife does not commit

16. Migaku Sato, trans., *Gospel according to Mark* and *Gospel according to Matthew* (Tokyo: Iwanami, 1995), 110–11 (my translation).
17. Ibid., 109.

adultery. In addition, from the context of the discourse (Mark 10:2, "Is it possible for a man to divorce his wife?") and from the tradition (Deut 24:1), we can tell that a husband divorces his wife of his own free will.

Now it has become clear that Sato has another view. He contends that a husband's divorcing his wife results in her committing adultery through her remarriage. I argue that it is the wife's adultery (having intercourse with another person) that, in the eyes of the society, produces the broken relationship of the original marriage. The Greek word used for "commit adultery" is *moicheuō* in its middle form, which grammatically shows active involvement of the subject. It may show that wives, when they are involved in relationships with other men, are more committed to their new relationships than those with their husbands and may show their desire to separate from their current husbands. It is clear that the second point Sato makes, that a wife is convicted of adultery if she marries another man after her husband divorces her, is not true.

Nor is Sato's statement correct that the only way for a divorced wife to survive is to be remarried, because remarriage is not the only option left for the divorced woman. In Mark 10:11-12, where the husband and wife are dealt with equally, we find it possible for a wife to divorce (*apolysai* in Greek) her husband. There are some who insist that the phrase does not go back to Jesus by arguing that it was impossible for wives to initiate divorces in the context of Judaism at the time of Jesus. However, since Bernadette Brooten published her study with results giving evidence that women could initiate divorces at that time, her thesis has been supported by many.[18] Therefore, it becomes difficult to deny the phrase as going back to Jesus himself. As a result, it becomes impossible to give complete assent to what Sato says about the divorced woman whose only option was to be remarried. Women who initiated divorce must have had some means to earn their daily bread.

Nevertheless, many widows and divorced women of the time were able to remarry. In fact, there were many women who died after giving birth, and therefore many of the divorced women were asked to remarry to replace the dead mothers.

---

18. Bernadette Brooten, "Könnten Frauen im alten Judentum die Scheidung betreiben? Über-legungen zu Mk 10,11-12 und 1Kor 7,1 10-11," *Evangelische Theologie* 42 (1982): 65–80.

My Contention

I think it is more natural to take the meaning of Jesus' statement in the following manner. A wife who is handed a letter of divorce by her husband without her consent as written in Deut 24:1 is possibly driven to committing adultery with another person because she has not followed the legitimate process of divorce with the approval of both. Her adultery is not in relation to her previous husband.

A husband who one-sidedly divorces his wife can not only motivate her to have a relationship with another man but is also in danger of committing adultery by engaging in a relationship with another woman. Thus, my interpretation turns out to be quite different from Sato's. Here I must raise another question on the translation of the term "divorce" (*apolysai/apolyō* in Greek) though I have used "divorce" so far following NRSV.

Not "Divorce" but "Throw Away"

Should we translate *apolysai/apolyō* "divorce"? The argument I deployed in the above section also depends on how we interpret/translate the word *apolysai.* The Japanese word used in Sato's translation, *Rien,* legally implies "dissolving adoption" and is popularly used for the separation of a married couple. In relation to our interest, we may note that couples who cannot bear a child adopt a boy with an expectation that he may continue their family lineage. If he cannot give birth to their heir, his adoption may be dissolved by his parents. There used to be a popular expression using the same word when a husband thrusts a note of divorce at his wife. Coincidentally, the situation that women of Japan experienced in the old days fits well with what Sato reads in the texts in the sense that separation or divorce could be initiated by the arbitrary will of husbands. The translated word may be effective to express the unilateral relationship of a husband with his wife, but if we look for a more appropriate translation that is faithful to the Greek word and able to be equally used for both woman and man, we had better use "throw away," "abandon," or "terminate unilaterally." I argue that *apolysai* has a particular meaning that is not what we generally think of or legally define as "divorce." In other cases in the Christian Testament, *apolyō* is also used in the sense "to set a distance," "annul a relationship," and "throw away." When "throw away" or "abandon" is used, it makes explicit that separation is not made as a result of the agreement of the two (see Mark 5:36, 45; 8:9).

In Deut 24:1, a husband writes his wife "a certificate of divorce." "Certificate" is in Greek *apostasion,* which means "abandonment" or "alienation," and the word may be used because there is no reciprocity in this kind of divorce. It also implies that the dissolution of the marriage could be done without reciprocal consent at all. Then another question comes up concerning what Greek term for "divorce" would have the same legal meaning in our regular usage today. I will deal with this issue later.

What Does Jesus' Reply Imply?

The Word apolyō

The word *apolyō* is used both in Jesus' response and in the question raised by the Pharisees. Actually, it is remarkable when we learn that Jesus makes use of the very word that has been used one-sidedly by men and applies it equally to both women and men. By putting both women and men on an equal level, he reverses the question and reveals the focus of the real issue.

From the text, it is plausible to say Jesus does not refer to "divorce and remarriage" in the sense that he is asked by the Pharisees. He has rather raised a different question about a series of behaviors to "throw away one's partner unilaterally and then seek to remarry," which could happen far more dominantly to men of the first century of Judea than to women.

Jesus surprisingly then prohibits such a practice by both women and men. The text that refers to both women and men is found only in Mark, the first of the four Gospels; this may have the highest possibility of coming from Jesus' mouth. Therefore, we need to take particular note of the point that this text is not simply prohibiting divorce. It is not simply prohibiting a husband from divorcing his wife at his arbitrary will, but is also prohibiting both the wife and the husband from the behavior of "throwing away her/his partner and seeking remarriage." "Throwing away one's partner" is not a divorce based on consent given by both sides. In such circumstances, without pursuing the legitimate process of divorce, if one seeks to remarry, it should then be denoted as committing adultery. This is how we should interpret Jesus' challenge and prohibition. The new meaning of adultery given by Jesus describes a situation when one partner in the marriage discards the other without their consent, to marry someone else.

Jesus' saying in 10:11-12, "Whoever divorces his wife and marries another commits adultery against her; and if she divorces her husband and marries another, she commits adultery" (NRSV), calls for still closer scrutiny. In the first half of the instruction referring to men, the phrase "against her" is added, while "against him" is not included in the last half referring to women. Sato comments that this is a reference to his previous wife and not the woman he seeks to remarry.[19] In this case, since the man has not executed his separation from his previous wife on a reciprocal basis, we can say that he commits adultery against both his previous wife and the new woman he marries. The reason the same thing is not repeated regarding the behavior of the wife may be found in the reality that she has the least chance to throw away her husband in the patriarchal society of first-century Judea.

Redefining the Concept

Then what do these words imply? The two actions of "throwing one's partner away" and "seeking remarriage" must have taken place at the same time because they together reveal the man's intention. A reason for these acts could be for a man to satisfy his lust. If such actions were not happening, Jesus would not need to challenge the practice. What surprises us in his saying is that he implies that the same could happen to women. Not only does he put women and men on an equal level as a part of God's creation, but he also warns both women and men that they could commit adultery. We might then infer that Jesus prohibits "divorce" when it is pursued with a desire to satisfy one's lust, so that Jesus might urge his followers to practice ascetic self-restraint in an eschatological hope that the reign of God is just around the corner.[20]

Creation Story: Theological Significance of Marriage

To the Pharisees who raise questions using the law as their shield, Jesus responds by drawing on phrases from Gen 1:27 and 2:24, which do not explicitly talk about divorce. I would like to draw attention to this notion and the texts.

---

19. Sato, *Mark*, 48.
20. If so, separation seeking for "ascetic self-restraint" and separation based on the consent of both sides, which are argued in 1 Cor 7:5 by Paul, are also taken to be realistic behavior in the eschatological hope for the pressing reign of God.

Mark records the discursive story just before the prohibition phrase "throw away one's partner and seek for remarriage" (10:2-9). It is Pharisees who challenge Jesus with the intention of testing him. "Is it possible for a husband to throw away his wife?" (my translation). After some conversation, Jesus indicates his answer by quoting and combining two phrases from Genesis (1:22 and 2:24 or 5:2). He says, "From the beginning of creation, 'God made them male and female.' For this reason a man shall leave his father and mother (and be joined to his wife), and the two shall become one flesh" (NRSV). The clause in parenthesis is set off because there is some uncertainty about whether it existed in the earliest text (such manuscripts as Sinaiticus, Vaticanus, and Athos omit it). Jesus further adds his own interpretation of the quotation. "So they are no longer two, but one flesh. Therefore what God has joined together, let no one separate" (*chōrizō* in Greek). According to this statement, Jesus absolutely prohibits divorce. We need to make it clear that his focus is on infringing on or turning against God's will through human selfishness. Nevertheless, we should take the word "separate" in this phrase as expressing "divorce with reciprocal consent," for it cannot mean otherwise on an egalitarian basis. I would like to emphasize that "separate" (*chōrizō*) has a very different meaning from "throw away" (*apolyō*).

While the Pharisees challenge him drawing on Deuteronomic law, which makes it possible for a husband to throw away his wife in a one-sided manner, Jesus announces the true intention of marriage. While they ask about the possibility of divorce, he makes his response based on a theological concept of marriage. It is, therefore, clear that we cannot decide whether Jesus legitimates divorce or not. The discourse centers on the issue caused by heterosexual marriage, but we cannot argue from this statement that Jesus limits sexual relationships only to those between heterosexual persons.[21] For certain, neither is it a teaching of the prohibition of divorce.

---

21. As we see in the Matthean version (Matt 19:9 "whoever divorces his wife, except for unchastity, and marries another commits adultery"), if *porneia* (translated as "unchastity"), can be the only reason for legitimizing "divorce," we should ask what kind of behavior *porneia* designates. Most scholars take it as sexual misconduct, and even equate it with adultery (Tom Hanks, *The Subversive Gospel* (Cleveland, Ohio: Pilgrim, 2001), 33; Martin, *Sex and the Single Savior,* 232 n. 29; Sato, *Mark,* 110). But since both Mark and Matthew list *porneia* alongside adultery (*moicheia*) in the list of immoral conduct (Mark 7:21-22; Matt 15:19), it is apparent that these are two different concepts. The word *porneia* derives from the verb *pernēmi*, meaning "to sell (especially slaves)," suggesting that *porneia* meant "to buy and sell for sexual relations," that is, to conduct prostitution. We should remember that where there

Jesus, who talks about the foundation of marriage by drawing on the creation story in Genesis, does not see divorce as realistic or possible. He cannot see "throwing away one's partner unilaterally and seeking to marry another" as a legitimate way of cancelling one's marriage.

In Mark, the cancellation of marriage that seemed one-sidedly possible for a husband was clearly transformed by Jesus. He put it on an equal level and made it possible for a wife to divorce her husband. It should be noted that Jesus thought it was a foundational aspect of marriage to see that both women and men were on equal footing. At the same time, he reinterpreted adultery, which used to be considered an infringement on a man's property. According to Jesus, adultery can happen when either the woman or the man throws away her/his partner and seeks another relationship with a new partner. Jesus' transformative attitude is epoch making. While he was strongly against throwing away or abandoning one's partner, it is not certain if he was also against divorce, which was executed reciprocally.

What Can We Learn from This Study?

To a discourse that began with a challenging question concerning throwing away one's wife, Jesus made a few points very clear. (1) Divorce cannot take place based on one party's desire alone. (2) Throwing away one's partner and seeking to marry another is adultery. (3) Adultery in this sense can happen to either the wife or the husband. (4) The theological foundation of marriage is in the will of God as intended in the creation story. Therefore, it essentially rejects human arbitrariness. (5) The possibility of divorce is not negated. (6) Sexuality is not negated. (7) Partners whom God ties together are not necessarily limited to heterosexual relations. This can be especially said in the case of Mark, as he never refers to any exception, unlike Matthew.[22] He

---

is no way for a wife to divorce her husband except running away from him, prostitution is one of the few means through which unmarried women could survive on their own. In Matthew, Jesus seems to insist that there is no reason to bind her to her husband, if the marriage has already failed and she resorts to prostitution. If so, we can say that Jesus is not against divorce.

22. In the Gospel of Matthew, the author thinks heterosexual relations more probable, as he not only refers to the exception phrase but also seriously discusses male lust (see Matt 5:27-28).

expands the concept of family/household to a community to which everyone is invited.

If we focus on God's will along with the theological concept that every human being is a part of God's creation, we can glimpse the possibility of accepting any two persons who commit to each other as partners. The two points Jesus shows are (1) to interpret partnership based on God's creation, and (2) to extend the traditional horizon of family/household to the extent that everyone is included equally. Following these ideas, we may be able to overcome the traditional boundaries that have been given or taught that did not allow us to see beyond heterosexual relations and to perceive diverse ways of marrying under the will of God or creating families. It is not possible to see in Jesus' teaching the idea that procreation is the only reason for sexual intercourse. On the contrary, in a fellowship that includes diverse persons as a family, sexual relations will become realistic for anyone—never married ones, currently unmarried ones, persons with diverse sexual orientations and gender identities. People should accept each other as persons on an equal level.

I must say this is very important for us Japanese Christians who are disturbed by the present situation of the churches in Japan, which hide in a deep mist the uniqueness and revolutionary quality of Jesus' movement. We must engage in gazing at the dimly lit texts of the Scriptures.

It is regrettable to see that the dominant–subordinate relationship of hierarchy between Christ and the church is already expressed in the Christian Testament (see, for example, 1 Cor 11:7-12). Furthermore, the patriarchal relationship of a husband with his wife is used as a metaphor to explain the relationship between Christ and the church (see 1 Cor 11:3; Eph 1:22; 4:16; Col 1:18; 2:19). Thus, we can trace the process of how quickly in early Christian church history heterosexual marriage began to be admired, confirming the subordinate position of wife to husband. Here we encounter a new question of whether it is appropriate to grasp the relationship between Christ and the church through the metaphor of the dominant–subordinate relationship of heterosexual marriage, but this has to be challenged at another time, as it is beyond our present concern. We may have to conclude that in the early church heterosexual marriage was already recognized as the only legitimate form of marriage. Even then, we cannot conclude that there were no other sexual relationships existent.

Conclusion

As Jesus boldly criticized the traditional way of life in his society and presented new definitions, we are surely asked to awaken our courage and assume our responsibility to ask what is the basic and urgent question to be asked by ourselves and our churches? We may be asked to grope about to discern where and how the will of God appears for us who are living in our churches today. It has become apparent that the church's interpretation of the texts of putting the strongest emphasis on heterosexual relationships was not true with Jesus and his followers. We must conclude that a "cultural reading" of marriage done consciously and unconsciously by Japanese churches needs thoroughgoing exegetical scrutiny. In addition, we must conclude that the so-called cultural reading of a text can abuse its original meaning. We have found profound, audacious ideas in the resources recorded in Mark. Though they are not abundant, they are powerful enough to overturn the skewed interpretation of the texts given by a culturally colored traditional interpretation of the texts. It may be very difficult for churches to undergo change, especially because their interpretations are in tune with traditionally accepted social conventions, but they need to be continually challenged.

It is encouraging to see the recent discoveries and studies of the *Gospel of Judas* in addition to other documents such as the writings from Nag Hammadi and the *Gospel of Mary*. They show the possibility of a variety of understandings and interpretations that are quite different from what we have learned in our canon. Churches are to be challenged to search for new ways through which we can accept the reality of diverse sexuality.

CHAPTER 9

The Relationship between John the Baptist and Jesus in the Gospel of Mark

A Postcolonial Interpretation from a Chinese Malaysian Context

Menghun Goh

In this article, I will show how the representation of John the Baptist changes over time in an honor-and-shame Jewish culture, especially in the broader context of power struggles in the Roman Empire.[1] I will focus my cross-cultural reading on Mark 1:9-11 and 2:18-22, which deal with John's relationship with Jesus. The language of power relations is important in my postcolonial interpretation, as the issue of center versus periphery is a very sensitive concern in Malaysian Chinese honor-and-shame society. For example, as a result of the British colonial policy in maximizing its profits from Malaysia's natural resources, the British alienated, stratified, and assigned the Malays, Chinese, and Indians (the three main races in Malaysia) to differ-

---

1. Bruce J. Malina, *The New Testament World: Insights from Cultural Anthropology,* rev. ed. (Louisville: Westminster John Knox, 1993), 33–38. For a critique of the static understanding of honor and shame that tends to relate honor with male and shame with female, see Elisabeth Schüssler Fiorenza, "The First Letter of Peter," in *A Postcolonial Commentary on the New Testament Writings,* ed. Fernando F. Segovia and R. S. Sugirtharajah (London: T&T Clark, 2007), 393–402; see also Louise Lawrence, "'For Truly, I Tell You, They Have Received Their Reward' (Matt 6:2): Investigating Honor Precedence and Honor Virtue," *Catholic Biblical Quarterly* 64 (2002): 687–702. Passages related to John in the Gospel of Mark are the following: 1:2-8 (John's baptism and prophecy); 1:9-11 (Jesus' baptism by John); 1:14 (Jesus' going to Galilee after John's incarceration); 2:18-22 (John's disciples and Pharisees questioning Jesus about his disciples' not fasting); 6:14-29 (the beheading of John); 8:27-30 (Is Jesus John?); 9:1-13 (Is John Elijah[?], although Mark does not spell it out as Matthew does); and 11:27-33 (the authority of John's baptism).

ent sociopolitical and economic roles along racial lines. While no one group can dominate the other easily, these groups do not work together either. This strategy of "divide and conquer" can then prevent collaboration against the British Empire. Among the Chinese, at least until the late 1980s, there are also various affiliations depending on which Chinese dialect one speaks. Born and raised in this kind of multicultural, multiracial, and multireligious environment, I naturally have become sensitive to the division and diversity around me.

With such sensitivity to disruption and conflict, I find Mark's portrayal of John rather ambiguous and ambivalent. My main inquiry in this article is this: If, as I will argue, Mark does *not* present John as recognizing Jesus' mission and as testifying for him, why do we have such a high regard for John in Christian traditions?[2] This is an important question for us Malaysian Chinese Christians. To what extent do Malaysian Chinese Christians simply accept and incorporate Western Christian traditions and interpretations of John into their own understanding of John in Mark? Is our portrayal of John colored by the Gospels of Matthew, Luke, and John? If so, are we projecting onto Mark our readings of the Gospels? Further, to what degree did the notion that Mark was an abbreviation of Matthew influence our interpretation of Mark? If we are indeed reading Mark's John the Baptist in light of Matthew's, at least before the scrutiny of modern biblical criticism, then are we not sidelining Mark and refusing to let Mark be Mark? What are we missing by refusing to let Mark be Mark? By ignoring the ambiguous and ambivalent portrayal of John's relationship with Jesus in Mark and adopting a "normalized" image of John, while Mark seems to be telling us a much more complicated picture, we are missing a teaching that is potentially most significant for us, in our Malaysian Chinese context, still framed and marked by (neo)colonialism.

---

2. This tremendous respect for John is visible in the Christian liturgical calendar, especially in the Eastern Orthodox Church, in which six feast days are associated with John. For details, see *The Menaion of the Orthodox Church,* trans. Isaac E. Lambertsen, 11 vols. (Liberty, Tenn.: St. John Kronstadt Press, 1999). Besides these feast days, the icon of John is also very prominent. "In larger [Orthodox] churches, the first row of icons almost always includes the icon of St. John the Forerunner and Baptist, placed immediately next to Christ's." Constantine Cavarnos, *Orthodox Iconography* (Belmont, Mass.: Institute for Byzantine and Modern Greek Studies, 1992), 23.

What Is a Postcolonial Interpretation?

At the risk of oversimplification, a postcolonial interpretation is concerned with how the center is established at the expense of the other.[3] It is an effort to decenter the center so that there can be either no one fixed center or, more realistically, many centers coexisting simultaneously. Hence, in my interpretation of John, I am not arguing for a more accurate portrayal of John within a collective honor-and-shame culture, but I am offering another potential image of John from my Chinese Malaysian interpretation.

The critique against the center is important, because it can prevent the normalization of certain sociopolitical structures and culture that demand that everything else be defined and operated in relation to the center.[4] Once a center is established, not only will all differing and dissident voices be systematically considered rebellious, illegal, and abnormal, but they will also be forced to express their complaints and protests through the voice and system created by the center. Consequently, the center becomes the indisputable rightful center, without feeling the need to justify its seemingly innate status and privileges. A postcolonial interpretation, however, does not aim simply to deconstruct and expose the unjust principle and relationship between the center and the margin/periphery. It also seeks to end this kind of inhumane relationship and to empower both the oppressed and the oppressor to move toward a more wholesome relationship in respecting each other's differences and letting the other be the other.[5]

Postcolonial Interpretation in Mark

For the purpose of my interpretation of John the Baptist in Mark, I will first look at the representation of power relations in the text. If the Gospel does

---

3. Fernando F. Segovia provides a comprehensive study of various scholars' different understandings of postcolonialism and its range of applications: "Mapping the Postcolonial Optic in Biblical Criticism: Meaning and Scope," in *Postcolonial Biblical Criticism: Interdisciplinary Intersections,* ed. Stephen D. Moore and Fernando F. Segovia (London/New York: T&T Clark International, 2005), 23–78.

4. This kind of strategic othering the other in the image and likeness of the center for the benefit of the center is prevalent in both politics and scholarship; see Edward W. Said, *Orientalism* (New York: Vintage, 1979).

5. Leela Gandhi, *Postcolonial Theory: A Critical Introduction* (New York: Columbia University Press, 1998), 122–40.

allude to the language of domination, resistance, and liberation, which I argue that it does, then how does Mark portray John's prominent religio-sociopolitical status in light of his own oppressed and persecuted community?[6] In postcolonial language, does Mark display a sense of attraction for and yet alienation from the John movement? Although Mark accepts John's authority (1:2-8; 11:27-33), he remains silent about John's recognition of Jesus' mission and even suggests dispute between John's disciples and the Jesus group (2:18).

Indeed, the complexity of power relations is reflected throughout the Gospel. Simon Samuel, for instance, argues that Mark 1:1—"The beginning of the good news of Jesus Christ (Son of God)"[7]—could have appealed to both Jewish and non-Jewish audiences, as words like "the beginning," "good news," "Christ," and "Son of God" had both Jewish eschatological and Roman imperialist connotations, related to the inauguration of a new era by a new king. According to Samuel, this verse is an indication of "a pro or anti-colonial response to Rome or as an ambivalent affiliative-disruptive postcolonial response to both the Roman colonial and the native Jewish nationalistic and collaborative discourses of power."[8] By showing different aspects of power relations in the beginning of the Gospel, Mark then tries to present an alternative community centering on "Jesus Christ, the Son of God" to an audience that was familiar with both Jewish and Roman sociopolitical ideologies, or at least with one of the two. At the same time, Mark's text is also ambivalent with this tactic; the Gospel can, thus, be read as both an affiliative and disruptive discourse vis-à-vis the powerful.

This form of resistance to the dominant group is made explicit also in Stephen Moore's analysis of Jesus exorcising the demon-possessed man in Gerasa (Mark 5:1-20). Moore argues that the name of the demon, "Legion,"

---

6. For evidence and arguments supporting John's honored status, see Mark 1:5-6; 11:32; Josephus, *Jewish Antiquities* 18.5.2 §§116–19; John P. Meier, *A Marginal Jew: Rethinking the Historical Jesus,* vol. 2, *Mentor, Message, and Miracles,* Anchor Bible Reference Library (New York: Doubleday, 1994), 19–20. On the subject of the minority status of Mark's community, see James A. Wilde, "A Social Description of the Community Reflected in the Gospel of Mark" (Ph.D. diss., Drew University, 1974); Ched Myers, *Binding the Strong Man: A Political Reading of Mark's Story of Jesus* (Maryknoll, N.Y.: Orbis, 2006).

7. All Bible quotations are my translations, unless indicated otherwise.

8. Simon Samuel, "The Beginnings of Mark: A Colonial/Postcolonial Conundrum," *Biblical Interpretation* 10, no. 4 (2002): 405.

in 5:9 is a hermeneutical key in the text to underline Roman colonial occupation of Palestine as a demonic possession that Jesus cast out.[9] Jesus' pronouncement in Mark, "the things of Caesar give to Caesar and the things of God give to God" (12:17), is another challenge to the empire because "in accordance with Israelite tradition and theology, everything belongs to God, nothing is due to Caesar."[10] This type of anticolonial discourse (6:14-28; 10:35-45; 12:13-17; 13:9; 15:1-26) is, however, subtle, compared to the harsh antagonism against local Jewish leaders and elites who were associated with the temple (Mark 13). This invective against the local ruling class (3:22-30; 7:5-13; 11:15-17; 12:9-12; 12:38-40; 13:1-31) is perhaps Mark's attempt to blame the empire's less powerful agents for social oppression, as they were a less threatening target at which to aim.[11]

By employing the symbolic imagery of the withered fig tree and the collapse of the heavenly bodies in Mark 13, and by portraying Jesus as "the Son of Man coming in clouds with great power and honor" (13:26) who sends his angels/messengers to gather "his chosen out of the four winds, from the end of the earth to the end of heaven" (13:27), Mark is then creating an alternative community to both the one offered by the Jewish local elites and the empire. The problem is, however, that the power structure of this community seems to mimic that of the community it seeks to overthrow. According to Moore, by depicting Jesus as the divine authority, Mark mirrors "Roman imperial ideology, deftly switching Jesus for Caesar,"[12] an imitation displaying the colonized's reaction of "simultaneous attraction and repulsion" toward the empire.[13] In short, as Mark tried to talk back to the empire, he replicated the empire's language and structure in presenting the Jesus group as the new

---

9. Stephen D. Moore, "Mark and Empire: 'Zealot' and 'Postcolonial' Readings," in *The Postcolonial Biblical Reader*, ed. R. S. Sugirtharajah (Malden, Mass./Oxford: Blackwell, 2006), 194 (emphasis original).

10. Ibid., 198.

11. Tat-siong Benny Liew also comments, "Since ancient Jewish apocalyptic writers, in the interest of self-preservation, tend to level their attacks at a more benign target than the Roman imperialists themselves, it is possible that Mark's verbal assault on the Jewish authorities is a similar tactic or 'scapegoating'" ("The Gospel of Mark," in *A Postcolonial Commentary on the New Testament Writings*, ed. Fernando F. Segovia and R. S. Sugirtharajah [London: T&T Clark, 2007], 110).

12. Moore, "Mark and Empire," 200.

13. Ibid., 198.

empire, an (unfortunate?) tactic Tat-siong Benny Liew also underlines from his diasporic interpretation of Mark.[14]

Reading Mark from an apocalyptic setting, Liew argues that, with Jesus being described as the Son of God, the Gospel is saying that no political or religious power can claim authority over the Jesus group. In fact, while Jesus is presented as an authority against his opponents when it comes to interpreting the Hebrew Bible, Jesus "as God's beloved Son and heir"[15] is not "subjected to the authority of Hebrew Scriptures. Jesus becomes his own authority to give pronouncements that ask for decision without discussion."[16] Hence, although Mark deconstructed Roman and Jewish leadership, he created another "hierarchical community structure . . . [with Jesus] at the pinnacle of the hierarchy of his household, just as the Gentile or Roman rulers are at the pinnacle of their hierarchy of power, 'lording over' and 'exercising authority over' (10:42) those who rank below them."[17] In his critique of Mark's imitation of Rome's ideology, Liew therefore comments:

> Authority is (over)powering. It demands the submission of everybody, and thus also the annihilation of those who do not submit. In other words, vindication must become vindictive. The problem is that by defeating power with more power, Mark is, in the final analysis, no different from the "might-is-right" ideology that has led to colonialism, imperialism and various forms of suffering and oppression. Mark's Jesus may have replaced the "wicked" Jewish-Roman power, but the tyrannical, exclusionary and coercive politics goes on.[18]

While the Gospel may have imitated the power language of the empire, we also need to consider the misunderstanding, questioning, and even rejection of Jesus' authority by his family (3:20-21), disciples (8:33), and others (1:45; 5:17; 6:3). Mark does not present a univocal (re)presentation. Therefore, Liew makes it clear that his interpretation comes from his "commitments and

---

14. Different from Samuel's reading of Mark, which assumes Mark's intention, Liew states very clearly that "no one can offer a positivist account of Mark's meaning. We perceive certain 'truths' of an ancient text through the lens of our personal commitments and current investments" ("Gospel of Mark," 105).
15. Liew, "Gospel of Mark," 113.
16. Ibid.
17. Ibid., 114.
18. Ibid., 117.

investments [that] are characterized by a diasporic sensibility that 'make[s] room for reciprocal critique and multiple commitments.' "[19] It seems, as Liew is aware, that his reading may offend others, especially ordinary readers who treat the Bible as the Holy Scripture.

As sociologist Peter Berger has argued, our society not only "structures, distributes, and co-ordinates [our] world-building activities"; it also guards the "order and meaning not only objectively, in its institutional structures, but subjectively as well, in its structuring of individual consciousness."[20] In other words, "the individual is socialized to *be* a designated person and to *inhabit* a designated world."[21] Thus, if "the individual becomes that which he is addressed as by others," can we be too critical in criticizing the mimicry of power language adopted by Mark?[22] Even if the Markan Jesus may have the ultimate authority in the *parousia,* his authority is still understood within the context of suffering and cross. In fact, it seems that, as Mark mimics the power language employed by the empire, he also exposes and, moreover, transforms the connotation of such power language. To some degree, to demand that the Gospel address all issues without using the language of its time can also be a colonizing move. At the same time, however, I also appreciate Liew's concern and critique because "colonial mimicry"—the replacement of one power structure with another of similar nature—will only extend the existing problem that marginalizes the other.

Given this power struggle language in Mark, we can say that the Gospel as a postcolonial writing was responding to and reflecting its tactics to deal with the imperial-colonial power. This postcolonial interpretation, however, is often sidelined in traditional North Atlantic scholarship. For to be aware of the oppressive power relations, we have to, at least, feel or experience the pain and suffering felt by the victims of marginalization caused by the center's domination. But, as Liew suggested, "because of the West's conventional identification with Rome, its habitual antagonism against Jewish cultures and its grandiloquent separation of politics and religion, Markan studies tend to focus on either first-century religious conflicts between Jews and Christians or other contemporary questions of 'faith.' "[23] But are politics and religion

---

19. Ibid., 105.
20. Peter L. Berger, *The Sacred Canopy: Elements of a Sociological Theory of Religion* (New York: Doubleday, 1967), 3, 7. 21.
21. Ibid., 16 (emphasis original).
22. Ibid.
23. Liew, "Gospel of Mark," 106.

always separated? In the ancient Mediterranean world, religion "was an over-arching system of meaning that unified political and kinship systems (including their economic aspects) into an ideological whole. It served to legitimate and articulate (or delegitimate and criticize) the patterns of both politics and family."[24] Moreover, as the term "religion" is a modern Western sociopolitical construct, can we then spiritualize the power relation in Mark and neglect the economic and sociopolitical conflicts between the center and the margin?[25]

A spiritualized interpretation, however, is *the* popular interpretation of John's relationship with Jesus among many Malaysian Chinese Christians. John is *always* portrayed as a very pious and self-denying forerunner and even a martyr in the line of duty preparing the path for Jesus. John might have doubted Jesus' mission in Matthew, but his doubt was for the benefit of his disciples so that Jesus could tell them that he was the Messiah. John might continue to have his own group of disciples working next to Jesus', especially in the Fourth Gospel, but there was no conflict between the John and Jesus movements, though we may wonder why the two were not combined as one. John's priestly family might be related to Jesus' poor family in Luke, and in an honor-and-shame communal society, the former should be of great help to the latter, but the absence of communication and relationship between the two families did not arouse much curiosity among Malaysian Chinese Christians, who also live in an honor-and-shame communal society. It appears that John and Jesus were treated as independent individuals apart from their communities. This kind of interpretation, focusing on individuals, is not uncommon in Western Christian traditions and North Atlantic scholarship. Malaysian Chinese Christians seem to have received, internalized, and made such interpretations their own, despite their own cultural and sociopolitical contexts.

John's Relationship with Jesus in Mark: A Postcolonial Interpretation?

A quick glance at the representation of John's relationship with Jesus in North Atlantic scholarship will show that scholars are mostly concerned with

---

24. Bruce J. Malina and Richard L. Rohrbaugh, *Social Science Commentary on the Synoptic Gospels* (Minneapolis: Fortress Press, 1992), 257.
25. Richard King, *Orientalism and Religion: Postcolonial Theory, India and 'The Mystic East'* (London/New York: Routledge, 1999), 35–61.

the historical *Sitz im Leben* and hence the original meaning(s) of the biblical texts. To some degree, this search for a scientific, critical, and objective interpretation of the texts reveals the uneasy, if not combative, relationship between the church and the state as well as between Christianity and non-European cultures and religions, a tension that we know became prominent following the European Enlightenment. But these emphases are foreign to my context, which focuses on communal-interpersonal relationship within an honor-and-shame culture, where one's success is tied to one's close relationship with others.

For instance, influenced by the European Enlightenment, which focused on scientific reasoning and natural laws, Reimarus argued that John and Jesus were two cousins planning a political scheme to establish an earthly reign of God. At Jesus' baptism, John "act[ed] as though he only became aware of his [that is, Jesus'] existence through divine revelation."[26] So, while John prepared people to accept Jesus' messiahship, Jesus in turn praised John highly and validated his divine mission.[27] Reading through the lens of suspicion about the authoritative role of church in society, Remairus thus interpreted John and Jesus as two collaborators trying to validate the legitimacy of each other.[28] While this indictment may be a bit too harsh, later scholars did point out that Jesus was initially part of the John's movement. Carl Kraeling, for example, argues that, as John's disciple, Jesus accepted his proclamation of "the imminence of the divine judgment and the need for decision, repentance and Abrahamic piety."[29] Different from John, however, Jesus believed

---

26. Since most scholarly work on John is tied to the quest for the historical Jesus, I will start with Reimarus's *Fragments,* which most scholars identify as marking the beginning of critical biblical scholarship on the quest of the historical Jesus. See Charles H. Talbert, ed., *Reimarus: Fragments,* trans. Ralph S. Fraser (Philadelphia: Fortress Press, 1970), 138.

27. Talbert, *Reimarus,* 139–44.

28. David Friedrich Strauss, however, objected that if John had known about Jesus' mission, he would not have asked whether he was the Messiah in Matt 11:3. John's recognition of Jesus' messiahship was, therefore, added by the Gospel (Strauss, *The Life of Jesus Critically Examined,* trans. George Eliot [New York: Macmillan, 1892], 222–27). Strauss also argued that Jesus, "attracted by the fame of the Baptist, put himself under the tuition of that preacher . . . after the imprisonment of John, carried on . . . the same work, never ceasing even when he had far surpassed his predecessor, to render him due homage" (p. 233).

29. Carl H. Kraeling, *John the Baptist* (New York: Charles Scribner's Sons, 1951), 136.

that "God's saving will was already in action."[30] In fact, instead of a fiery judgment, as preached by John, Jesus was proclaiming God's mercy in God's judgment.[31] This sharp difference in understanding God's judgment seems to suggest that John did not really recognize and acknowledge the messiahship of Jesus.[32] In spite of this different theology, Jesus still respected John (Mark 11:27-33). Here, we can see that scholars try to maintain a still-good relationship between John and Jesus, despite their separation. However, in a communal society, what does a separation between two groups connote? Maurice Goguel, therefore, suggests an ugly split between the two. As Jesus considered "the message of John the Baptist was incomplete and therefore ineffective,"[33] John saw Jesus as "an unfaithful disciple and almost a renegade."[34] The two may go their own ways, but what about their disciples? How would the society view the groups?

Across the aisle from scholars who assert that Jesus was initially a disciple of John, Günther Bornkamm and Joan Taylor argue otherwise. Bornkamm wrote, Jesus "did not begin his work as a disciple of John and did not directly continue John's work. . . . he never opposed him. He acknowledged John and related his own vocation with that of the Baptist."[35] In fact, John played an important part in the Jesus movement despite the fact that the difference between them in the eschatological time line was "like that between the eleventh and the twelfth hours"[36]—John as the crucial link between "the time of preparation for the end and Jesus the bringer of the

---

30. Ibid., 153.

31. Meier, *Marginal Jew,* 2:9. According to Robert Webb's sociohistorical reading, John was a "leadership popular prophet" who had a group of disciples around him, including Jesus. While John proclaimed the imminent judgment and restoration by the expected figure, he was not anticipating the end of the world. See Robert L. Webb, "John the Baptist and His Relationship to Jesus," in *Studying the Historical Jesus: Evaluation of the State of Current Research,* ed. Bruce Chilton and Craig A. Evans, New Testament Tools and Studies 19 (Leiden/New York: Brill, 1994), 179–229, here 223.

32. Meier, *Marginal Jew,* 2:21. This argument was also made by Charles H. H. Scobie, *John the Baptist* (London: SCM, 1964), 213.

33. Maurice Goguel, *Jesus and the Origin of Christianity,* trans. Olive Wyon, vol. 2 (New York: Harper & Bros., 1960), 275–76.

34. Ibid., 276.

35. Günther Bornkamm, *Jesus of Nazareth,* trans. Irene and Fraser McLuskey with James M. Robinson from the third edition (New York: Harper & Bros., 1960), 49–50.

36. Ibid., 45.

time of rejoicing."[37] Likewise, Joan Taylor thinks that, although "Jesus was without a doubt deeply impressed by John and sought to follow his example and his teaching, bringing the same message of the coming of the kingdom of God and urgency of repentance," "it cannot be argued that Jesus simply continued John's message as a disciple; Jesus was a 'prophet' in his own right, legitimated by God (in his own experience) at his immersion by John." Hence, Jesus seems to "believe that he and John were acting in union as agents of God."[38]

Whether Jesus was a disciple of John and whether the split between John and Jesus was hostile or not, we cannot treat John and Jesus apart from their communities, especially when "individual becomes that which he [or she] is addressed as by others."[39] If John and Jesus were on good terms with each other, the two groups should be on good terms as well. After all, John was a very honorable teacher or prophet in the society; otherwise Mark would not have begun his Gospel with him, let alone have Jesus recognize his mission and accept his baptism.[40] Yet the existing tension between the movements of John and Jesus is considerable.

John's role in Mark, in comparison with that in the other canonical Gospels, was relatively short and was curtailed rather early (1:14). John functions more like a symbolic figure with an ephemeral stage appearance. Even when John the forerunner was said to have testified for Jesus (1:7-8), Mark does not indicate that he recognized Jesus as "the one stronger than me [who] comes after me" (Mark 1:7). The spiritual vision and voice in Mark 1:10-11 were addressed to Jesus alone, personally. The good news may begin with John and hence indicates his tremendous importance as the herald of the good news, but John does not seem to know that Jesus was the Messiah. So, what was Mark trying to say about John, as it seems rather ambiguous? Focusing on Mark 2:18-22, I wonder whether the Gospel, in an honor-and-shame

---

37. Ibid., 50.

38. Joan E. Taylor, *The Immerser: John the Baptist within Second Temple Judaism* (Grand Rapids/Cambridge: Eerdmans, 1997), 50,12, 293.

39. Berger, *Sacred Canopy,* 16.

40. Walter Wink (*John the Baptist in the Gospel Tradition*, Society for New Testament Studies Monograph Series 7 [Cambridge: Cambridge University Press, 1968], 2), argues that "[r]esurrection, death, suffering, ministry all lead back to the forerunner, and through John even the Old Testament prophecies become a part of the 'beginning of the Gospel of Jesus Christ'" (p. 5).

culture, was trying to, albeit suggestively (and perhaps reflecting a particular historical situation), group John's disciples and the Pharisees together as a foil to the Jesus movement.

A Postcolonial Contextual Interpretation of John

I emphasize the values of honor and shame in my postcolonial interpretation because the place of honor, and hence the public or divine recognition of one's status, plays a huge role in the construction and maintenance of center versus margin. To observe this power relation in Mark, we need to consider the role of honor in the Gospel. First of all, the fact that John had his own disciples signifies that the John and Jesus groups were not working together; if they were, there would be only one group of disciples, called either John's or Jesus' disciples. As Bruce Malina points out, people "define themselves rather exclusively in terms of the groups in which they [are] embedded; their total self-awareness emphatically depends upon such group embeddedness."[41] Members within the same group "owe loyalty, respect, and obedience of a kind which commits their individual honor without limit and without compromise."[42] It is, therefore, interesting to read that, in the Fourth Gospel, John's two disciples followed Jesus only after John's testimony of Jesus (John 1:35-36; cf. 3:22-26); in this way, the integrity and honor of both the John movement and the Jesus movement could be preserved.

Once we understand how in-groups and out-groups function in a communal society, then the term "disciple" in Mark 2:18, as Robert Bratcher pointed out, "should be taken not to use a word that means only 'students' or 'learners,' as though they were students in school. 'Followers' or 'helpers' or even 'apprentices' would be preferable."[43] In fact, the word "disciple" (*mathētēs*) shows the intimate relationship and loyalty between the teacher and student of the group. Joan Taylor argues that in the New Testament, *mathētēs* "always implies the existence of a personal attachment which shapes the whole life of the one described as *mathētēs* and which in its particular-

---

41. Malina, *The Social World of Jesus and the Gospels* (London/New York: Routledge, 1996), 41.
42. Malina, *New Testament World*, 45.
43. Robert G. Bratcher, *A Translator's Guide to the Gospel of Mark* (London/New York/Stuttgart: United Bible Societies, 1981), 26.

ity leaves no doubt as to who is deploying the formative power."[44] Therefore, "the control of the *mathētēs* by the man to whom they have committed
themselves extends in the NT to the inner life."[45] This picture of the disciples closely related and influenced by their teacher also corresponds to my
understanding of an honor-and-shame society. In a Confucian saying, "even
if someone is your teacher for only a day, you should always regard him as
your father for the rest of your life." Given this understanding of honor, we
can then examine whether Mark portrays John as testifying for Jesus, or as
a part of the Jesus movement, or as leading a movement subjugated under
the Jesus movement.

Was John Part of the Jesus Movement?

While the academy is generally neutral in its assessment of John, Christianity at the popular level is never ambiguous about its veneration of him.
John's fate is even said to forecast Jesus' fate in which the passion of John is
described as the model for the passion of Jesus.[46] In his literary study of the
characters in Mark, Jack Dean Kingsbury wrote,

> In Mark's story, then, John is the forerunner of Jesus who readies Israel
> for Jesus' coming. As forerunner, however, John is more than merely
> the temporal predecessor of Jesus. Indeed, in his own person and fate
> he foreshadows the person and fate of Jesus. To illustrate, both John
> and Jesus are sent by God in fulfillment of OT prophecy (1:2-3). As
> end-time agents of God, both discharge their ministries in the time of
> the gospel. Both proclaim a message summoning Israel to repentance.
> Both gather disciples. Both attract huge throngs of people (1:5; 3:7-8).
> Both utter words of prophecy (1:7-8). Both are repudiated by the reli-
> gious authorities of Israel. Both are delivered up to their enemies. And
> both die unjustly and disgracefully at the hands of rulers who permit
> themselves to be manipulated by others. *To know of John is to know in
> advance of Jesus.*[47]

---

44. Taylor, *Immerser,* 441–42.
45. Ibid., 442.
46. Morna D. Hooker, *Not Ashamed of the Gospel: New Testament Interpretations of the Death
of Christ* (Grand Rapids: Eerdmans, 1994), 47–52.
47. Jack Dean Kingsbury, *Conflict in Mark: Jesus, Authorities, Disciples* (Minneapolis: Fortress Press, 1989), 33 (emphasis mine).

From the point of view of literary analysis, John may serve as a forecast to what will happen to Jesus. But seen through a postcolonial lens, such an interpretation can be problematic, especially when we treat this literary representation of John as a reflection of history as if, historically, Jesus was predestined to follow John's fate. Or, put the other way around, John's suffering is a pious model for Malaysian Chinese Christians to imitate since even Jesus himself did it. Such an interpretation among the oppressed may condone, if not support, the inevitability of suffering. Moreover, it can wrongly suggest that John's life and death were nothing but a script pointing to the life and death of Jesus.

From a cultural reading, I interpret that such association of Jesus' life with that of John reflects Mark's attempt to connect or juxtapose the unknown life of Jesus with that of the better-known life of John so that the brutal and shameful crucifixion of Jesus could be explained in a positive light like the beheading of John, a death considered by many to be the result of his righteousness, according to Josephus (*Jewish Antiquities* 18.5.2 §§116–19). Thus, our interpretation differs from literary analysis, which can be traced back to Willi Marxsen's argument that "the entire Gospel of Mark is to be understood from the end backward."[48] Mark could be portraying a different John, a John possibly not part of the Jesus movement, a John not necessarily used as an exemplar for preparing the path of Jesus. This rereading of John seems to be more fitting; otherwise, the fact that John also had disciples would not make sense in a collective honor-and-shame culture.

We may argue that the inclusion of John's disciples is to show to John's disciples that they should follow John to be part of the Jesus movement, but this argument does not consider honor-and-shame values. If we say that John was part of the Jesus movement and that his disciples were not, we are suggesting that John was an ineffective teacher who had no honor and authority; otherwise his disciples would have followed his instructions and not questioned Jesus' teaching. But if John was portrayed as such an incapable figure, then why would Mark want to put him right at the beginning of the Gospel? Hence, the most we can be sure of is that John, a popular and respected religious figure, was depicted in the Gospel as related to the Jesus movement.

---

48. See Wink, *John the Baptist*, 1.

Given the high social and religious status of John, it is not odd for the Gospel to have someone of John's stature baptize Jesus, regardless of whether he recognized Jesus' mission or not. Linking the Jesus movement with John could of itself gain some standing for Mark's oppressed community. This association with John's authority in the society is seen also in Jesus' rhetorical retort to the chief priests, scribes, and elders when they questioned his authority (11:27-32). Mark tells us that the religious leaders were hesitant to answer Jesus' question about John's authority for baptizing. If they denied John's authority, they would be rejecting his honor, which according to the public, came from God. To do so in public would only bring shame to themselves as incapable of recognizing something so basic that everyone knew (11:32). John's authority was, thus, affirmed.

In the light of collective honor-and-shame values, we can then say that, in Mark, John was not part of the Jesus movement. Just as Jesus had his own disciples, so did John. John, at best, was only loosely related to the Jesus movement. This imagery, however, changes tremendously in the other canonical Gospels.

Tensions Reflected in the Redaction of Mark 1:9-11 by Other Canonical Gospels

Mark may not be concerned with the implication of Jesus' baptism; other Gospels and early church fathers certainly are. This gradual change of stance toward John's relationship with Jesus seems to mark the power struggle in the early church trying to ensure Jesus' superiority to John, which we do not find in Mark. Mark 1:9-11 simply says that John baptized Jesus and that the heavenly voice was addressed only to Jesus, "You [singular] are my son the beloved, in you [singular] I have taken delight" (1:11). By portraying Jesus as the "Christ, the Son of God" in the beginning of Jesus' gospel (1:1) and having the heavenly voice further reinforcing Jesus' identity, Mark shows that John's baptism was also divinely commissioned; otherwise Jesus "Christ, the Son of God" would not be baptized by him. In other words, Mark indicates that John's repentant baptism into the forgiveness of sins was also part of Jesus' gospel. John was, thus, linked to the gospel of Jesus.

Matthew, however, has to make sure that the heavenly voice was addressed to John and the public as well (Matt 3:17). The contrast between

John baptizing people in water for repentance (3:11) and the one more powerful than he (that is, Jesus) baptizing in the Holy Spirit and fire suggests that the nature of these two baptisms was different. Hence, when according to Matthew, John would have prevented Jesus from being baptized, even though this act rightly shows his acknowledgment of Jesus as more powerful than he, John was mistaken about the nature of Jesus' baptism and authority. [49] If the baptism was related to bearing the fruits of repentance, of which Jesus must have had more than enough, how could John have stopped Jesus from being baptized? No wonder Jesus had to teach John and nudge him, "permit it now; for it is proper for us in this way to fulfill all righteousness" (3:15), as the time has already changed and the kingdom of heaven is really here (3:2). John's authority is subsumed under Jesus' as Jesus appears to know much better about his mission than John himself does.

In Luke, the differences can be striking when we consider the passage immediately preceding Luke 3:21-22. In 3:20, Herod the tetrarch puts John in prison. In v. 21, "As all the people were baptized, and as Jesus was baptized [*baptisthentos*] and praying [*proseuchomenou*] the heaven was opened." Compared to Mark and Matthew, the baptism scene in Luke is rather fast. Luke pays little attention to the baptism; the focus is on Jesus, prayer, and the Holy Spirit.[50] Darrell Bock also points out that the temporal order in the sequence of the verbs of baptism (*baptisthentos*) and prayer (*proseuchomenou*) in v. 21 "shows that the only ongoing event at the time of heavenly voice was the prayer. . . . Thus, in contrast to Matt. 3:14-15, Luke makes no point about why Jesus should get baptized."[51]

In the Fourth Gospel (John 1:29-34), the difference is even more noticeable. We do not have Jesus' baptism. In 1:29-31, the Gospel has John testifying for Jesus:

---

49. As W. D. Davies and Dale C. Allison Jr. point out, scholars have spilled much ink over this redaction of Matthew from Mark and have offered a wide range of theories and explanations (*A Critical and Exegetical Commentary on the Gospel according to Saint Matthew*, vol. 1, *Introduction and Commentary on Matthew I–VII*, International Critical Commentary, 3 vols. (Edinburgh: T&T Clark, 1988), 321–23.

50. Indeed, "Luke makes clear that the important event followed the actual baptism." Darrell L. Bock, *Luke*, vol. 1, Baker Exegetical Commentary on the New Testament 3 (Grand Rapids: Baker, 1994), 336.

51. Ibid., 336.

Behold, the lamb of God, who lifts up the sin of the world. This is the man of whom I said, "after me comes a man who was ahead of me because he was before me." I did not know him, but for this reason I came baptizing with water so that he may be revealed to Israel.

After hearing John's confession, we may expect John to baptize Jesus, but such was not the case. John went on to testify for Jesus in 1:32-34:

I have seen the spirit coming down like a dove from the heaven and it remained upon him. And I did not know him, but the one who sent me to baptize in water said to me, "upon whom you see the spirit coming down and stay upon him, he is the one baptizing in holy spirit." And I have seen and I have testified that he is the son of God.

Without Jesus' baptism, how could John recognize Jesus as the one who will baptize in holy spirit? Jesus' baptism was, therefore, only implied. Note also the exact repetition of "I did not know him" in vv. 31 and 33, as if the Gospel tried to stress the impartiality and validity of John's witnessing. Was such a solemn disclaimer related to John's emphatic denial of his Elijah identity, which flatly contradicted Jesus' assertion of John being Elijah in the other Gospels? The fact that the Fourth Gospel, unlike the Synoptics, has John narrate the theophany is also incredible! But what transpired between Mark and the other Gospels that made them so insecure about Jesus' baptism by John?

This uneasiness is even more visible in the non-canonical Gospels, such as the *Gospel of the Nazoreans,* the *Gospel of the Hebrews,* the *Gospel of the Ebionites,* and the *Infancy Gospel of James.*[52] For instance, in the *Gospel of the Nazoreans,* when Jesus was invited by his mother and brothers to be baptized by John, he replied, "What sin have I committed that I should go and be baptized by him? Unless what I have said is a matter of ignorance." Early church fathers also tried to rationalize Jesus' baptism to show that he is without sin and that he is not inferior to John.[53] Justin in *Dialogue with Trypho* 88, for example, says that Jesus' baptism was "for the sake of the human race, each having sinned individually"; Ignatius of Antioch and Gregory of

---

52. W. Barnes Tatum, *John the Baptist and Jesus: A Report of the Jesus Seminar* (Sonoma, Calif.: Polebridge, 1994), 88–92.
53. Kilian McDonnell, *The Baptism of Jesus in the Jordan: The Trinitarian and Cosmic Order of Salvation* (Collegeville, Minn.: Liturgical, 1996), 19–28.

Nazianzus justified the baptism as to hallow the water; Jerome said that it was "for a future remission, which was to follow through the sanctification of Christ." Hippolytus reasoned that the baptism was for our sake, otherwise the heavens would have been shut; and Augustine argued that "no baptism was necessary for Christ, but he freely received the baptism of a servant to draw us toward his baptism."[54]

Given these early responses, it is really remarkable that the Gospel writer himself was not concerned with the implications of Jesus' baptism. On top of that, Mark did not feel the need to have John recognize Jesus' mission either. Since Mark already states that Jesus was "Christ, Son of God" and that the Gospel was Jesus' good news (1:1), Mark seems content to connect as many people as possible with his Gospel, as long as they are not against it.

Interpreting Mark 2:18-22 in Light of Mark 1:9-11

Mark's tendency to connect more people to the gospel is visible also in 2:18-22. While Mark is ambiguous about the antagonists' identity, Matthew simply spells it out that they were John's disciples and others. In Mark, this is the only place that shows the potential dispute between John's disciples and the Jesus group.

> And the disciples of John and the Pharisees were fasting. And they came and said to him, "Why are the disciples of John and the disciples of Pharisees fasting, but your disciples are not fasting?" (Mark 2:18)

Notice that in Greek, the subject of *erchontai kai legousin autō* is not indicated. It can mean "some people" as most English translations offer.[55] In Matt 9:14, however, the text clearly says that it was John's disciples who questioned Jesus about his disciples' non-fasting behavior: "Then the disciples of John came to him saying, 'Why do we and Pharisees fast much, but your disciples do not fast?'" From an honor-and-shame culture, when one questioned

---

54. Thomas C. Oden and Christopher A. Hall, eds., *Mark,* Ancient Christian Commentary on Scripture 2 (Downers Grove, Ill.: InterVarsity, 1998), 11.
55. Adela Yarbro Collins argues that the subject "is not the disciples of John or the Pharisees, but is indefinite. This conclusion is supported by the formulation of the question, which refers to those groups without identifying the speakers with either of them" (*Mark: A Commentary,* Hermeneia [Minneapolis: Fortress Press, 2007]), 197.

the disciples' behavior, one also questioned the teacher's teaching ability and authority. Hence, Matthew makes it clear that it was John's disciples challenging Jesus' authority. Furthermore, W. D. Davies and Dale C. Allison suggest that by not putting John's disciples and the Pharisees together, as we have in Mark, Matthew tries to make John's disciples "the third story in a row in which a different religious group has shown itself to be at cross purposes with Jesus—the scribes in 9:1-8, the Pharisees in 9:9-13, the disciples of John the Baptist in 9:14-17."[56] In short, John's disciples were challenging the piety and devotion of the Jesus movement.

While the account in Luke is similar to Mark in not indicating who questioned Jesus, it makes a sharper distinction between the John and Jesus groups, as the questioning happened right in the middle of a great banquet (Luke 5:29). In fact, the issue was, "the disciples of John are fasting frequently and making prayers, so are the [disciples] of Pharisees, but your [disciples] are eating and drinking" (5:33).[57] The irony and contrast could not be more obvious! In other words, Jesus' movement, unlike John's group and the Pharisees, did not act like a pious movement focusing on God. Moreover, in the parable of the new-old garment, Lukan language is sharper than that of Matthew and Mark. In 5:36, Luke adds a new description:

> No one after tearing a piece away from the new garment puts it upon the old garment; if he does, he will tear the new and the piece from the new will not match the old.

The focus is clearly on not tearing the new. The emphasis is on taking care of the new. Verse 39 further makes this concern explicit: "And no one after drinking old wine wants the new for he says, 'the old is good.'" Luke then underlines "the strong tendency to prefer the old" among the scribes and Pharisees.[58] But the point is that the new should, in the first place, not be mixed with the old, lest it be adulterated.

---

56. Davies and Allison, *Matthew,* 108.
57. Given the setting in Luke, the questioning seems to still take place in the banquet, and hence the question was probably asked by the Pharisees and the scribes. Robert C. Tannehill, *The Narrative Unity of Luke-Acts: A Literary Interpretation,* vol. 1, *The Gospel according to Luke,* Foundations and Facets (Philadelphia: Fortress Press, 1986), 173–74.
58. Ibid., 174.

Given this short comparison, it seems that the ambiguous identity of the antagonists in Mark 2:18-22 was not insignificant. By putting the disciples of John and the disciples of Pharisees together (2:18), even if Mark may be criticizing John's disciples in a roundabout way—given that the Pharisees were portrayed negatively in the Gospel—he only did so subtly. [59] In fact, the parables of the new-old garment and wine and wineskin do not seem to criticize John's group. Hence, the leaving out of the antagonists' identity may not be accidental if, according to Joanna Dewey, Mark 2:1—3:6 was a "well-worked-out deliberately constructed chiastic structure"[60] with the center at Mark 2:18-22 (our pericope) which centers at Mark 2:20, "but the days will come when the bridegroom is snatched away from them, and then they will fast on that day."

If the theme of suffering is also the focus for the entire Gospel, which Martin Kähler famously describes as "a passion narrative with an extended introduction," and if the passion of John is set to forecast the passion of Jesus, according to literary criticism, then why is this potential conflict between John's disciples and the Jesus group put together in Mark 2:18-22, where the center is about Jesus' death?[61]

Concerning John's death in Mark 6:14-29, while the account seems to cut off the flow of the twelve disciples' successful missionary work (6:7-13 and 6:30) to suggest that "violent death may result from missionary activity," John's death was also related to Jesus' reputation.[62] Instead of reading John's death as pointing toward Jesus', reading from an honor-and-shame culture, I interpret the mention of John's death here in Mark as an attempt to explain Jesus' dishonorable treatment in his hometown (6:1-6). In other words, Jesus'

---

59. Taylor argues that if the goal of John, as a well-respected and influential immerser and teacher of righteousness, was to teach Jewish people to obey Torah, then the Pharisees would hardly be hostile toward John; the Pharisees "may well have accepted that John was a 'good man,' as Josephus did at the end of the first century" (*Immerser,* 211).

60. Joanna Dewey, "The Literary Structure of the Controversy Stories in Mark 2:1—3:6," in *The Interpretation of Mark,* ed. William Telford, Issues in Religion and Theology 7 (Philadelphia: Fortress Press; London: SPCK, 1985), 112.

61. Martin Kähler, *The So-Called Historical Jesus and the Historic, Biblical Christ,* ed. and trans. Carl E. Braaten, Seminar Editions (Philadelphia: Fortress Press, 1964), 80.

62. Yarbro Collins notes that although this relationship between the disciples' missionary work and suffering "may or may not have been intentional on the part of the evangelist . . . the connections may well have been made by some ancient readers, just as they are by some modern readers" (*Mark,* 303, 296).

suffering and rejection by people were not unlike the treatment of John. If the more famous John could die such a shameful death, then Jesus' shameful crucifixion was not too shocking. Again, this attempt to link the less famous, and perhaps suspicious, movement of the Jesus group with that of John was Mark's endeavor to tell his community that they were equally honorable, if not more!

Interpreting from the Margin: Self-preservation and Growth

What Mark did with Jesus' baptism and the potential dispute between John's disciples and the Jesus movement can be seen as a survival tactic. This survival tactic is not opportunistic.[63] Rather, it helps to clarify unfounded rumors so that people would not reject and even persecute Mark's community outright simply because of the hearsay that they might have encountered. In other words, if John is related to the Jesus movement, how terrible could the Jesus movement be?

With Mark being the earliest written Gospel, and hence perhaps the least developed community compared to the ones of the other canonical Gospels, it would be wise for Mark's oppressed community to garner as much support as possible, at least sympathy, from various groups. As is readily recognizable in my context, it would be a dangerous move to fix and draw clear boundaries from other groups and isolate oneself from them. As long as Mark's community did not need to compromise too much of its core identity, Mark would try to work with as many groups as possible. Jesus' comment "Whoever is not against us is for us" (9:40) is a case in point. Hence, even if there might be tensions and differences between the John and Jesus movements, there was no need to spell out the differences, especially if the groups are not too different from Mark's community. Such compromise and negotiation are visible in Mark's ambiguity and sometimes ambivalence. Thus, even though John did not recognize Jesus, the Markan Jesus still respected John's divine

---

63. Here, I am thinking of Sharon D. Welch, *A Feminist Ethic of Risk,* rev. ed. (Minneapolis: Fortress Press, 2000). Referring to Mildred D. Taylor's works (*Roll of Thunder, Hear My Cry,* and *Let the Circle Be Unbroken*), Welch comments on the Logans that "because of the costs and extreme risks of resistance, the Logans teach their children that it is important to choose their battles carefully. Not to resist means death, yet to resist continually would be impossible, also bringing death. They have to learn to resist in such a way that they maintain their self-respect and lay the groundwork for further struggle" (*Feminist Ethic,* 79–80).

mission (11:27-32). As Jesus' parable says, new wine for new wineskin and old wine for old wineskin (2:22). Let the new be new; let the old be old. From my contextual perspective this is a significant feature of the text.[64]

Another significant feature of the text is Jesus' retort to the scribes-Pharisees: "Those who are well have no need of a physician, but those who are sick; I have come to call not the righteous but sinners" (2:17). In other words, Mark's community proclaimed and identified itself with the oppressed. Mark was not only a Gospel for instructing Christians; it was also for recruiting them (13:9-11). Given the pervasiveness of imperial cultic practices, it might be difficult for a minority group to maintain its own identity in the midst of all these threats. But, if the interventionist preaching of the gospel was a "pocket of resistance" to shatter boundaries of systemic oppression in the Markan community, as Brian Blount argues, then Mark could rally much support and rapport among the oppressed, who were tired, disillusioned, and disaffected by the oppressive authority.[65] Indeed, throughout Mark the stories of "exorcisms, healings, unusual authority, and hyperbole of people flocking in from everywhere represent the crossing of boundaries that oppress the readers in Mark community."[66] By associating the Jesus group with the oppressed, which most likely constituted the majority of the population, Mark spoke to the hearts of the many.[67] With the Jesus group seen as supportive of the oppressed, then, Mark could at least gain credibility and moral support from various groups that were oppressed in the society.

The ambiguity of John's relationship to Jesus is, I would argue, tactical in an honor-and-shame communal society, where groups that are related tend to help each other as much as possible. In trying to create a breathing space among dominant forces, Mark perhaps also tried to show the divine authority of the Jesus group by placing John at the beginning of his Gospel. And as we have seen earlier, most scholars agree that John was a significant figure

---

64. Matthew 12:30, on the other hand, has Jesus say, "Whoever is not with me is against me, and whoever does not gather with me scatters." An identical saying is found also in Luke 11:23. Luke 9:50, however, also has the parallel saying to Mark 9:40, within the parallel story.

65. Brian Blount, *Go Preach! Mark's Kingdom Message and the Black Church Today*, Bible and Liberation Series (Maryknoll, N.Y.: Orbis, 1998), 5–10.

66. Ibid., 92.

67. K. C. Hanson and Douglas Oakman, *Palestine in the Time of Jesus: Social Structures and Social Conflicts* (Minneapolis: Fortress Press, 1998).

in the society. Josephus's account of John in his *Jewish Antiquities* 18.5.2
§§116–19 shows that John was so highly regarded "in the eyes of the people
that they explained the defeat of Herod's army as a vindication of John's
goodness, virtue, and righteousness." For Mark, it appears that whether John
recognized Jesus as the Son of God was not as important. An implied association and relatedness between the John and Jesus groups were good enough
to incorporate John into the gospel of Jesus.

As a threatened minority group, Mark probably was not concerned with
polemics against other groups that might be of possible help to his cause. In
fact, it would not be wise for the Markan community to pick a fight with
many groups and hence further alienate itself from the society at large. For
its survival and cultivation of good relationships with other groups, Mark's
community would need to be tactical in picking its fights. As Liew puts it,
"since ancient Jewish apocalyptic writers, in the interest of self-preservation,
tend to level their attacks at a more benign target than the Roman imperialists themselves, it is possible that Mark's verbal assault on the Jewish authorities is a similar tactic of 'scapegoating.' "[68] Furthermore, I argue that among
Jewish authorities, Mark tries to align himself with people-popular and
respected groups, among which was the John group, so as not to antagonize
anyone unnecessarily.

Examining how different Gospels redact Mark 2:18-22 and Mark 1:9-11,
we see how the representation of John changes over time in an honor-and-
shame Jewish culture, especially in the context of power struggles in the
Roman Empire. This interpretation of John shows how negotiation is made
in culling support and how collaboration is formed in carving out breathing
space in the midst of dominant forces. Given my Chinese Malaysian cultural
background, I show that this tactic is not a stranger to a minority group
striving to maintain its identity while trying to keep up a good relationship
with other groups as much as possible. This postcolonial interpretation of
John in the Gospel of Mark is, then, also my contextual interpretation of
John. In a multiracial and multireligious nation like Malaysia, such tactics
are not uncommon in forming alliances with as many other groups as possible. In fact, in a recent general election in March 2008, collaborations were
even formed among traditionally less friendly groups, setting aside party-

---

68. Liew, "Gospel of Mark," 110.

line differences, so that a more unified front could be achieved as a viable alternative to the government. Within this collaboration, a new major party was formed to integrate the Malays, Chinese, Indians, and others into key positions within the organization, and hence, presenting a new possibility that a party of all races could indeed be created. In many ways, this party is providing an alternative vision to the current government, which is formed by different parties along racial lines. As a result of this tactic, the opposition parties managed to prevent the government from acquiring the majority rule in the parliament.[69] The problem, however, is that once these parties, which were not friendly with each other, gain more power and status, they may again define more clearly their party-line philosophies. Hence, the tenuous collaboration that was formed before and after the general election can be very unstable and ambiguous.[70]

For the Gospel of Mark, even though the collaboration is tied to survival, it is not opportunistic; it is about preaching and spreading the gospel. It is not about making over the group's values just so that we can gain benefit from such association with John! A certain compromise can be made, but it cannot jeopardize one's core identity. If ambiguity and ambivalence are merely for self-preservation, then Mark would not have forewarned his community to be bold by bracing themselves against brutal persecutions. Mark would not have encouraged his community to endure until the end in doing God's will (3:35). In fact, Mark would not have stressed that honor comes not from people but from God (8:33-38). This honor, in Mark, is about the cross and suffering: "If anyone wants to follow after me, let him deny himself and take up his cross and let him follow/obey me" (8:34). Indeed, in the midst of suffering, the Markan community is still asked to obey the two most important commandments: to love God wholly and to love one another as one will love oneself (12:29-31). This tactic of survival is clearly more than self-preservation. It is about expanding the boundary and horizon

---

69. For details, see http://www.nytimes.com/2008/03/09/world/asia/09malaysia.html?ref =asia, http://www.nytimes.com/2008/03/15/world/asia/15malay.html?ref=asia, and http:// www.nytimes.com/2008/02/10/world/asia/10malaysia.html?fta=y.

70. In the case of John, the ambiguous relationship between the John and Jesus groups became more clearly defined as Christian communities gradually became more established in society. And as the John group continued to exist alongside the Jesus group, as we see in the Pseudo-Clementine writings, association with John was not only less helpful but also problematic.

of one's heart, one's worldview, and one's group. While it teaches us not to undertake unnecessary suffering, it emboldens us to take up our own crosses when our core identity in loving God and loving others is adulterated by dishonorable tactics.

For Malaysian Chinese Christians, what is our core identity? We are Christians but we are also Malaysian Chinese. We may feel that our hybrid identity causes us to form as many alliances as possible so that our voices can be heard. As Christians, we may feel that our interpretation of the Bible is inferior to Western interpretations. But as Christians, our honor comes not from people but from God. As this honor is tied to loving God wholly and loving each other, how can we love if we cannot be honest with God, with our culture, and with our curiosities and questions about the Bible? A postcolonial contextual interpretation of John's relationship with Jesus then teaches us, Malaysian Chinese Christians, not to discredit our contextual interpretations outright. *And* it teaches us not to discredit Western and other interpretations either. Rather, it teaches us to respect, as Jesus respected John's divine mission even if John might not have recognized his. Indeed, it teaches us to seek God's honor by being honest with God, with ourselves, and with others in our search for a better understanding of the biblical texts, ourselves, and of one another.

CHAPTER 10

Contextual Reading of Mark and North Atlantic Scholarship

Daniel Patte

Self-conscious contextual biblical interpretations acknowledge and affirm the role of the interpreters' contexts in shaping the interpretations and conversely the role of these interpretations in shaping, addressing, and transforming the interpreters' contexts. Such self-conscious contextual biblical interpretations transform the relationship of academic biblical studies with interpreters of the Bible in other circles, including in other academic fields (for example, theology, homiletics), in the churches, in the culture and society, in literature and the arts. It goes without saying that, for me, these transformations are positive developments.

This is not to say that contextual interpretations are a new phenomenon in scholarly circles. As I will argue, any critical biblical interpretation is necessarily contextual. But this contextuality is muted, hidden, or not made explicit. Why is it not acknowledged? How can it be acknowledged?

Struggling with this question will help us envision strategies for developing self-conscious contextual practices. In this essay, I suggest how a didactic practice of self-conscious contextual biblical interpretations affects theological education, by transforming the relationship between critical biblical studies and homiletics. I will illustrate these points through references to the Gospel of Mark.

My Context

What is the context from which I read the Gospel of Mark?

I could say many things about my context as a French person living in North America, after two years in Congo; about being raised in a French Huguenot family during World War II, and studying theology in Montpellier and Geneva. I could speak of myself as a visitor and teacher in southern Africa and the Philippines.

All these experiences marked me and my reading of Mark. But I cannot deny the fact that my primary context is and has been academia—or more specifically the North Atlantic academia (a phrase that I use as shorthand for "Western European and North American academia").[1]

For most North Atlantic biblical scholars, saying that my reading of Mark is done from (or in) a North Atlantic academic context is simply nonsensical. Good scholarship is "a-contextual," isn't it? It establishes an interpretation of the Bible that transcends all contexts, establishing the truth about the text. The scholarly morality of knowledge demands a rejection of contextual interpretations as illegitimate; to interpret contextually is to read pre-understandings *into* the biblical text, instead of weeding out these wrong understandings from the interpretations.[2]

Thus, strangely enough, my *contextual* reading of Mark takes place in the context of an academy that denies the contextual character of its own interpretations and rejects contextual studies as illegitimate and implausible—although they might be exotic curiosities.

---

1. I am in my fortieth year of teaching undergraduate, seminary, and graduate courses in New Testament studies. I have been a regular participant in and contributor to the meetings of the SBL (Society of Biblical Literature) and also of the AAR (American Academy of Religion), as well as of the SNTS (*Studiorum Novi Testamenti Societas*), and the *Colloquio Ecumenico Paolino*. Yet the North Atlantic scholarly societies and the dialogue with other biblical and theological "scholars"—a term that I understand in its primary meaning as designating "those who study" the Bible and theology—are only a part of my academic context, often in tension with the other parts of my academic context, which involve, as discussed below, studying the history of the reception of biblical texts, including their receptions by Christian believers (and my students) who are reading these texts as Scripture in their specific contexts.

2. See Van A. Harvey's brilliant analysis of scholarly morality of knowledge in *The Historian and the Believer: The Morality of Historical Knowledge and Christian Belief* (New York: Macmillan, 1966).

Yet, as I pay attention to this context, I can recognize how this anti-contextual context and our responses to it frame our interpretations of the Gospel of Mark. If we ignore this anti-contextual context, its effects can potentially be quite problematic. It drives our interpretations blindly; we fail to be critical, as we give up the control of our interpretations and of the ways in which they affect others. But if, in an effort to call all interpreters to exercise critical control over our interpretations and to assume responsibility for our teaching, we acknowledge that this context is anti-contextual, we discover that, when we acknowledge it, this anti-contextual context can fruitfully shape our teaching and pedagogy, transform for the better our view of the academy and of its role in theological education, even as this anti-contextual context is transformed by the very fact that its role in interpretation becomes apparent.

Let me try to clarify this tangled web by retelling the story of my personal trajectory. This story might help readers to see the problem that needs to be addressed more clearly so that these transformations can take place in a fruitful way.

In this anti-contextual context of academia, how did I become convinced of the importance of contextuality in biblical studies—including scholarly, critical biblical studies? How did I become convinced of the contextual character of all North Atlantic academic biblical interpretations, including the most technical exegeses and (especially) those that deny their contextual character? How did I become convinced that specialized scholarly biblical interpretations are advocacy interpretations (usually androcentric and/or patriarchal interpretations) as much as feminist, African American, or Latino/a interpretations are? How did I become convinced that acknowledging the contextual character of one's biblical interpretation is an urgent matter of accountability in the field of biblical studies (as I have argued[3] and illustrated[4] elsewhere)?

Learning hermeneutical and semiotic theories, beneficial as it was, did not truly help in this transition. Decades of studies of hermeneutical theories

---

3. Daniel Patte, *Ethics of Biblical Interpretation: A Reevaluation* (Louisville: Westminster John Knox, 1995). See also Elisabeth Schüssler Fiorenza, *Rhetoric and Ethic: The Politics of Biblical Studies* (Minneapolis: Fortress Press, 1999).
4. Daniel Patte, *Discipleship according to the Sermon on the Mount: Four Legitimate Readings, Four Plausible Views of Discipleship, and Their Relative Values* (Harrisburg, Pa.: Trinity Press International, 1996).

and semiotics—including Heidegger, Bultmann, Gadamer, and Ricoeur in hermeneutics, and Eco and Greimas in semiotics—had made clear to me and many others that there is no interpretation without pre-understandings—and these pre-understandings are contextual, of course. Yet, like most biblical scholars, I continued to conceive of the hermeneutical process as a two-step process: a "scientific," a-contextual exegesis describing "what the text meant," followed by a contextual "hermeneutical" application envisioning "what the text means for today" (an unduly simplistic pattern derived from Krister Stendahl's balanced proposal, and achieving exactly the opposite of what Stendahl intended). With the help of structural semiotics, I argued for a plurality of legitimate and plausible interpretations in my studies both of Paul's letters and of the Gospels and in my teaching. Nevertheless, until the early 1990s, I carefully avoided acknowledging the contextuality of my interpretations—even though in theory I knew they were contextual. The question is: Why this implicit denial of contextuality? And why did I finally acknowledge the contextual character of biblical interpretations in the early 1990s?

Obviously, what prevented me from recognizing the role of contextuality in my biblical interpretations was not a lack of theoretical knowledge. I had all the hermeneutical and semiotic theoretical knowledge I needed. The problem was the stigma attached to contextuality in critical biblical interpretation. In the scholarly community, it was/is shameful to acknowledge that one's interpretation could have been influenced by one's context. A contextual interpretation is tainted! It is not pure enough! It is biased. It is irrational, if not fundamentalist or superstitious. It is shameful.

Overcoming the Stigma Attached to Contextuality in Critical Biblical Interpretation

A stigma cannot be overcome by theoretical knowledge (about hermeneutics); it is an ideological or convictional problem—as my experience illustrates. Now, as Louis Althusser aptly defined it, an "ideology is a representation of the imaginary relationship of individuals to their real conditions of existence."[5] This means that ideological or convictional perceptions, such

---

5. Louis Althusser, *Essays on Ideology* (London: Verso, 1984).

as this stigma, can be overcome only when the worldview (the representation of the imaginary relationships in life)[6] that this stigma reflects is confronted with incongruous "real conditions of existence"—that is, by realities that are incompatible with the ideology and can no longer be ignored. The stigma attached to contextuality in biblical studies can be overcome only through such a shock treatment.

The knee-jerk perception that contextual interpretations are illegitimate, implausible, and invalid can first be confronted *with* the reality that our interpretations are always didactic discourses; we are always interpreting for an audience—or better, dialogically *with* an audience—whether this audience includes other biblical scholars for/with whom we are writing, or students in our classes. An interpretation needs to have an audience, and thus it needs to be contextual in order to be meaningful (and thus plausible) and valuable (and thus valid).

When this reality of the didactic character of our biblical interpretation is made apparent, the question becomes: How do we, biblical scholars, relate to our audience? To other biblical scholars? To other colleagues who read the Bible? To our students?

When these questions are raised, it soon appears that denying the contextual character of our interpretation leads us to *lacking professional respect for other biblical scholars*. I gently made this observation on a panel regarding a commentary[7] in which an author wrote more than one thousand times that another scholar was "wrong" or "misinterpreted" the biblical text—as if this other commentator did not have a wide range of knowledge and was incompetent. Why not acknowledge the contextuality of their respective interpretations? This other scholar was also on the panel, defending himself. The responses from both panelists were puzzled comments; of course, we respect each other's scholarship. "Do you really?" was my reply. "Why do you need to deny the didactic character of your interpretations? Are you not seeking to address the needs and questions of two different audiences and thus you chose

---

6. The worldview or ideology can also be viewed as a mythical system (Claude Lévi-Strauss), a cosmos (Peter Berger), a semantic universe (A. J. Greimas), or, as I prefer, a system of convictions. The distinctions among these, important as they are, are not relevant here.

7. Since this is meant as an illustration, not an attack, I will not give names.

to emphasize different aspects of the text?" But the puzzlement lingered. More is needed for a shift of paradigm.

When we remember that the audience for our biblical interpretations includes our colleagues in other theological fields (for example, in theology, ethics, pastoral care, and homiletics), it soon becomes clear that to deny the contextual character of our interpretations is also *to show a lack of professional respect for our colleagues in other fields.* I was utterly astounded when a theologian complained that we, biblical scholars, constantly use a veto power against other fields, telling theologians and homileticians, in effect, that their interpretations are illegitimate as long as they do not conform to the results of critical biblical scholarship, results that we promulgate. For this theologian, this lack of professional respect for colleagues was the direct result of the biblical scholars' efforts to reach a universal truth—the only true meaning of the text that should be adopted by all in all contexts. Even when we, biblical scholars, acknowledge that this universal truth is always out of reach (in line with a Kantian transcendental method, arguing that this is a reaching-out-toward-without-ever-grasping), the results of our "scientific" interpretations forcefully deny the legitimacy of any interpretation, especially contextual interpretations, that dare to diverge from our own. Thus, we implicitly adopt a condescending attitude vis-à-vis theologians, homileticians, and other colleagues.[8] Are we not expecting theologians and homileticians to take our a-contextual scholarship as a model they should follow? Are we not showing a lack of professional respect for our colleagues in other fields by denying the contextual character of our interpretations? We never meant to do so. But the puzzlement lingers. Still more is needed for a shift of paradigm.

The shock treatment that challenged for me the stigma attached to contextuality in biblical studies occurred in the classroom—an appropriate place for biblical interpretations that are didactic in character! This stigma attached to contextuality was most directly challenged when I was confronted with our students' incongruous "real conditions of existence." I have long carried

---

8. It is also denying any value to the interpretations of the Bible through the centuries that our colleagues in church history study. This even applies to New Testament studies. For instance, of course, the interpretation of Isa 40:3 in Mark 1:2ff. is valueless; it is merely a "popular . . . oral conflation of prophecies" (as a biblical scholar wrote; implying it is "worthless," and "we know better") (footnote ad loc. in *The New Oxford Annotated Bible,* 3rd ed., ed. Michael Coogan (New York: Oxford University Press, 2001).

as a badge of honor the objections of my students who complained that my teaching destroyed their faith. Good! Their dogmatic or fundamentalist readings of the Bible needed to be shaken up, as mine had been. But, I was stopped in my tracks in the late 1980s and early 1990s, when I was told in no uncertain terms by students, colleagues, and other authorities (including African authorities) that my teaching—a teaching of "a-contextual" critical biblical studies—was *condoning patriarchalism, sexism, racism, apartheid, colonialism.*

Of course, my spontaneous reaction was to hide behind the text: "I cannot help it if the text is patriarchal, sexist, anti-Jewish, racist, colonialist, imperialist. Following a scientific model, I have to present what the text says; then the readers and students have to draw whatever conclusions they want regarding how to apply 'what the text said' to their lives today." But the puzzlement lingered. I could not deny the reality of sexism, of racism, of anti-Semitism, of apartheid, of colonialism, and their disastrous effects. The weight of evidence was too much. For me, somewhere in Africa, the paradigm shifted.

I will spare my reader nearly twenty years of learning from many people around the world, and from undergraduate, divinity, and graduate students in my classes, in order to go directly to the main conclusions that we progressively reached with the groups of colleagues involved in the Romans through History and Cultures SBL seminar (1998–2008),[9] then with the seventy scholars who developed the *Global Bible Commentary*,[10] and now the group of colleagues involved in the Contextual Biblical Interpretation SBL Group.[11] Then I will briefly review the didactic strategies that follow from these conclusions.

First Conclusion: Critical biblical studies must account for, and assume responsibility for, the effects they have in life.

Interpretation of the Bible always matters. Biblical interpretations often have, for better or worse, very powerful effects on the readers and people around them. This conclusion presupposes two things:

---

9. Leading to Romans through History and Cultures, a ten-volume book series at Continuum.
10. Daniel Patte et al., eds., *Global Bible Commentary* (Nashville: Abingdon, 2004).
11. Out of which the book series Texts @ Contexts is developed.

1. We have a choice among several interpretations, and thus are responsible for our choice and its effects. This is what hermeneutical and semiotic theories have long argued; the meaning of any given text is not contained in the text-as-container; meaning is produced in multiple ways in the dialogue between the text and its readers.

2. The interpretations of biblical texts are all the more powerful in the life context of their interpreters, because for believers these texts are Scripture, that is, words-to-live-by.[12]

Second Conclusion: Critical biblical scholars should take conscientious preachers, rather than scientists, as models for their scholarship.[13]

This was a surprising discovery that arose from the group studying the reception of Paul's Letter to the Romans.[14] In order to compare these different interpretations of Romans, we recognized that we needed to make distinctions among three separate, but intertwined, interpretive choices:

1. *Analytical interpretive choices*—that is, foregrounding one aspect of the text perceived as *more significant* than other textual features. Most individual readers commonly make these choices spontaneously out of their particular aesthetic, cultural sense. Biblical scholars do so by choosing to use one of the dozens of exegetical methods, each foregrounding one aspect of the text as particularly significant.[15]

---

12. Interpreters who are not believers almost necessarily take into account that these texts are Scripture for believers, even if their goal is to deny any scriptural authority to these texts.

13. This is viewing scientists as aiming at bias-free, a-contextual descriptions. Actually, this common model used in historical-critical biblical scholarship would be questioned by scientists involved in theoretical scientific research.

14. In what follows, I quote freely from Grenholm and Patte, "Overture: Reception, Critical Interpretations, and Scriptural Criticism," in *Reading Israel in Romans* (New York: Continuum, 2000), 1–54.

15. Paula Gooder (*Searching for Meaning: An Introduction to Interpreting the New Testament* (Louisville: Westminster John Knox, 2008) illustrates twenty-three methods, from traditional criticisms (various forms of historical criticism, concerned with one kind or another of textual features pointing "behind the text") to various forms of literary criticism (focused on textual features pointing to inner-textual relationships) and to various kinds of reception criticisms (focused on textual features that affect readers in various ways). For a shorter listing of these methods, see also Daniel Patte, Monya Stubbs, Justin Ukpong, and Revelation Velunta, *The Gospel of Matthew: A Contextual Introduction for Group Study* (Nashville: Abingdon, 2003), 54–57. The choice of certain features of the text as "particularly significant" reflects the inculturation of the individual reader and her/his identity; aesthetic, literary, moral, historical perspectives are cultural, even as these resist a particular culture.

2. *Contextual interpretive choices*—through which the interpreters choose to relate the biblical text to certain aspects of their concrete life contexts, using the text as a lens to assess their contextual situation and to recognize the relational problems that need to be addressed; and seek to identify the teaching that this text might (or might not) have for this life context. The "choice" of a context and contextual problem frames the interpretation, and vice versa, the text as interpreted transforms the view of the context and its problems.

3. *Theological/hermeneutical interpretive choices*—through which the interpreters choose to emphasize a particular theological theme as constructed and delimited on the basis of the interpreters' religious perspective and experience.[16] Conversely, through a theological interpretive choice, the text challenges, refines, or supports the theological pre-understandings of the interpreters.

These different interpretive choices and their roles in any biblical interpretation became much clearer when we recognized that conscientious preachers are the model that critical biblical scholars need to emulate. Indeed, such preachers assume responsibility for their interpretations by self-consciously making these three types of choices.

a. *Analytical interpretive choices* Preachers closely read and analyze the biblical text by consulting several commentaries and other critical studies of the text; looking not for one but for several legitimate and plausible interpretations. Preachers presuppose that they have a choice among several interpretations—whether they ultimately make this choice by themselves or with a group (as in what is known as a roundtable pulpit).

b. *Contextual interpretive choices* As conscientious preachers develop their sermons, they seek to *discern how this scriptural text engages the life of their parishioners* by addressing actual needs in their life contexts— relational needs of various kinds.

c. *Theological/hermeneutical interpretive choices* Furthermore, as conscientious preachers conceptualize the teaching of the text and their sermons, they strive to identify theological categories that account for

---

16. These religious experiences are broadly understood to include secular experience, and the most religious of experiences, namely, the silence or absence of God.

the way in which the text relates to the religious experiences of Christian believers—their own and those of their parishioners (experiences of both the presence or absence of the divine). [17]

As they make these three different choices, conscientious preachers implicitly or explicitly (in a roundtable pulpit) read the biblical texts "with others"—usually they read with the scholars whose commentaries they consult and with the parishioners to whom they will preach (whether these parishioners are present in spirit in the preachers' study or more directly present in the flesh in a roundtable pulpit group).[18]

Third Conclusion: Critical biblical scholars, following the model of conscientious preachers, should make explicit that they read the biblical text as Scripture.

Obviously preachers read the biblical text as Scripture. But do critical biblical scholars read the biblical text as Scripture? A chorus of scholarly voices responds: "Of course not! This is not what we are doing!" Yet I want to affirm that most critical biblical exegeses are shaped by an awareness that the biblical texts are read as Scripture by believers, all the more so when they seek to debunk certain interpretations of these biblical texts. Thus, the most "scientific" abstract exegeses cannot and do not ignore the fact that biblical texts are functioning as Scripture for believers. But the stigma of contextual readings surfaces again as soon as one suggests that critical biblical scholars

---

17. It is essential to recognize that the dreadful experiences of total vulnerability in the absence of God are genuine religious experiences. See Cristina Grenholm, *Barmhärtig och sårbar: En bok om kristen tro på Jesus* (Stockholm: Verbum, 2004) (first edition 1999).

18. For me, preachers who pretend that they did not make any of these choices are theologically and ethically problematic preachers (although they might be great orators). These poor preachers strive to read the Bible in the splendid isolation of their ivory towers from which they come to dispense the true, authoritative meaning of the biblical text that their parishioners should passively receive from them. Rather than "reading with others" (their parishioners), these questionable preachers take shortcuts by "reading for others"—claiming to have the only true and possible reading, positing that others are ignorant subalterns who cannot read correctly by themselves. "Reading for others" (or "speaking for others") is one of the attitudes that Gayatri Spivak denounced as a colonialist attitude. Gayatri Spivak, "Can the Subaltern Speak?" in *Marxism and the Interpretation of Culture,* ed. Cary Nelson and Lawrence Grossberg (Urbana: University of Illinois Press, 1988), 277–313 For the adaptation of her categories in biblical studies, see Gerald O. West, *Contextual Bible Study* (Pietermaritzburg: Cluster Publications, 1993), 14–17.

read and should explicitly read the biblical texts as Scripture. The primary reason is an amazingly reductionist view of scriptural reading. Following Wilfred Cantwell Smith's remarkable study *What Is Scripture? A Comparative Approach,* a phenomenological perspective soon shows that as words-to-live-by, Scripture has necessarily many roles for believers. [19] Choosing one of these roles of Scripture is actually making one of the theological interpretive choices that any interpretation of a religious text involves, as believers relate biblical texts to their life contexts.

Some of the distinct roles that Scriptures play for believers can be signaled by common metaphors. As a "lamp to my feet and light for my path" (Ps 119:105), Scripture provides (individual) believers with knowledge of what is good and evil, a sense of direction for their lives, and thus also doctrinal instructions. As the rule of the community (or *canon,* in its etymological meaning) for assessing behavior, Scripture provides the community of believers with knowledge of God's will and shapes the believers' moral life, so that the community/church might fulfill its mission.

Both the preceding roles of Scripture posit that believers search Scripture for inspired (moral and doctrinal) "knowledge"; the inspired, infallible Word is identified with the "content" of the text ("what the text says"). These roles of Scripture are most common in the North Atlantic world, so much so that often they are taken to be the only ones, or as the literal readings of biblical texts. But they are not.

- As good news or as warning (which a rule of the community can also be), Scripture motivates believers to do God's will in response either to the good news of God's love or to threats of punishment. Then the inspired, infallible Word is the motivation conveyed by the text (rather than the knowledge of God's will, as above).
- As book of the covenant ("Testament"), Scripture conveys to the community of believers a vision of their identity and vocation as members of God's people; by entering the story of God's people, believers participate in this story and gain a true sense of relationship to others, to the world, and to God.

---

19. Wilfred Cantwell Smith, *What Is Scripture? A Comparative Approach* (Minneapolis: Fortress Press, 1993).

- As corrective lenses and prophecies being fulfilled, Scripture conveys to the community of believers a vision of God's interventions in their present life experiences; believers can recognize that the Scriptures are fulfilled (a role of Scripture strongly emphasized by the Gospels and Paul).
- As empowering word, Scripture is a performative word through which powerless people are transformed and empowered to be agents of the kingdom (as the poor are in the beatitudes).
- As holy Bible, Scripture is itself a divine manifestation; the encounter with the holy through Scripture iconoclastically shatters the believers' previous convictions.

When this diversity of roles of Scripture is recognized (there are other roles beyond those outlined above), it becomes clear that, as they make explicit the contextual character of their interpretation, critical biblical scholars should make explicit how they relate the biblical texts to certain present-day life contexts; or—and this amounts to the same thing—how their critical studies relate the biblical texts to the believers' way of reading these texts as words-to-live-by—either denouncing certain scriptural uses (and abuses) of the text or positively proposing alternative scriptural readings. This is why, in our effort to represent the work of the Romans through History and Culture group, Cristina Grenholm and I have proposed to call this process of self-conscious contextual biblical interpretations "Scriptural Criticism."

A Pedagogical Practice of Contextual Biblical Interpretation

A self-conscious practice of contextual biblical interpretation calls for different pedagogical strategies in critical biblical studies, since it is a matter of training our students—whether seminarians, undergraduates, or doctoral candidates—to emulate conscientious preachers. Let me simply tell how I envision and practice my teaching of critical biblical studies.

First, we need to recognize that the role of the teacher changes. I am no longer in the classroom to impart the right interpretation of the text and to correct the students' wrong interpretations. I am joining my students in their reading; I am reading with my students. What makes me a teacher is that I know many more readings of the given text than my students do, because I have "read with" many more people—and not because I have the true critical interpretation that my students should adopt. My other skill comes from my practice of self-conscious contextual biblical interpretation.

Emulating the preachers, our students need to learn to "read with others." One strategy for this is to envision the class as a roundtable seminar (as in the roundtable pulpit) in which all the participants (students and teacher) are invited to read with each other, respecting each reading. This requires us to abandon the traditional Enlightenment pedagogical model through which students should be viewed as empty containers who need to be filled up with a knowledge content—and our sense that they should be wiped clean of their wrong knowledge so as to be made into blank slates upon whom the scholars would write the true interpretation. Of course, this is following pedagogical strategies long developed elsewhere, heeding the basic notions of Paulo Freire's *Pedagogy of the Oppressed*.[20] Far from being *tabulae rasae*, students bring to the table their contextual understandings of the Bible. At first, students resist expressing their understanding of the teaching of the text for a certain context—they came to class to correct their wrong readings of the Bible, didn't they? But they soon cooperate. Then, as they compare their interpretations with each other—taking note of the differences—they can begin to recognize the contextual character of their interpretations, not as a problem but as a necessary part of any fruitful interpretation.

As they compare their different contextual interpretations of a given text by reading with each other, participants in the seminar readily recognize that they have made certain contextual interpretive choices; that is, spelling out how their interpretation envisioned the biblical text as addressing a particular concrete problem in a particular life context. Similarly, once prompted, they readily recognize in a preliminary way some of the theological/hermeneutical interpretive choices they have made, at first the kind of role of Scripture

---

20. Paulo Freire, *Pedagogy of the Oppressed,* trans. Myra Bergman Ramos (New York: Herder & Herder, 1970; rev. ed.: New York: Continuum, 1993). Beside his predecessors in Latin America since the sixteenth century, see also Ivan Illich, *Deschooling Society* (New York: Harper & Row, 1971); F. Ross Kinsler, *The Extension Movement in Theological Education: A Call to the Renewal of the Ministry*, rev. ed. (Pasadena: William Carey Library, 1981), as well as F. Ross Kinsler, ed., *Ministry by the People: Theological Education by Extension* (Geneva: World Council of Churches; Maryknoll, N.Y.: Orbis, 1983) and *Diversified Theological Education: Equipping All God's People* (Pasadena: William Carey International University Press, 2008).

they envisioned, but also that they have construed in a certain way a certain theological theme that they related to the text.

At this point, it is often helpful to discuss other self-conscious contextual interpretations of the given biblical text, such as sermons and the growing number of published contextual interpretations.

On the Gospel of Mark, I found particularly helpful the little book of contextual interpretations by Ched Myers, Karen Lattea, et al., *Say to This Mountain: Mark's Story of Discipleship;* Brian K. Blount, *Go Preach! Mark's Kingdom Message and the Black Church Today;* diverse feminist interpretations, such as Mary Ann Tolbert, "Mark," in *The Women's Bible Commentary,* as well as those by Hisako Kinukawa and Musa Dube in the *Global Bible Commentary.*[21]

Also, I find it most helpful to alert the participants to the fact that self-conscious contextual interpretations use different strategies. Among various emphases are (1) inculturation, especially in the reader's conception of theological themes and/or perception of what is most significant in a text; (2) liberation, where the reader is primarily concerned with the contextual choices, and socioeconomic and political issues; (3) inter(con)texts, that is, reading a biblical text together with a text from the interpreter's context, which also affects the conception of themes and/or perception of what is most significant in a text; and (4) sacramental/liturgical settings, which obviously affect the theological choices, but also in the process both the analytical and the contextual choices.

As members of the roundtable seminar take note of the differences of these interpretations among themselves and with their own, they become more and more aware of the contextual and theological interpretive choices they have made. They also are aware that there are differences regarding the features of the texts that are viewed as most significant, and that there are analytical interpretive choices.

---

21. Ched Myers, Karen Lattea, et al., *Say to This Mountain: Mark's Story of Discipleship* (Maryknoll, N.Y.: Orbis, 1996); Brian K. Blount, *Go Preach! Mark's Kingdom Message and the Black Church Today,* Bible and Liberation Series (Maryknoll, N.Y.: Orbis, 1998); Mary Ann Tolbert, "Mark," in *The Women's Bible Commentary,* ed. Carol A. Newsom and Sharon H. Ringe (London: SPCK; Louisville: Westminster John Knox, 1992), 263–74. Also helpful are some of the essays reproduced in *A Feminist Companion to Mark,* ed. Amy-Jill Levine and Marianne Blickenstaff (Cleveland: Pilgrim, 2004).

Yet they remain concerned: Are these various self-conscious contextual interpretations properly grounded in the biblical text? Explanations about semiotic and hermeneutical theories showing that legitimate meaning-effects are appropriately produced through the dialogue between text and readers on the basis of various features of the text do not suffice (if indeed they are helpful at all). What becomes convincing for participants is to study a plurality of divergent scholarly interpretations of the biblical text, as they are asked to respect all these critical biblical interpretations (rather than playing these scholars against each other) by underscoring that each of these biblical scholars has demonstrated scholarly skills in linguistics, in historical studies of various kinds, in rhetoric, and in literary studies. They are asked to pay close attention to the critical analytical methods each used (identifying these methods with the help of books such as *Mark and Method: New Approaches in Biblical Studies,* edited by Janice Capel Anderson and Stephen D. Moore[22]); these scholars have made different analytical interpretive choices.

The participants are then invited to recognize the differences among the conclusions drawn from these different interpretations—for example, by focusing on their various ways of interpreting central themes, such as parables or kingdom. For instance, what are the differences between a redaction-critical interpretation of Mark (for example, in the commentary by John R. Donahue and Daniel J. Harrington, *The Gospel of Mark*), a critical literary interpretation of Mark (in Mary Ann Tolbert's *Sowing the Gospel*), a sociopolitical interpretation (for example, in Ched Myers's *Binding the Strong Man*), a narrative-political interpretation of Mark (as in Richard A. Horsley's *Hearing the Whole Story*), and a history of religion/ritual studies interpretation (as in Nicole Wilkinson Duran's, *Power of Disorder*).[23]

These scholarly interpretations for the most part deny their contextual character. But now members of the roundtable seminar discover that their

22. Janice Capel Anderson and Stephen D. Moore, eds., *Mark and Method: New Approaches in Biblical Studies* (Minneapolis: Fortress Press, 1992).

23. John R. Donahue and Daniel J. Harrington, *The Gospel of Mark,* Sacra Pagina 2 (Collegeville, Minn.: Liturgical, 2002); Mary Ann Tolbert, *Sowing the Gospel: Mark's World in Literary-Historical Perspective* (Minneapolis: Fortress Press, 1989); Ched Myers, *Binding the Strong Man: A Political Reading of Mark's Story of Jesus* (Maryknoll, N.Y.: Orbis, 1988); Richard A. Horsley, *Hearing the Whole Story: The Politics of Plot in Mark's Gospel* (Louisville: Westminster John Knox, 2001); Nicole Wilkinson Duran, *The Power of Disorder: Ritual Elements in Mark's Passion Narrative,* Library of New Testament Studies 378 (New York: Continuum, 2009).

own contextual interpretation posited an understanding of the themes in Mark similar to one of these interpretations and that they can use this interpretation as a companion scholar to support more fully and refine their own interpretation—especially their analytical and theological choices. And they discover that other participants in the roundtable seminar do the same thing with other companion scholars. Different scholarly interpretations are associated with different contextual interpretive choices, even though they want to claim that they are context free.

Then, participants in the roundtable seminar can draw two conclusions from these observations.

1. While we cannot pretend to guess what is the context from which and for which given scholarly interpretations have been written, it becomes apparent that for each critical biblical interpretation the critical method used is readily associated with a certain kind of context and of contextual problems.

2. Since each participant in the roundtable seminar now recognizes that her/his interpretation is the result of a series of choices—analytical, contextual, and theological interpretive choices—among plausible and legitimate alternatives, she/he has to assume responsibility for his/her interpretation. Thus, each has the ethical obligation of assuming responsibility for her/his choice of interpretation—because biblical interpretation always matters and affects people and their lives. The question is: For the given context (including all those who will be directly or indirectly affected by this interpretation— and therefore often for a broader context than originally envisioned), among all these interpretations, which is the best interpretation?

This involves asking about each interpretation: What specific needs does it effectively and successfully address or fail to address in the context under consideration? What problematic effects does it have (or could it potentially have) in this specific context and in a broader context? Who benefits from this interpretation? Who is hurt (or neglected) by this interpretation?

There are also religious/theological questions that must be raised explicitly (rather than being hidden). These interpretations posit different roles of this text as Scripture for Christian believers and emphasize different theological views (with which the interpreter identifies or which she/he rejects). The question is: What is the role of Christian convictions and values in one's choice of one interpretation as better than the others for this context?

Ultimately, practicing self-conscious critical biblical studies by emulating conscientious preachers is a matter of the morality of knowledge. Yet, instead of a morality of knowledge conceived as accountability exclusively to the scientific guild, it is a morality of knowledge conceived as accountability to the broader community of all the readers of the Bible (including the scholarly guild) and all those who are affected by biblical interpretations all around the world.[24]

---

24. See again Harvey, *Historian and the Believer.*

BIBLIOGRAPHY

Althusser, Louis. *Essays on Ideology.* London: Verso, 1984.

Anderson, Janice Capel, and Stephen D. Moore, eds. *Mark and Method: New Approaches in Biblical Studies.* Minneapolis: Fortress Press, 1992.

Aono, Tashio, trans. *The Pauline Letters.* Tokyo: Iwanami, 1996.

Arai, Sasagu. *Jesus Christ.* Tokyo: Koudan-sha, 1979.

Bailey, James L. "Experiencing the Kingdom as Little Children: A Rereading of Mark 10:13-16." *Word & World* 15 (1995): 58–67.

Bal, Mieke. "Myth à la Lettre: Freud, Mann, Genesis and Rembrandt, and the Story of the Son." In *Discourse in Psychoanalysis and Literature*, edited by S. Rimmon-Kenan, 57–89. London: Methuen, 1987. Repr. In *A Feminist Companion to Genesis*, edited by A. Brenner, 343–78. Sheffield: Sheffield Academic, 1993.

Banana, Canaan Sodindo. *The Church and the Struggle for Zimbabwe: From the Program to Combat Racism to Combat Theology.* Gweru, Zimbabwe: Mambo, 1996.

Barr, David L. *New Testament Story: An Introduction.* 3rd ed. Belmont, Calif.: Wadsworth, 2002.

Barton, Stephen C. *Discipleship and Family Ties in Mark and Matthew.* Society of New Testament Studies Monograph Series 80. Cambridge/New York: Cambridge University Press, 1994.

Bassler, Jouette M. "Community Disagreements: Contested Gender Roles." In *Conflict and Community in the Corinthian Church*, edited by J. Shannon Clarkson, 21–34. New York: Women's Division, General Board of Global Ministries, United Methodist Church, 2000.

Berger, Peter L. *The Sacred Canopy: Elements of a Sociological Theory of Religion.* New York: Doubleday, 1967.

Best, Ernest. *Disciples and Discipleship: Studies in the Gospel according to the Mark.* Edinburgh: T&T Clark, 1986.

Blount, Brian K. *Can I Get a Witness? Reading Revelation through African American Culture.* Louisville: Westminster John Knox, 2005.

———. *Cultural Interpretation: Reorienting New Testament Criticism.* Minneapolis: Fortress Press, 2005.

———. *Go Preach! Mark's Kingdom Message and the Black Church Today.* Bible and Liberation Series. Maryknoll, N.Y.: Orbis, 1998.

Bock, Darrell L. *Luke.* Vol. 1, *1:1—9:50.* Baker Exegetical Commentary on the New Testament 3. Grand Rapids: Baker, 1994.

Bornkamm, Günther. *Jesus of Nazareth.* Translated by Irene McLuskey and Fraser McLuskey with James M. Robinson. New York: Harper & Bros., 1960.

Bourdillon, Michael. *The Shona Peoples: An Ethnography of the Contemporary Shona, with Special Reference to Their Religion.* Shona Heritage Series 1. Gweru, Zimbabwe: Mambo, 1982.

Bratcher, Robert G. *A Translator's Guide to the Gospel of Mark.* London/New York/Stuttgart: United Bible Societies, 1981.

Bravo Gallardo, Carlos. *Jesús, hombre en conflict: El relato de Marcos en América Latina.* Santander: Sal Terrae, 1986.

Brooten, Bernadette. "Konnten Frauen im alten Judentum die Scheidung betreiben? Überlegungen zu Mk 10,11-12 und 1 Kor 7,10-11." *Evangelische Theologie* 42 (1982): 65–80.

———. "Zur Debatte über das Scheidungsrecht der jüdischen Frau." *Evangelische Theologie* 43 (1983): 466–78.

Brown, Nina. "Edward T. Hall, Proxemic Theory." http://www.csiss.org/classics/content/13. Accessed October 26, 2009.

Bultmann, Rudolf. *The History of the Synoptic Tradition.* Translated by John Marsh. New York: Harper & Row, 1963.

Cavadini, John C., ed. *Miracles in Jewish and Christian Antiquity: Imagining Truth.* Notre Dame Studies in Theology 3. Notre Dame: University of Notre Dame Press, 1999.

Cavarnos, Constantine. *Orthodox Iconography.* Belmont, Mass.: Institute for Byzantine and Modern Greek Studies, 1992.

Chavunduka, Gordon L. "Traditional Medicine and Christian Beliefs." In *Christianity South of the Zambezi,* edited by M. F. C. Bourdillon. Zimbabwe: Mambo, 1977.

Chung, Chung-wha, ed. *Korean Classical Literature.* London/New York: Kegan Paul International, 1989.

Cohen, A. *Everyman's Talmud.* New York: Schocken, 1975. Especially on "Children," 170–72.

Collins, Adela Yarbro. *Mark: A Commentary.* Hermeneia. Minneapolis: Fortress Press, 2007.

Collins, Raymond F. *Divorce in the New Testament.* Good News Studies 38. Collegeville, Minn.: Liturgical, 1992.

Cook, Guillermo, and Ricardo Foulkes. *Marcos.* Comentario bíblico Hispanoamericano. Miami: Caribe, 1990.

Countryman, L. William. *Dirt, Greed, and Sex: Sexual Ethics in the New Testament and Their Implications for Today.* Minneapolis: Fortress Press, 2007.

Daneel, M. L. *Old and New in Southern Shona Independent Churches.* Vol. 1, *Background and Rise of the Major Movements.* The Hague: Mouton, 1971.

Davies, W. D., and Dale C. Allison Jr. *A Critical and Exegetical Commentary on the Gospel according to Saint Matthew.* Vol. 1, *Introduction and Commentary on Matthew I–VII.* International Critical Commentary. 3 vols. Edinburgh: T&T Clark, 1988.

Dewey, Joanna. "The Literary Structure of the Controversy Stories in Mark 2:1—3:6." In *The Interpretation of Mark,* edited by William Telford. Issues in Religion and Theology 7. Philadelphia: Fortress Press; London: SPCK, 1985.

Donahue, John R., and Daniel J. Harrington. *The Gospel of Mark.* Sacra Pagina 2. Collegeville, Minn.: Liturgical, 2002.

Dormandy, Richard. "The Expulsion of Legion: A Political Reading of Mark 5:1-20." *Expository Times* 111, no. 10 (2000): 335–37.

Duran, Nicole Wilkinson. *The Power of Disorder: Ritual Elements in Mark's Passion Narrative.* Library of New Testament Studies 378. New York: Continuum, 2009.

Eagleton, Terry. *Literary Theory: An Introduction.* Minneapolis: University of Minnesota Press, 1983.

Edelstein, Emma J., and Ludwig Edelstein, eds. *Asclepius: A Collection and Interpretation of the Testimonies*. Baltimore: John Hopkins Press, 1945.

Fanon, Frantz. *The Wretched of the Earth*. New York: Grove, 1968; French original, 1961. A newer edition is translated by Richard Philcox. New York: Grove, 2004.

Fenkl, Heinz Insu. "Reflections on Shamanism." In *New Spiritual Homes: Religion and Asian Americans,* edited by David K. Yoo. Honolulu: University of Hawaii Press, 1999.

Focant, Camille. *L'evangile selon Marc.* Paris: Cerf, 2004.

Freyne, Sean. *A Galiléia, Jesus e os Evangelhos.* São Paulo: Loyola, 1996. Original 1988.

Gabriel, Peter. "Not One of Us." From the third album entitled *Peter Gabriel.* Mercury Records, 1980.

Gandhi, Leela. *Postcolonial Theory: A Critical Introduction.* New York: Columbia University Press, 1998.

Gelfand, Michael. *Shona Religion: With Special Reference to the Makorekore.* Cape Town: Juta, 1962.

Goguel, Maurice. *Jesus and the Origin of Christianity,* vol. 2. Translated by Olive Wyon. New York: Harper & Bros., 1960.

Gooder, Paula. *Searching for Meaning: An Introduction to Interpreting the New Testament.* Louisville: Westminster John Knox, 2008.

Goss, Robert E. *Queering Christ: Beyond Jesus Acted Up.* Cleveland: Pilgrim, 2002.

Grenholm, Cristina. *Barmhärtig och sårbar: En bok om kristen tro på Jesus,* rev. ed. [Merciful and Vulnerable: Contemporary Christian Faith in Jesus] Stockholm: Verbum, 2004.

Grenholm, Cristina, and Daniel Patte. "Overture: Reception, Critical Interpretations, and Scriptural Criticism." In *Reading Israel in Romans: Legitimacy and Plausibility of Divergent Interpretations.* Romans through History and Cultures Series. Harrisburg, Pa.: Trinity Press International, 2000.

Gundry, Robert H. *Mark: A Commentary on His Apology for the Cross.* Grand Rapids: Eerdmans, 1993.

Hanks, Tom. *The Subversive Gospel: A New Testament Commentary on Liberation.* Cleveland, Ohio: Pilgrim, 2001.

Hanson, K. C., and Douglas E. Oakman. *Palestine in the Time of Jesus: Social Structures and Social Conflicts.* Minneapolis: Fortress Press, 1998.

Harvey, Van A. *The Historian and the Believer: The Morality of Historical Knowledge and Christian Belief.* New York: Macmillan, 1966.

Hays, J. Daniel, and Donald A. Carson. *From Every People and Nation: A Biblical Theology of Race.* New Studies in Biblical Theology 14. Downers Grove, Ill.: InterVarsity, 2003.

Hays, Richard B. "Paul on the Relation between Men and Women." In *A Feminist Companion to Paul,* edited by Amy-Jill Levine, 137–47. Feminist Companion to the New Testament and Early Christian Writings 6. London: T&T Clark International, 2004.

Herzog, William R. *Prophet and Teacher: An Introduction to the Historical Jesus.* Louisville: Westminster John Knox, 2005.

Hinkelammert, Franz. "El asesinato es un suicidio: De la utilidad de la limitación del cálculo de utilidad." In *Pasos,* no. 74. San José, Costa Rica: Departamento Ecuménico de Investigaciones, 1997.

Hollenbach, Paul W. "Jesus, Demoniacs, and Public Authorities: A Socio-Historical Study." *Journal of the American Academy of Religion* 49, no. 4 (1981): 567–88.

Hooker, Morna D. *The Gospel according to Saint Mark.* Black's New Testament Commentaries. London: A. & C. Black, 1991.

———. *Not Ashamed of the Gospel: New Testament Interpretations of the Death of Christ.* Grand Rapids: Eerdmans, 1994.

Horsley, Richard A. *Hearing the Whole Story: The Politics of Plot in Mark's Gospel.* Louisville: Westminster John Knox, 2001.

———. *Jesús y el Imperio: El Reino de Dios y el nuevo desorden mundial.* Estella: Verbo Divino, 2003.

———. "'My Name Is Legion': Demon Possession and Exorcism as Responses to Roman Domination." Paper presented at the Society of Biblical Literature annual meeting, 2007.

———, ed. *Paul and Empire: Religion and Power in Roman Imperial Society.* Harrisburg, Pa.: Trinity Press International, 1997.

Horsley, Richard A., with John S. Hanson. *Bandits, Prophets and Messiahs: Popular Movements in the Time of Jesus.* Minneapolis: Winston, 1985.

Howard, J. Keir. "New Testament Exorcism and Its Significance Today." *Expository Times* 96, no. 4 (1985): 105–9.

Howard, Virgil, and David B. Peabody. "Mark." In *The International Bible Commentary: A Catholic and Ecumenical Commentary for the Twenty-*

First Century, edited by William R. Farmer et al., 1331–67. Collegeville, Minn.: Liturgical, 1998.

Johnson, Luke Timothy. *The Writings of the New Testament: An Introduction.* Rev. ed. Minneapolis: Fortress, 1999.

Josefo, Flavio. [Flavius Josephus]. *Historia de las guerras de los judíos I y II.* Buenos Aires: Alabastros, 1943.

Kähler, Martin. *The So-Called Historical Jesus and the Historic, Biblical Christ.* Edited and translated by Carl E. Braaten. Seminar Editions. Philadelphia: Fortress Press, 1964.

Kazen, Thomas. "Son of Man as Kingdom Imagery: Jesus between Corporate Symbol and Individual Redeemer Figure." In *Jesus from Judaism to Christianity: Continuum Approaches to the Historical Jesus,* edited by Tom Holmén. Library of New Testament Studies 352. London/New York: T&T Clark, 2007.

Kelber, Werner. *The Kingdom in Mark: A New Place and a New Time.* Philadelphia: Fortress Press, 1974.

Keller, Mary. *The Hammer and the Flute: Women, Power, and Spirit Possession.* Baltimore: Johns Hopkins University Press, 2002.

Kendall, Laurel. *Shamans, Housewives, and Other Restless Spirits: Women in Korean Ritual Life.* Studies of the East Asian Institute. Honolulu: University of Hawaii Press, 1985.

Kiely, Harry C. "The Demon of Addiction: Jesus Answers Our Cry for Spiritual Deliverance: A Bible Study on Mark 5:1-20." *Sojourners* 25 (1996): 26–29.

Kim, Chongho. *Korean Shamanism: The Cultural Paradox.* Hants, England: Ashgate, 2003.

Kim, Jean Kyoung. *Women and Nation: An Intercontextual Reading of the Gospel of John from a Postcolonial Feminist Perspective.* Biblical Interpretation Series 69. Leiden/Boston: Brill, 2004.

Kim, Seung-Kyung. "Family, Gender, and Sexual Inequality." In *Modern Korean Society: Its Development and Prospect,* edited by Hyuk-Rae Kim and Bok Song, 131–57. Berkeley: Regents of the University of California, 2007.

King, Richard. *Orientalism and Religion: Postcolonial Theory, India and 'The Mystic East.'* London/New York: Routledge, 1999.

Kingsbury, Jack Dean. *Conflict in Mark: Jesus, Authorities, Disciples.* Minneapolis: Fortress Press, 1989. Spanish trans. *Conflicto en Marcos: Jesús, autoridades, discípulos.* Córdoba: El Almendro, 1989.

Kinukawa, Hisako. "Mark." In *Global Bible Commentary,* edited by Daniel Patte et al., 367–78. Nashville: Abingdon, 2004.

———. *Women and Jesus in Mark: A Japanese Feminist Perspective.* Bible and Liberation Series. Maryknoll, N.Y.: Orbis, 1994.

Kittel, Gerhard, and Gerhard Friedrich, eds. *Theological Dictionary of the New Testament,* vols. 1, 3, 4, and 7. Translated by G. W. Bromiley. 10 vols. Grand Rapids: Eerdmans, 1966–82.

Kittredge, Cynthia Briggs. "Christian Interpretations of Marriage and Slavery." In *Conflict and Community in the Corinthian Church,* edited by J. Shannon Clarkson, 53–65. New York: Women's Division, General Board of Global Ministries, United Methodist Church, 2000.

Koo, Hagen. "The Korean Stratification System: Continuity and Change." In *Modern Korean Society: Its Development and Prospect,* edited by Hyuk-Rae Kim and Bok Song, 36–62. Berkeley: Regents of the University of California, 2007.

Kraeling, Carl H. *John the Baptist.* New York: Charles Scribner's Sons, 1951.

Kwok, Pui-lan. *Discovering the Bible in the Non-Biblical World.* Bible and Liberation Series. Maryknoll, N.Y.: Orbis, 1995.

Lawrence, Louise. " 'For Truly, I Tell You, They Have Received Their Reward' (Matt 6:2): Investigating Honor Precedence and Honor Virtue." *Catholic Biblical Quarterly* 64 (2002): 687–702.

Lebacqz, Karen. "Appropriate Vulnerability: Sexual Ethics for Singles." In *Sexual Ethics and the Church: After the Revolution: A Christian Century Symposium,* edited by John J. McNeill et al. Chicago: Christian Century Foundation, 1989.

Liew, Tat-siong Benny. *Politics of Parousia: Reading Mark Inter(con)texually.* Biblical Interpretation Series 42. Leiden/Boston: Brill, 1999.

MacDonald, Margaret Y. "Virgins, Widows, and Wives: The Women of I Corinthians 7." In *A Feminist Companion to Paul,* edited by Amy-Jill Levine, 148–68. Feminist Companion to the New Testament and Early Christian Writings 6. London: T&T Clark International, 2004.

Malina, Bruce J. *The New Testament World: Insights from Cultural Anthropology.* Rev. ed. Louisville: Westminster John Knox, 1993.

———. *The Social World of Jesus and the Gospels.* London/New York: Routledge, 1996.

Malina, Bruce J., and Richard L. Rohrbaugh. *Social Science Commentary on the Synoptic Gospels.* Minneapolis: Fortress Press, 1992.

Marcus, Joel. *Mark 1–8: A New Translation with Introduction and Commentary.* Anchor Bible 27. New York: Doubleday, 2000.

Martin, Dale B. *Sex and the Single Savior: Gender and Sexuality in Biblical Interpretation.* Louisville: Westminster John Knox, 2006.

Mateos, Juan. *Marcos 13: El grupo cristiano en la historia.* Madrid: Cristiandad, 1987.

Mbiti, John S. *African Religions and Philosophy.* New York: Anchor, 1970.

McDonnell, Kilian. *The Baptism of Jesus in the Jordan: The Trinitarian and Cosmic Order of Salvation.* Collegeville, Minn.: Liturgical, 1996.

Meier, John P. *A Marginal Jew: Rethinking the Historical Jesus.* Vol. 2, *Mentor, Message, and Miracles,* Anchor Bible Reference Library. New York: Doubleday, 1994.

The Menaion of the Orthodox Church. Translated by Isaac E. Lambertsen. 11 vols. Liberty, Tenn.: St. John Kronstadt Press, 1999.

Meyers, Carol L. "Women in the Period of the Hebrew Bible." In *The Women's Bible Commentary,* edited by Carol Newsom and Sharon H. Ringe, 244–51. London: SPCK; Louisville: Westminster John Knox, 1992.

Muzorewa, Gwinyai Henry. *An African Theology of Mission.* Lampeter: Edwin Mellen, 1990.

Myers, Ched. *Binding the Strong Man: A Political Reading of Mark's Story of Jesus.* Maryknoll, N.Y.: Orbis, 1988.

———. *O Evangelho de São Marcos.* São Paulo: Paulinas, 1992.

Nam-dong, Suh. "Towards a Theology of Han." In *Minjung Theology: People as Subjects of History,* edited by Commission on Theological Concerns of the Christian Conference of Asia. Maryknoll, N.Y.: Orbis, 1981.

Nasimiyu-Wasike, Anne. "Christianity and the African Rituals of Birth and Naming." In *The Will to Arise: Women, Tradition and the Church in Africa,* edited by Mercy Amba Oduyoye and Musimbi R. A. Kanyoro, 40–53. Maryknoll, N.Y.: Orbis, 1992.

The New Oxford Annotated Bible. 3rd ed. Edited by Michael Coogan. New York: Oxford University Press, 2001.

Newsom, Carol A., and Sharon H. Ringe, eds. *The Women's Bible Commentary.* Expanded ed. Louisville: Westminster John Knox, 1998.

Neyrey, Jerome H., S.J. "Miracles, in Other Words: Social Science Perspective on Healings." In *Miracles in Jewish and Christian Antiquity: Imagining Truth,* edited by John C. Cavadini. Notre Dame Studies in Theology 3. Notre Dame: University of Notre Dame Press, 1999.

Nickelsburg, George W. E. *Ancient Judaism and Christian Origins: Diversity, Continuity, and Transformation.* Minneapolis: Fortress Press, 2003.

Nouwen, Henri J. M. *The Wounded Healer: Ministry in Contemporary Society.* Garden City, N.Y.: Doubleday, 1972.

Oden, Thomas C., and Christopher A. Hall, eds. *Mark.* Ancient Christian Commentary on Scripture 2. Downers Grove, Ill.: InterVarsity, 1998.

Okure, Teresa. "The Will to Arise: Reflections on Luke 8:40-56." In *The Will to Arise: Women, Tradition and the Church in Africa,* edited by Mercy Amba Oduyoye and Musimbi R. A. Kanyoro, 50–56. Maryknoll, N.Y.: Orbis, 1992.

The Oxford Classical Dictionary. Edited by Simon Hornblower and Antony Spawforth. 3rd rev. ed. Oxford/New York: Oxford University Press, 2003.

Paris, Peter J. *The Spirituality of African Peoples: The Search for a Common Moral Discourse.* Minneapolis: Fortress Press, 1995.

Patte, Daniel, ed. *Cambridge Dictionary of Christianity.* Cambridge: Cambridge University Press, 2010.

————. *Discipleship according to the Sermon on the Mount: Four Legitimate Readings, Four Plausible Views of Discipleship, and Their Relative Values.* Harrisburg, Pa.: Trinity Press International, 1996.

————. *Ethics of Biblical Interpretation: A Reevaluation.* Louisville: Westminster John Knox, 1995.

Patte, Daniel, et al., eds. *Global Bible Commentary.* Nashville: Abingdon, 2004.

Patte, Daniel, Monya Stubbs, Justin Ukpong, and Revelation Velunta. *The Gospel of Matthew: A Contextual Introduction for Group Study.* Nashville: Abingdon, 2003.

Penner, Todd C., and Caroline Vander Stichele, eds. *Her Master's Tools? Feminist and Postcolonial Engagements of Historical-Critical Discourse.* Global Perspectives on Biblical Scholarship 9. Atlanta: Society of Biblical Literature, 2005.

Perkins, Pheme. "The Gospel of Mark." In *The New Interpreter's Bible*, 8:507–734. 12 vols. Nashville: Abingdon, 1995.

Pesch, Rudolf. "The Markan Version of the Healing of the Gerasene Demoniac." *Ecumenical Review* 21 (1971): 349–76.

Reid, David. *New Wine: The Cultural Shaping of Japanese Christianity.* Berkeley: Asian Humanity Press, 1991.

Reimarus, Hermann Samuel. *Reimarus: Fragments.* Edited by Charles H. Talbert. Translated by Ralph S. Fraser. Philadelphia: Fortress Press, 1970.

Rhie, Deok Joo. *Pioneer Women in Korean Church: Struggles for Freedom and Liberation in the Time of Evangelization and Western Civilization.* In Korean. Seoul: Hong Sung Sa, 2007.

Rhoads, David, et al., eds. *From Every People and Nation: The Book of Revelation in Intercultural Perspective.* Minneapolis: Augsburg Fortress, 2005.

Robbins, Vernon K. "Pronouncement Stories and Jesus' Blessing of Children: A Rhetorical Approach." *Semeia* 29 (1983): 405–19.

———. *The Tapestry of Early Christian Discourse: Rhetoric, Society and Ideology.* London/New York: Routledge, 1996.

Said, Edward W. *Orientalism.* New York: Vintage, 1979.

Samuel, Simon. "The Beginnings of Mark: A Colonial/Postcolonial Conundrum." *Biblical Interpretation* 10, no. 4 (2002): 405–419.

Sato, Migaku, trans. *The Gospel according to Mark.* Tokyo: Iwanami, 1995.

———. *The Gospel according to Matthew.* Tokyo: Iwanami, 1995.

Sato, Migaku, and Sasagu Arai, trans. *The Gospel according to Luke and Acts.* Tokyo: Iwanami, 1995.

Schüssler Fiorenza, Elisabeth. "The First Letter of Peter." In *A Postcolonial Commentary on the New Testament Writings,* edited by Fernando F. Segovia and R. S. Sugirtharajah, 393–402. London: T&T Clark, 2007.

———. *In Memory of Her: A Feminist Theological Reconstruction of Christian Origins.* New York: Crossroad, 1983.

———. *The Power of the Word: Scripture and the Rhetoric of Empire.* Minneapolis: Fortress Press, 2007.

———. "Text and Reality—Reality as Text: The Problem of a Feminist Historical and Social Reconstruction Based on Texts." *Studia Theologica* 43 (1989): 19–34.

Scobie, Charles H. H. *John the Baptist*. London: SCM, 1964.

Segovia, Fernando F. *Decolonizing Biblical Studies: A View from the Margins*. Maryknoll, N.Y.: Orbis, 2004.

———. "Mapping the Postcolonial Optic in Biblical Criticism: Meaning and Scope." In *Postcolonial Biblical Criticism: Interdisciplinary Intersections*, edited by Stephen D. Moore and Fernando F. Segovia, 23–78. London/New York: T&T Clark International, 2005.

———, ed. *Reading from This Place*. Vol. 1, *Social Location and Biblical Interpretation in the United States*. Minneapolis: Augsburg Fortress, 1995.

Segovia, Fernando F., and Mary Ann Tolbert, eds. *Reading from This Place*. Vol. 2, *Social Location and Biblical Interpretation in Global Perspective*. Minneapolis: Augsburg Fortress, 1995.

Smith, Wilfred Cantwell. *What Is Scripture? A Comparative Approach*. Minneapolis: Fortress Press, 1993.

Soares-Prabhu, George M. "Anti-Greed and Anti-Pride: Mark 10:17-27 and 10:35-45 in the Light of Tribal Values." In *Voices from the Margin: Interpreting the Bible in the Third World,* edited by R. S. Sugirtharajah. New ed. Maryknoll, N.Y.: Orbis, 1995.

Spivak, Gayatri. "Can the Subaltern Speak?" In *Marxism and the Interpretation of Culture,* edited by Cary Nelson and Lawrence Grossberg, 277–313. Urbana: University of Illinois Press, 1988.

Strauss, David Friedrich. *The Life of Jesus Critically Examined*. Translated by George Eliot. New York: Macmillan, 1892.

Tabor, James D. *The Jesus Dynasty: The Hidden History of Jesus, His Royal Family, and the Birth of Christianity*. New York: Simon & Schuster, 2006.

Tácito, Cayo Cornelio. [Tacitus]. *Anales*. México: Porrúa, 1991.

Tannehill, Robert C. *The Narrative Unity of Luke-Acts: A Literary Interpretation*. Vol. 1, *The Gospel according to Luke*. Foundations and Facets. Philadelphia: Fortress Press, 1986.

Tatum, W. Barnes. *John the Baptist and Jesus: A Report of the Jesus Seminar*. Sonoma, Calif.: Polebridge, 1994.

Taylor, Joan E. *The Immerser: John the Baptist within Second Temple Judaism*. Grand Rapids/Cambridge: Eerdmans, 1997.

Theissen, Gerd. *La redacción de los evangelios y la política eclesial.* Estella: Verbo Divino, 2002.

―――. *Sociology of Early Palestinian Christianity.* Translated by John Bowden. Philadelphia: Fortress Press, 1978.

Tolbert, Mary Ann. *Sowing the Gospel: Mark's World in Literary-Historical Perspective.* Minneapolis: Fortress Press, 1996.

Turner, Victor. *The Ritual Process: Structure and Anti-Structure.* The Lewis Henry Morgan Lectures 1966. London: Routledge & Kegan Paul, 1969. Reprint, Chicago: Aldine, 1995.

Ukpong, Justin. "Inculturation Hermeneutics: An African Approach to Biblical Interpretation." In *The Bible in a World Context: An Experiment in Contextual Hermeneutics,* ed. Walter Dietrich and Ulrich Luz. Grand Rapids: Eerdmans, 2002.

United Nations Development Program. *El conflicto, callejón con salida: Entender para cambiar las raíces locales del conflicto.* Informe Nacional del Desarrollo Humano para Colombia, 2003. Bogota: UNDP, 2003.

Vena, Osvaldo D. *Evangelio de Marcos.* Miami: SBU, 2008.

―――. *The Parousia and Its Rereadings: The Development of the Eschatological Consciousness in the Writings of the New Testament.* Studies in Biblical Literature 27. New York: Peter Lang, 2001.

―――. "The Rhetorical and Theological Center of Mark's Gospel." In *Los caminos inexhauribles de la Palabra,* edited by Guillermo Hansen. Buenos Aires: Lumen/ISEDET, 2000.

Waetjen, Herman C. *A Reordering of Power: A Sociopolitical Reading of Mark's Gospel.* Minneapolis: Fortress Press, 1989.

Watson, G. R. *The Roman Soldier.* Ithaca, N.Y.: Cornell University Press, 1969.

Webb, Geoff R. *Mark at the Threshold: Applying Bakhtinian Categories to Markan Characterisation.* Biblical Interpretation Series 95. Leiden/Boston: Brill, 2008.

Webb, Robert L. "John the Baptist and His Relationship to Jesus." In *Studying the Historical Jesus: Evaluation of the State of Current Research,* edited by Bruce Chilton and Craig A. Evans, 179–229. New Testament Tools and Studies 19. Leiden/New York: Brill, 1994.

Weeden, Theodore J. *Mark: Traditions in Conflict.* Philadelphia: Fortress Press, 1979.

West, Gerald O. *Contextual Bible Study.* Pietermaritzburg: Cluster Publications, 1993.

Wilde, James A. "A Social Description of the Community Reflected in the Gospel of Mark." Ph.D. diss., Drew University, 1974.

Wink, Walter. *John the Baptist in the Gospel Tradition.* Society for New Testament Studies Monograph Series 7. Cambridge: Cambridge University Press, 1968.

Wire, Antoinette Clark. *The Corinthian Women Prophets: A Reconstruction through Paul's Rhetoric.* Minneapolis: Fortress Press, 1990.

Wordelman, Amy L. "Women in the Period of the New Testament." In *The Women's Bible Commentary*, edited by Carol Newsom and Sharon H. Ringe, 390–96. London: SPCK; Louisville: Westminster John Knox, 1992.

Wrede, William. *The Messianic Secret.* Translated by J. C. G. Greig. Cambridge: J. Clarke, 1971.

Yano, Kazue. "The 'Problems' in Contemporary Marriage: What TFR 1.29 Tells Us." *News Letter* 29 [Center for Feminist Theology and Ministry in Japan, 2006].

———. "Re-reading Ruth through Marriage and the Family." *News Letter* 14 [Center for Feminist Theology and Ministry in Japan, 2002].

Zvobgo, Edison. *The Struggle for Zimbabwe.* Harare: Zimbabwe Publishing, 1981.

AUTHOR INDEX

SCRIPTURE INDEX

ANCIENT AND OTHER EXTRA-BIBLICAL SOURCES INDEX